AS MEDIA STUDIES:
The Essential Introduction for WJEC

Developing key topics in depth and introducing students to the notion of independent study, this full-colour, highly illustrated textbook is designed to support students through their WJEC AS in Media Studies. Individual chapters cover the following key areas:

- textual analysis: visual, technical and audio codes
- textual analysis: narrative and genre codes
- approaches to representation
- approaches to audience response
- case studies on: gender, ethnicity, age, issues and events, national and regional identity
- passing MS1: media representations and receptions
- production work, evaluation and report

Specially designed to be user-friendly, *AS Media Studies: The Essential Introduction for WJEC* includes activities, key terms, case studies and sample exam questions. It introduces the course, tackles useful approaches to study, key content covered in the specification, and guides the student in approaching and planning the exam and production work through analysis, prompts and activities.

Antony Bateman is Head of Media and Film Studies at Bingley Grammar School and has previously been Rochdale 14–19 Creative and Media Diploma Programme Director. He is co-author of *A2 Media Studies: The Essential Introduction for WJEC* (2010).

Sarah Casey Benyahia is a teacher and examiner of Film and Media Studies. She is currently Head of Film at Colchester 6th Form College. She is the author of *Teaching Contemporary British Cinema* (2005), *Teaching TV and Film Documentary* (2008), *The Crime Guidebook* (2011) and co-author of *A2 Media Studies: The Essential Introduction for WJEC* (2010), *AS Film Studies: The Essential Introduction* (2nd edition, 2008) and *A2 Film Studies: The Essential Introduction* (2nd edition, 2009).

Claire Mortimer is an Assistant Examiner for the WJEC board and has worked as a Media and Film Studies teacher for many years. She is currently Head of AS Media Studies and a Lecturer in Film Studies at Colchester Sixth Form College. She is the author of the Routledge Film Guidebook, *Romantic Comedy* (2010).

Peter Wall is Chair of Examiners for both GCE Media Studies and GCSE Media Studies for a major Awarding Body. He is co-editor of *Media Studies: The Essential Resource* (2004), *Communication Studies: The Essential Resource* and *Film Studies: The Essential Resource* (2006), co-author of *AS Media Studies: The Essential Introduction* (3rd edition, 2008), *A2 Media Studies: The Essential Introduction for WJEC* (2010) and *Framework Media: Channels* (2004) and author of *Media Studies for GCSE* (2007).

The *Essentials* Series

This series of textbooks, resource books and revision guides covers everything you need to know about taking exams in Media, Communication or Film Studies. Working together the series offers everything you need to move from AS level through to an undergraduate degree. Written by experts in their subjects, the series is clearly presented to aid understanding with the textbooks updated regularly to keep examples current.

Series Editor: Peter Wall

AS Communication and Culture: The Essential Introduction, Third Edition
Peter Bennett and Jerry Slater

A2 Communication and Culture: The Essential Introduction
Peter Bennett and Jerry Slater

Communication Studies: The Essential Resource
Andrew Beck, Peter Bennett and Peter Wall

AS Film Studies: The Essential Introduction, Second Edition
Sarah Casey Benyahia, Freddie Gaffney and John White

A2 Film Studies: The Essential Introduction, Second Edition
Sarah Casey Benyahia, Freddie Gaffney and John White

Film Studies: The Essential Resource
Peter Bennett, Andrew Hickman and Peter Wall

AS Media Studies: The Essential Introduction for AQA, Third Edition
Philip Rayner and Peter Wall

A2 Media Studies: The Essential Introduction for AQA, Second Edition
Antony Bateman, Peter Bennett, Sarah Casey Benyahia, Jacqui Shirley and Peter Wall

AS Media Studies: The Essential Introduction for WJEC
Antony Bateman, Sarah Casey Benyahia, Claire Mortimer and Peter Wall

A2 Media Studies: The Essential Introduction for WJEC
Antony Bateman, Peter Bennett, Sarah Casey Benyahia and Peter Wall

AS Media Studies: The Essential Revision Guide for AQA
Jo Barker and Peter Wall

A2 Media Studies: The Essential Revision Guide for AQA
Jo Barker and Peter Wall

Media Studies: The Essential Resource
Philip Rayner, Peter Wall and Stephen Kruger

AS MEDIA STUDIES:
The Essential Introduction for WJEC

Antony Bateman, Sarah Casey Benyahia, Claire Mortimer and Peter Wall

Routledge
Taylor & Francis Group

LONDON AND NEW YORK

First published 2011
by Routledge
2 Park Square, Milton Park, Abingdon, Oxon OX14 4RN

Simultaneously published in the USA and Canada
by Routledge
711 Third Avenue, New York, NY 10017

Routledge is an imprint of the Taylor & Francis Group, an informa business

British Library Cataloguing in Publication Data
A catalogue record for this book is available from the British Library

Library of Congress Cataloging-in-Publication Data
  AS media studies: the essential introduction for WJEC /
  Antony Bateman . . . [et al.].
    p. cm. — (The essentials series)
  Includes index.
  1. Mass media. I. Bateman, Antony, 1970–
  P90.A225 2011
  302.23—dc22   2010050318

ISBN13: 978–0–415–61334–7 (pbk)
ISBN13: 978–0–203–81433–8 (ebk)

Typeset in Folio and Bauhaus by
Keystroke, Station Road, Codsall, Wolverhampton
Printed by Bell & Bain Ltd., Glasgow

CONTENTS

ILLUSTRATIONS

ACKNOWLEDGEMENTS

The images listed below have been reproduced with kind permission. While every effort has been made to trace copyright holders of these images, and to obtain permission for reproduction, this has not been possible in all cases. Any omissions brought to our attention will be remedied in future editions.

Images

1.7	Fifteen camera shots © Gill Branston and Roy Stafford
1.16	*(What's The Story) Morning Glory?* Oasis album cover. Photo © Michael Spencer Jones
1.20	*The Economist*, June 2010 © The Economist Newspaper Limited
1.21	Original (unedited) cover photograph from *The Economist*, June 2010 © Win McNamee/Getty Images
1.22	Joe Frazier © Time Inc. January 1 1971 Photo by John Shearer/Time & Life Pictures/Getty Images
1.26	Light positioning diagram © www.indyblog.com
1.27	*Into the Woods* theatre poster © Georgetown Globe Musical Productions
1.28	*The Times*, 'Top banker won't budge over £17m pension pot' © The Times/nisyndication.com
1.30	O2 Money in partnership with Natwest, advert created by VCCP
1.31	Toyota Touch advert © Country Hills Toyota
1.32	Example of newspaper formatting (*The Guardian*) © Copyright Guardian News & Media Ltd 2010
2.9	Anti-Blair/anti-war demonstration © AP/Press Association images
3.2	Edited version of original Conservative poster: 'Airbrushing you can believe in' © www.mydavidcameron.com
3.3	*Hello* magazine, 2 August 2010 © Hello!
4.1	Hayden Panettiere on the cover of *Company Magazine*, September 2009, Company © The National Magazine Company Ltd
4.2	*Harper's Bazaar*, October 2010 © National Magazine Company

4.4 Volkswagen Polo advert © Volkswagen Group Japan KK

4.5 Volkswagen Passat advert © Volkswagen Group

4.6 *Daily Mirror*, Friday, 13 August 2010 'Love & Pride' © Mirrorpix

5.1 Danny LaRue © Evening Standard/Stringer/Getty Images

5.2 *Men's Fitness*, May 2010 © Copyright Dennis Publishing Ltd

5.3 *Kerrang*, 9 October 2010 © Bauer Consumer Media Ltd

5.4 David Beckham © Barry King/WireImage/Getty Images

5.5 Cristiano Ronaldo © Eduardo Parra/WireImage/Getty Images

5.6 Zac Efron © Michael Caulfield/WireImage/Getty Images

5.9 Starsky and Hutch © SPELLING/GOLDBERG/THE KOBAL COLLECTION

5.10 *Zoo*, 5–11 March 2010 © Bauer Consumer Media Ltd

5.16 Natasha Kaplinsky © Dave Hogan/Stringer/Getty Images

5.17 J.K. Rowling © Daniel Barry/Stringer/Getty Images

5.23 Fiat billboard advert (with graffiti). Used with the permission of Jill Posener

5.24 The Spice Girls © Dave Benett/Getty Images

5.26 Women for Equality march, 1970s © Archive Photos/Stringer/Getty Images

6.3 *Asian Woman*, Summer 2010 © Jayson Emerald Media Corporation Ltd

6.7 Beyoncé Knowles: L'Oreal accused of 'whitening' singer in cosmetics ad, Mark Sweney, 8 August 2008 © Guardian News & Media Ltd

7.14 Madonna in January 1998 © S. Granitz/WireImage/Getty Images

7.15 Madonna in May 2008 © Daniele Venturelli/WireImage/Getty Images

8.1 Musicians of the Romanes Gypsy circus play in Paris © Photograph: Bertrand Langlois/AFP/Getty Images

9.1 7/7 tube bombings © AP/Press Association images

9.2 *Guardian*, 'Comprehensives lose out to elite schools in race for coveted A*' © Copyright Guardian News & Media Ltd 2010

9.6 The *Sun*, 'Beckhams' Staff Massacre' © The Sun/nisyndication.com

10.2 *Essex Life* magazine, August 2009 © Archant Life Ltd

10.4 The *Sun*, 'Their finest hour (and a half)' © The Sun/nisyndication.com

10.5 *New York Post*, Sunday, 13 June 2010. Used with permission of NYP Holdings Inc. Photo © Michael John/AP/Press Association Images

12.1 *Harper's Bazaar*, October 2010 © National Magazine Company

12.3 *FHM*, October 2010 © Bauer Consumer Media Ltd

12.4 Example student storyboard (1) © Courtesy of Amy Roberts

12.5 Example student storyboard (2) © Courtesy of Milly Dawson

12.6 180° rule diagram © Media Education Wales

12.9 Example student print production work – poster (1) © Courtesy of Liam Mahon

12.10 Example student print production work – poster (2) © Courtesy of Liam Mahon

12.11 Example student print production work – DVD cover © Courtesy of Liam Mahon

Text

Chapter 4

'Multi-tasking media consumption on rise among Britons, says Ofcom study' by Graeme Wearden (19 August 2010) © Copyright Guardian News & Media Ltd 2010

Chapter 8

'Beckham Studies? You're Hired!' by Ellis Cashmore (14 August 2008) © Sky News (online)

'Roma gipsy who fled Czech Republic is the new face of British policing' by Christian Gysin (5 April 2008) © Daily Mail/Solo Syndication Ltd

'Gypsy circus is next on France's expulsion list' by Lizzy Davies (26 September 2010) © Copyright Guardian News & Media Ltd 2010

Chapter 12

Extract from the script of *Waterloo Road*, series 1, episode 1 written by Ann McManus and Maureen Chadwick. The full script can be read online at www.bbc.co.uk/writersroom/insight/downloads/scripts/waterloo_road_s01e01.pdf.

INTRODUCTION

Why a textbook?

It might seem odd that in the twenty-first century the academic textbook is still going; that it hasn't been replaced by a more interactive internet-based form easily downloadable as an app. This seems even odder when the textbook is for media studies; a new and innovative course which challenges some of the more traditional approaches of longer-established subjects. It is the case though that a textbook – designed to be used alongside a companion website and all the resources of the internet – is still capable of fulfilling a specific need for students (and interested readers): that of providing reliable information, being a challenging and stimulating presence and hopefully inspiring you to continue your study to A2 and beyond. This description could also apply to the role of the teacher and that is deliberate; the aim of the book is to support you in your AS level study, to be an additional resource which will reinforce your classroom knowledge, explain areas you might find challenging and guide you in developing your understanding.

One of the drawbacks, however, of discussing the media in the form of a textbook is that even the most seemingly up-to-date examples from TV, music, magazines and websites very quickly seem old and nearly forgotten – clearly a published book can't keep changing in the way that new technology can. Therefore it is best to approach the examples in the case studies as an illustration of how to analyse texts, a way of practising your skills through an illustrated example. Good practice would be to use your own examples to keep your discussion of the media contemporary and relevant. To help you with this the book is complemented by a website: www.asmediastudies.co.uk contains up-to-date examples which couldn't be included in the book itself. The website will also offer detailed guidance on production work which has become an increasingly important element of the AS course worth 50% of the marks for the qualification.

How to use this book

The book is structured to follow the WJEC specification and to take account of your development as a learner in what might well be a new subject for you. Therefore chapters 3 and 4 provide the foundation for the course through the introduction of the two dominant theoretical concepts, Representation and Audience, before applying these approaches to detailed case studies which follow the areas provided by the WJEC. The rationale for this approach is to move from the key approaches which provide media studies with its theoretical underpinning to then testing how these theories can be applied to contemporary media texts. This idea of testing the theory is central; we don't assume that theories discussed will always be valid or particularly useful, it is up to you to apply and evaluate approaches. This strategy is particularly important because of the constantly changing nature of the media. Many of the theories which are still used in media studies were developed in the mid-twentieth century when the media really only referred to TV, radio, cinema and newspapers. The huge changes in new technology and its effect on the relationship between individuals and the media are likely to affect the usefulness of even the most respected and influential theories.

Structure and content: theories and case studies

The order of the chapters in this textbook are organised to 'teach' the WJEC specification; chapters 1–11 should provide all the content you need to successfully pass the exam unit. Chapter 12 focuses on the practical production and written components for the coursework unit.

Throughout the book the chapter content is broken up by boxes, tables and illustrations. This is partly a function of the design layout – being faced with a wall of black type can be off-putting for a reader – but it is also to encourage a more independent response from the reader; many of the boxes are designed to get you to bring forward your own examples, develop a theory further, etc.:

- Activity boxes: each time a new theory, approach or idea is introduced an activity has been designed to help you test your knowledge and understanding. These will range from posing a question for you to consider to worksheets requiring detailed responses.
- Information boxes: these provide explanations of specialist terms, information about theories and theorists, background context for issues of representation, etc. If a term or idea is used in the text which you are not familiar with, then it is likely to be explained in an information box.

Part 1 is the foundation of the book providing the most important tools that you need for your study of the media. Chapters 1 and 2 introduce the techniques of textual analysis, the main approach to analysing or 'reading' the media. This is divided into the different media language codes (visual, technical and audio) and the organising codes of narrative and genre. Each chapter uses a wide variety of media texts to define specialist terms, explain the technical consideration behind media forms and content as well as to give examples of textual analysis in practice. The ability to read a text with detailed reference to the relevant codes is crucial in developing your understanding of the media; everything you do in the rest of the course will be based on the assumption that you understand the codes and conventions of contemporary media whether that is analysing representations or responding to an unseen text in the exam.

The following chapters, 'Approaches to representation' and 'Approaches to audience response' introduce the theoretical framework for WJEC media studies which examine how and why particular groups and places are represented in the media. In turn this leads to a study of how audiences respond to those representations, either as individual spectators, a group or mass. Each chapter provides an overview and definition of the relevant theories and applies them to contemporary media examples. The concept of ideology is also introduced in these chapters suggesting that the media – through its representations – has an ideological function in society. This position underpins the analysis of representation in Part 2.

The WJEC specification identifies five areas of representation which have to be studied at AS – gender, ethnicity, age, issues and events, and national and regional identity – and these are used to structure Part 2. Each chapter focuses on one area of representation and the aim for each is to:

- provide context and history for each area of representation
- consider why each area of representation is important to study
- summarise relevant theories
- identify the use of familiar stereotypes as a way of introducing issues and debates
- apply audience theory to examples of representation.

To conclude Part 2, Chapter 11, 'Passing MS1' suggests techniques for performing successfully in the exam with practical suggestions for revision, preparation and how to structure your responses. A 'mock' exam is provided with some suggestions for the kind of response we think examiners would expect; there is also another example on the companion website.

Structure and content: creative work

The coursework element of the AS course has equal weighting with the exam unit, and success in the coursework will rely in part on your understanding of the codes and conventions, media theory studied in Part 1. The coursework is a chance to demonstrate this knowledge through production work rather than essay writing; it is therefore integrated with the more theoretical aspects of the course. It is also a chance to develop new skills in the context of media technology and to be creative. In Part 3, Chapter 12, 'Production work, evaluation and report', provides a detailed breakdown of everything which is required to help you understand the different elements for coursework success, including:

- what the coursework involves; pre-production, production and report
- effective research strategies
- planning your pre-production and production work
- effective approaches to the production task
- evaluation of your production
- writing the report
- examples of successful production work.

It is understood that despite the reasons for structuring the book as we have, you may not use it chronologically but rather for checking definitions, looking for particular case studies and examples, confirming the guidelines and requirements for the coursework unit, etc., and the book will work very well with that approach too. If you have any comments about how you use the book, which sections you found useful or confusing, etc., then we would welcome your (constructive!) feedback via the website; this will help us to improve our work in the future.

Finally we would like to take this opportunity to thank all those people who have been involved in the production of this book. This includes the colleagues and students at our institutions who have discussed, tested and questioned media theories, texts and approaches to delivering the subject, as well as suggesting diverse and interesting examples to look at. We would like to pay particular thanks to Aileen Storry, our editor at Routledge who has provided expertise, great patience and humour throughout. Our thanks are also due to her colleague Emily Laughton and our copy editor Janice Baiton for their diligence and patience during the production process. We are also very grateful to Pete Wall the series editor who has always provided expert and encouraging feedback on our work.

part **1**

THEORIES AND APPROACHES

TEXTUAL ANALYSIS: VISUAL, TECHNICAL AND AUDIO CODES

1

In this chapter we will look at:

■ What is meant by the term 'media text' and take a basic look at responding to media products by using both a critical approach and your own independent appreciation, understanding and enjoyment

■ How codes are used to create meaning in media

■ What deconstruction of media texts is

■ Ways in which meaning is created visually and through sound in the media

■ A checklist of general points for text analysis.

Responding to the media: the basics

As you commence your GCE in Media Studies, there is one thing which has probably dawned on you already: you will need to write about media products, or 'texts' as they are known in the subject. The word 'text' is usually associated with something which is written down or printed. In a magazine, for example, the text is usually taken to mean the writing which, together with the graphics, diagrams and images, are the main components of every magazine you can imagine. In Media Studies, however, the word refers to any media product such as a television programme, film, advertisement, newspaper article, video game, web page, photograph or radio programme. In the case of printed media, the word 'text' refers not just to the writing but to the images which accompany the writing as well.

Media 'texts' form an important part of the study of media; indeed, it could be argued that studying them and considering the messages and meanings they contain lie at the centre of the entire subject. As media students at AS level, you will need to be able to respond to a range of media texts, or as we said earlier, you will need to write about them and so there are a few approaches which you should adopt to this for studying the subject with WJEC.

- **Enjoyment and appreciation of media texts**. This is largely a personal response to a text but it is much more than simply saying whether you like it or not. Enjoyment cannot really be learned, although by appreciating a text you can begin to enjoy it. The clever use of colour, language, sound, camera-work, etc. can all lead to appreciation irrespective of whether you enjoy the text and would choose to consume it in your own time. Appreciation of a text therefore is literally saying what is excellent, good or poor about a text and saying why you have arrived at this opinion.
- **Critical understanding**. This is a slightly more theory-led or concept-led response. As you study elements and media types in the subject, you will discover that there is a wealth of information and theory about how media texts communicate and the effect they have on their audiences. These are useful to know in order to adopt a critical understanding of texts but poorly applied theory and using a theory or other analytical tools simply for the sake of it or to add gravitas to your answer is often worse than not using a theory at all, so use theory and perspectives wisely and with caution.
- **Exploring technology and the production processes**. This can be quite theoretical and use some technical terms but there is also scope for your own personal response on, for example, how effectively technology is used and how a media product has been produced.
- **An independent approach**. It isn't so much knowledge that is the key to success in Media Studies; it is more what you do with that knowledge. Be independent when you are researching and finding things out and autonomously forming your own opinions and your own views and presenting them in an effective way.

One of the main areas through which we are able to understand how media texts create meaning is through the use of codes and our ability to decode the messages. This may sound like it is getting a little complex; however, you already employ codes in understanding language. Indeed, you are able to read and make sense of this sentence because you are employing a set of codes which dictate how the English language operates. Letters are combined to make words, these words form sentences, and the sentences make paragraphs. If you were reading a book written in French, you would find that the paragraphs and sentences are structured in much the same way as they are in English. The letters too would be familiar but the way in which these letters are combined to make the words follow a different code, that of the French language, and so unless you could read and speak French or to give it the correct media term to 'decode' the words, the meaning behind the words would remain unknown.

In much the same way that we read words, sentences and paragraphs, we also learn to 'read' and understand media texts. Much of the communication which takes place in media texts does so by means other than verbal communication, such as the writing or the dialogue. Image, the use of colour, body language, costume and accent are all examples of non-verbal communication which help us to understand the key messages in a media product. Look at the CK advertisement in Figure 1.1 and consider how much of the communication in the text comes non-verbally.

Figure 1.1 Calvin Klein advert

The advertisement for CK Free is clearly trying to tell the audience something. But what? As an advertisement, how effective is it in communicating its messages?.

The actual meaning behind the CK Free advert is not definite, but we know enough about the codes in operation to be able to understand quite a lot about this text. Non-verbally, the model is dressed in a type of clothing and is adopting a pose which suggest that he is relaxed; his sunglasses (designer and expensive) suggest luxury – perhaps he is on holiday or maybe he is lucky enough to enjoy this lifestyle permanently. The presence of an image of the product in the bottom right-hand corner and the verbal text informing us that it is a new fragrance from Calvin Klein are all codes which combine to tell us that the text is an advertisement for a man's fragrance. This is perhaps an obvious conclusion but, upon deeper analysis, it is the associated meaning which reveals the most interesting reading of this text. Rather than simply saying that there is a new fragrance for men called CK Free which is now available in all good retail outlets, the text is using images to portray an enviable way of life and suggests that, by owning this product, you are taking steps towards achieving this way of life. In fact, the 'selling' of a way of life in advertisements is very widespread. This fragrance could have been advertised by showing it on the shelf in a dark and dingy basement bathroom but to do this would not be providing the right association with a certain way of life in the eyes of those who see the advert, and so a more luxuriant and desirable way of life is being used to advertise the product.

Maybe at this point you are a little confused or overwhelmed because we have introduced so early in the book some technical-sounding vocabulary and concepts but don't worry, it's not all terminology and theory. In fact answers which are laden with theory and terminology may reflect the fact that the writer can learn and remember a lot of information, and can reproduce it in an exam or an essay but they are not actually desirable as they miss the one aspect which forms the most satisfying part of the subject – your personal response. The key is to get the balance right between your use of theory, established tools of analysis and your own response. Going back to the CK advert, it is true to say that there are some technical codes at work here, such as the use of lighting to illuminate the area around the model's eyes, but you should also give consideration to whether you feel it is an effective advert or not, and give a reason for your answer. This you can do without using any theories or analytical tools.

Responding to the media: technical codes

When asked to respond to something or to analyse it, say, a certain item or event, it is understandable that you might think that you are being asked to simply 'write about' the topic in question. In fact this is more or less exactly what you are being asked to do but there needs to be a focus in your response. If you are analysing a media product, as you will certainly be asked to do several times throughout your career as a student of the subject, if you lack focus, then you run the risk of being too descriptive. Awarding bodies do not reward these answers well at any level but especially so at AS level where more focused responses which look at how media affects us, which show a more critical response and which address the key issues of the media text more fully are demanded. A criticism is not simply picking faults with or otherwise explaining how much you dislike something; a criticism in Media Studies is a more balanced expression of understanding the nature of something, a way in which you get to grips with exactly what you see is going on in the product or products you are analysing.

Let us start here with a simple activity aimed at building your confidence in talking about media texts in a critical way.

ACTIVITY

Compare these two homepages from two different newspaper websites. Don't worry about being too technical at this stage; your analysis can at this point be entirely your personal response. Consider the following:

- How do the two homepages differ from each other?
- How are they the same?
- What kinds of people do you think each is intended to be read by?
- How effective are they in capturing the spirit of the newspapers upon which they are based? (You may need to get hold of a copy of these paper versions if you don't know anything about them.)

Figure 1.2 The *Sun* online homepage

Figure 1.3 The *Guardian* online homepage

A useful way you can focus when answering is to regard your analysis as a deconstruction, literally taking the text to pieces and accounting for or explaining the relevance and importance of the main constituent parts, such as the verbal communication, the use of colour, sound, lighting, the position and movement of the camera, the performance of the actors or presenters, the setting, the layout and how people, places or 'things' are being represented in the text. In order to produce an effective deconstruction, it is a good idea to become familiar with two very simple analytical tools, in this case key terms widely used by Roland Barthes, which are in standard practice in image analysis: denotation and connotation.

The denotation, or the signifier, refers to the physical part of a text such as the use of the colour red or the way someone is dressed. The connotation or the signified is the meaning behind the denotations – for example, the colour red could be used to connote danger, passion or horror. Most of the time, groups of students tend to agree on the denotation but readings of the connotations are very much open to interpretation. In the earlier CK advertisement, for example, the connotations of the model wearing sunglasses range from making him look cool and trendy to the possibility that he has glaucoma or simply that he is wearing them because it is sunny. The main thing is to convince an examiner that your connotation is plausible and to give your reasons for arriving at this conclusion, or to put it more simply, to provide an independent, critical and personal response. Given the history of sunglasses being associated with looking cool, the most likely meaning behind the sunglasses in the CK advert would be that it adds coolness to the model and places this association in the minds of the audience in connection with the product.

ACTIVITY

What are the denotations and connotations of the uses of colour in the following film poster?

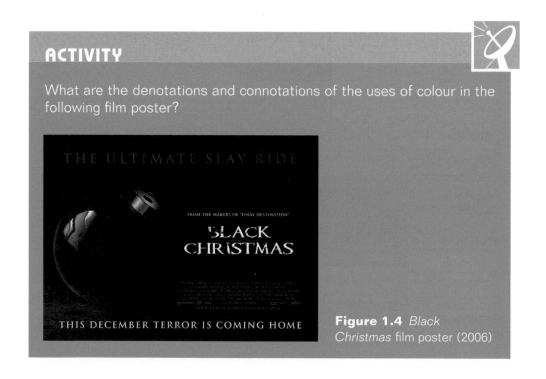

Figure 1.4 *Black Christmas* film poster (2006)

Why are red and black the most prominent colours for horror film posters?

■ Conduct some research into horror film posters; the website http:// uk.movieposter.com is useful for this, and find out the common features of horror posters regarding the use of colour, images and construction.
■ Using a DTP package such as Microsoft Publisher or Adobe Photoshop, design your own horror film poster.

Visual codes and audio codes

In this section we are going to look more closely at technical codes, specifically visual codes and audio codes. Visual codes tend to refer predominantly to camera-work, the use of lighting, and editing in audio visual media texts and graphic design elements for print-based or interactive media. Audio codes, literally sounds, are the other area of technical codes and will be considered later in the chapter. Lighting too has relevance to both moving and printed images and is examined in the static texts section later.

INFORMATION BOX

There is a lot more work taking place in a TV studio besides that of the presenter. The camera operators, sound recordists and floor managers are involved in the technical side of production.

Figure 1.5
Live television
studio recording

Moving texts

CAMERAWORK

Perhaps the most logical place to start when looking at moving images is with the camerawork. Moving images in media rely upon the use of a camera to create a large part of the intended meaning. Although many amateurs approach moving image practical work with a 'point the camera and press record' kind of approach, professionals spend a lot of time planning every shot and deciding how best to use the camera to create the desired effect. This is a good example of how meaning is created through a form of non-verbal communication; in Figure 1.6, from the BBC show *Dr Who* the shot of The Doctor on the left forces the viewer to concentrate upon the setting and the environment the character is in. In effect, this long shot helps to set the scene but in the close-up shot on the right, the viewer is asked to focus upon the facial expressions and to decipher the meaning behind the look – in this case the most likely connotation is uncertainty, trepidation or revulsion. A similar effect is achieved through the use of cropping a still image, a technique which is looked at in more detail later in this section. Although these two shots are of the same scene, the choice of shot is important in helping to communicate meaning to the viewers.

Figure 1.6 *Doctor Who*

Figure 1.7 shows some of the shots which camera operators may employ in creating different meanings. These shots are found in a wide range of media, especially in TV and film work. The decisions about which shots to use will usually be taken collaboratively between the cinematographer, whose job it is to consider both the camerawork and the lighting, the director and the production designer.

ACTIVITY

Watch a 5-minute extract of a fictional drama show on TV such as a soap opera and make a note of how many different shots are used. What reasons are there for using the shots chosen?

AS MEDIA STUDIES: THE ESSENTIAL INTRODUCTION FOR WJEC

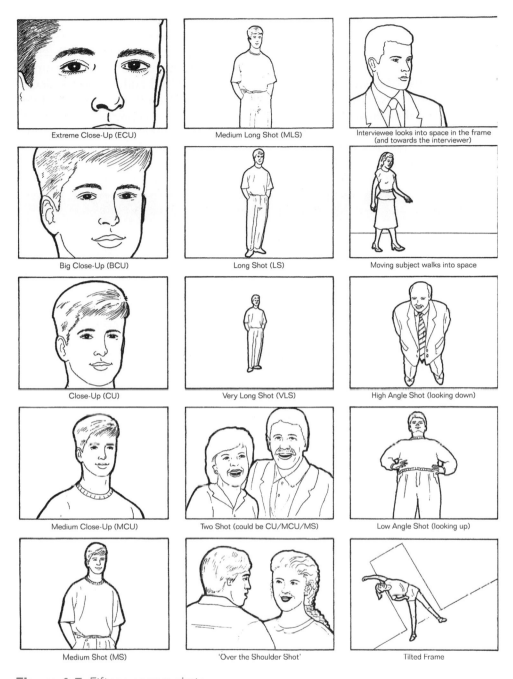

Extreme Close-Up (ECU)

Medium Long Shot (MLS)

Interviewee looks into space in the frame
(and towards the interviewer)

Big Close-Up (BCU)

Long Shot (LS)

Moving subject walks into space

Close-Up (CU)

Very Long Shot (VLS)

High Angle Shot (looking down)

Medium Close-Up (MCU)

Two Shot (could be CU/MCU/MS)

Low Angle Shot (looking up)

Medium Shot (MS)

'Over the Shoulder Shot'

Tilted Frame

Figure 1.7 Fifteen camera shots

Cameras in audio-visual media products are seldom stationary and the movement of a camera can contribute to the creation of meaning, and terms such as *zoom*, *pan* or *tilt* in connection with camera movements are fairly well known. A longer list of the main camera movements is shown in the following table. These camera movements together with the choice of shot, lighting and editing form a kind of language through which audiences make meaning. When these are considered together with the actual subject being filmed and how that is presented, the complete visual package is called the *mise en scène*, a French term which has its origins in the theatre and which means literally placing on stage or in the scene – in other words, what you can see in the camera frame.

Moving camera shots	
Track shot	Here, the camera is mounted on a trolley, which moves along tracks (similar to train tracks). This enables smooth movement and is used, for example, to follow people while they are walking.
Dolly shot	For these shots, the camera is mounted on a tripod on wheels. It is then moved closer in or further out from the action. It is often used to explore the environment or focus attention on a person or a detail.
Zoom	In these shots, the camera itself remains still and the 'zoom' facility on the lens is used to bring a distant image into view in the case of a zoom in or to go from a close-up of the subject outwards in the case of a zoom out.
Crash zoom	The same as a zoom except the movement into or out of the action by the zoom facility on the lens takes place very quickly.
Pan	The camera moves horizontally from side to side.
Tilt	The camera moves vertically up and down.
Steadicam	This is a relatively new invention and is frequently used in sports coverage where the camera operator needs to move, such as along the touchline of rugby or football games. The camera operator wears a body brace to which the camera is attached. This allows the shot to be smooth and free from sudden bumps or jerks and is used to follow the action where cameras on dollies or tracks couldn't go. The camera operator in Figure 1.8 uses a steadicam whilst filming at an outdoor event. The result is smooth, flowing images irrespective of whether he is running or walking.

Figure 1.8 The steadicam allows a camera operator to move smoothly whilst filming

Of course being able to identify the movement of a camera or the choice of a shot and to correctly identify it is only really half the story. To do this is simply to provide a denotation and, as we have seen, that is nothing more than a description. In an analysis, when your job is to deconstruct a text, you would also need to be able to give a reason for that choice of shot. A crash zoom, for example, where the camera zooms either towards or away from the subject very quickly is usually done for dramatic effect, and the most common reason for a very long shot is as a means of establishing a scene and letting the audience know where the programme or a scene within it is set.

A TV programme which is set in the same location for each episode will usually employ an establishing shot in the opening sequence to act as a visual reminder to the audience of the setting and the location.

These TV shows each establish the setting in their opening sequences.

Figure 1.9 *Emmerdale* opening credits

Figure 1.10 *Frasier* opening credits

Figure 1.12 *CSI: NY* opening credits

Figure 1.11 *Eastenders* opening credits

EDITING

We often hear of actors' performances being left on the cutting room floor and the belief that the editor has the power to remove or alter the performance of an actor in a film or a TV show is not misplaced. However, editors usually do not work alone; instead they work under the guidance of and often actually with the director to create the finished product. So important is the job of the editor that some film directors, among them Clint Eastwood and the late Stanley Kubrick, actually edit their films as well as direct them.

The power wielded by the editor is neatly summarised by Thelma Schoonmaker who has edited all the films of Martin Scorsese since 1980: 'You get to contribute so significantly in the editing room because you shape the movie and the performances' (Nguyan, 2005). This is not only the case with film but also with TV, whether it is fictional media such as a drama or a sitcom or non-fictional reality TV or documentary.

In the case of a live broadcast, the editor must decide which shot to use from those available from the cameras being used to film the programme at the very moment that programme is being broadcast, with no opportunity to revisit the editing to improve or correct it. A good example of this is found in current affairs programmes such as the BBC's *Question Time*. The images in Figure 1.13 show some of the different camera shots which are available during a programme and the editor must choose the most appropriate shot for whatever is happening at that moment.

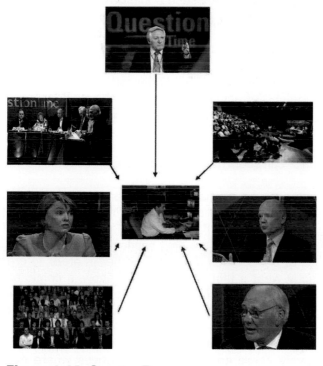

Figure 1.13 *Question Time*

The main function of editing in a moving media text is to construct a narrative in an understandable way so that the audience may apply meaning to what they see and this is as true in non-fictional texts as it is in fictional media. This can be summarised as a kind of cause-and-effect relationship between scenes. A scene of a person shooting an arrow, for example, ought to be followed by the consequences of that shot; likewise in a news bulletin, a scene of a journalist reporting a flood will probably be followed by a shot of the consequences of that flood. In their influential book *Film Art* (1996), Bordwell and Thompson call this a spatial consideration of the editing process. The shot of the arrow being fired may well be followed by a shot of a person falling to the ground. These two shots may show entirely different events and the 'victim' may not have been hit by the arrow we see fired at all, but by placing the two shots together we assume a 'spatial co-existence', that the person fell as a result of the arrow being shot; this would be because both the archer and the 'victim' were 'spatially' close. The editor who places these two shots together is partly responsible for the creation of a narrative.

Bordwell and Thompson (1996) also see that the editing process has other considerations which are the generally accepted convention in creating meaning:

- Rhythmic considerations, which are concerned with the pacing of a text or part thereof. In an exciting chase sequence, the editor will seek to heighten the suspense of the scene by not having any one shot on screen for more than a split second or else the rhythm of the scene could be lost. For this same reason, dreamy sequences are usually characterised by longer shots.
- Graphic considerations relate to how the two shots are connected to each other visually. These could be by means of juxtaposition or a contrast such as from light to dark, happy to sad, loud to quiet, etc. or by continuity, light to light, happy to happy, loud to loud and so on. Juxtaposition, or the placing of contrasting images together, is effective in heightening the experience. Have you ever come out of the cinema in the middle of the afternoon on a sunny day? It seems so much brighter than normal because the sunlight is juxtaposed with the darkness your eyes have become accustomed to in the cinema. Similarly, a scene of horror can seem more horrific if it is preceded by a scene of happiness.
- Temporal considerations such as spatial considerations relate to the use of 'syntagms' in media products. A character may fire a gun but our full understanding of the meaning behind this is only finalised when we see the consequences of that shot, typically in the next scene. These sequences, or 'syntagms' are a series of signs which are put together in order to create meaning, which is exactly what a film or fictional TV show, a comic book, computer game or even this very sentence consists of. The most straightforward way to approach this is by considering a narrative as 'linear' or that events happen in chronological order, hence time is running as we would expect and these narratives might be said to have a standard syntagmatic arrangement. Alternatively, there are non-linear narratives where events do not take place chronologically and the syntagmatic arrangement of the narrative is more complex and more confusing.

Editors can also manipulate the passing of time in the text when considering temporal matters. Elliptical editing is when the events take up less time on screen than they would in reality and overlapping editing is a process by which in repeating part or all of a shot, often from different angles, the event is expanded to occupy more time than it would in reality. For an excellent example of this, watch the scene in *The Terminator* (1984) where the petrol tanker driven by Arnold Schwarzenegger as the Terminator explodes.

Further to these considerations of space, time rhythm and graphics, there is a kind of language which different edits communicate and which the editor needs to follow, particularly in fictional media. Over time, the consecutive and persistent use of these edits in fictional media has led to an understanding between producers and audiences as to what messages are trying to be communicated through an edit.

Some of the most common examples of this are found at the beginning and the conclusion of a text. At the start, we are quite often introduced to the establishing shot by a scene which fades in from black; likewise at the end of the text a scene will often fade out to black. This is editing parlance for telling us that the narrative is starting or ending depending upon which part we are watching. Fades in and out of black are also used throughout the text to inform us that there is a time break between scenes or a break in direction of the narrative and the commencement of a new sub-narrative, so it is the editor's way of telling us that a new chapter in the narrative is starting.

The wipe shot, which is used extensively by the producers of the *Star Wars* films (where a shot moves across the screen in any direction and replaces its preceding shot), is often used as a way of saying to the audience that while one scene is happening, the other is too. This is used in the same way that an author might use the word 'meanwhile' to link to scenes from a novel.

INFORMATION BOX

i

This freeze frame shows a wipe shot from *Star Wars Episode IV: A New Hope* (1977) in which the scene with the spaceship at the top is replaced by the scene in the desert below. This is used here by the editor to say to the audience 'meanwhile . . .' between the shots.

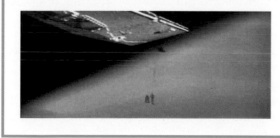

Figure 1.14 *Star Wars Episode IV: A New Hope* screenshot (1977)

Cuts, which are the most common form of edit in film and TV, simply show one shot being replaced by another. Finally, a dissolve is where one shot is replaced by the next but both appear momentarily on the screen together to again suggest a passing of time, but usually less time than that of a fade through black. The dissolve is similar to an author using the phrase 'later that day'.

A **DISSOLVE**, used frequently to suggest a passing of time or to suggest that a character may be dreaming and temporarily, both the character's face and the topic of the dream appear on the screen at the same time.

Figure 1.15 Example of a 'dissolve' screenshot

1. Watch a TV show of your choice and consider the following:

   ■ What edits can you identify in the programme?
   ■ Why have these edits been used?
   ■ What contribution to your understanding of the text has been made by the use of edits?

2. Analyse the editing in the opening credit sequence of *Coronation Street*.

   ■ How does the editing in the opening credits contribute to the overall feel of the programme and create meaning (you might also consider the visual images and the music as well)?

This shows how editing is concerned both with the construction of a narrative and with communicating how different shots interact with each other to create meaning for the audience. Of course, not everything is as simple as that and once you have established a set of 'rules', you can subvert those rules and do something completely different, and there are many examples of edits being used in a much more random and unpredictable way. The film makers of the French New Wave movement of the 1950s and 1960s demonstrated their 'rebellion' against the established conventions of film language by using unusual editing: fades where there would otherwise be cuts, cuts when none were required, iris editing (where the shot ends with a circle of black moving in from the edges of the screen to remove the shot in an ever-decreasing circle) and fades through black mid-way through a section of a shot. In more modern times, the TV show *Lost* and the *Kill Bill* films use editing to create a complex syntagmatic arrangement whereby events do not occur chronologically.

As GCE media students, your task is to be able to identify how meaning is created in the moving texts you are deconstructing, and perhaps after reading this section you may be surprised by how much of that meaning is derived from the editing and the camerawork as opposed to the narrative and the action you see.

ACTIVITY

We have now looked at camera shots, movement and editing. This activity is designed to get you thinking about how all three of these combine to create meaning.

Watch an extract from a film or TV show. Do not use one where little is happening, such as two characters simply talking to each other; find one where there is a lot of action and things happening. (You could use the opening car chase sequence from the 2008 James Bond film *Quantum of Solace* at http://www.youtube.com/watch?v=QXJiYV9 K77Q.) Concentrate upon the movements of the camera, the shots and the editing rather than on what is actually happening in the scene.

- What effect does the editing, movement of the camera and the shots have on the scene?
- Why are these used?
- How do the editing, camera movements and shots enhance the enjoyment the audience feels when watching the scene?

Static texts

PHOTOGRAPHY

Photography is an important part of media products, especially magazines, fashion shoots, printed advertisements, marketing campaigns and newspapers. Modern cameras have made photography considerably easier for the majority of people compared to how things used to be and the idea of 'point-and-press' and images visible on digital viewfinders are largely responsible for this. Thanks to digital photography, photographs are immediately available to be viewed and the days of taking your film to the nearest chemist and waiting up to a week for your photographs to be returned have gone. Professional photographers will usually use digital equipment but automatic focusing, shutter speeds, flashes and light adjustments are likely to be used by the pro, or indeed the keen amateur, as both wish to retain control over these to produce a variety of effects in their work. Most compact cameras which we use to take our holiday photographs will automatically focus on the main subject the camera is pointed towards and facial recognition is widely available on many cameras to ensure that if the shot is of a person, they are in focus. It is not always the case that a photographer will want the subject at the foreground of the image to be in focus, as is the case on the CD packaging for the Oasis album *(What's The Story) Morning Glory?* where it is the background which is in sharp focus. This is not normally the effect desired by photographers.

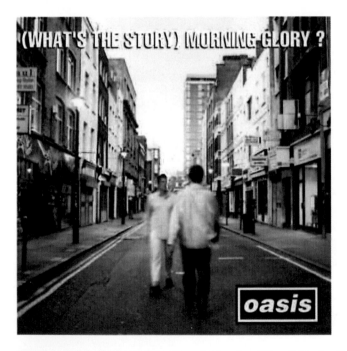

Figure 1.16 *(What's The Story) Morning Glory?* Oasis album cover

Photo © Michael Spencer Jones

There has been much debate in recent years about how modern computer programs can facilitate the manipulation of images. Even fairly simple software which is fitted as standard on most home computers can allow images to be changed so that people's appearances can be altered, and therefore the potential exists to actually change the message in some way. Such practices are widely used in the world of magazines, fashion photography and advertisements. The image in Figure 1.17 shows how the photograph of Keira Knightley on the left has been manipulated to create the image on the right which was used on a poster for the film *King Arthur*.

INFORMATION BOX

Spot The Difference! The image used on the poster for the film *King Arthur* has been changed in a number of ways from the actual photograph which was taken. There are subtle changes in the shape of the mouth and the eyes, the skin looks to have more of a sheen and the overall colour is warmer. The most pronounced difference, however, are the larger breasts digitally 'given' to Keira Knightley in the manipulated image.

Figure 1.17 *King Arthur* film poster (2004) – original (unedited) image of Keira Knightley and final (airbrushed) version

In the case of adverts for beauty products it is understandable that the appearance of a model needs to be 'perfect' but it is the nature of this 'perfection' which raises serious issues for us as media students. The result of the airbrushed images of both male and female models which we see in magazines and advertisements, with perfect skin, hair and bodies, is that the audience is given a very narrow representation where only people who conform to this narrow stereotype of perfection are seen as acceptable. A walk down any high street in any town in the world will reveal the true range of humanity with people of all shapes, sizes, appearances and features and yet generally the representations of people in media texts are more narrow in scope.

The film poster for the 2009 film *Crossing Over* in Figure 1.18 has been manipulated so as to change one of the messages, in this case to imply that one of the actors, Harrison Ford, is younger than his 67 years at the time the film was released. A still image from the film shows Ford in a more accurate and somewhat older light (Figure 1.19).

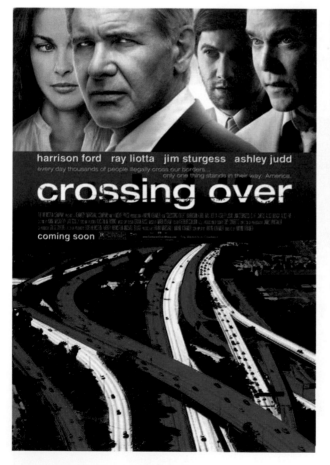

Figure 1.19 *Crossing Over* screenshot (2009)

Figure 1.18 *Crossing Over* film poster (2009)

Even when such cosmetic manipulation is absent in images, it is still possible to manipulate the image in much simpler ways. Photographs in newspapers are often cropped, which means that they are cut in size or that an element from the photograph is removed. This practice can simply be so that the image fits into the available space, but the process of cropping can change the message as is the case in Figure 1.20. Below is the cover from *The Economist* magazine from June 2010 which shows a pensive-looking President Obama on a beach in Louisiana close to the site of the oil leak which affected the Gulf of Mexico. If we consider a connotation of Obama's body language, his looking down would suggest a person deep in thought, contemplating or one faced with hardship or a huge problem. The *New York Times* in its Media Decoder column referred to the image as 'the ideal metaphor for a politically troubled president', presumably because he looked alone and anxious as he considered one of the worst environmental disasters in American history.

Figure 1.20
The Economist,
June 2010

Figure 1.21 Original (unedited) cover photograph from *The Economist*, June 2010

However, he wasn't alone and the real photograph shown in Figure 1.21 potentially tells a totally different story. In fact, the president was on the beach with two other people: Admiral Thad Allen of the US Coastguard and local resident Charlotte Randolph who appears to be talking to the president. Given the height difference between the two, it is perfectly plausible that Obama has lowered his head so that he can hear more clearly or, since the image on the cover is also cropped in size and does not reveal the fact that there are items on the ground, he may simply be looking at them. In a later email to the *New York Times*, the deputy editor admitted that the image had been cropped but claimed that this was not to make a political point, but simply that to have unknown people on the cover would have confused the readers. Whatever the reasoning behind the decision, the cover tells a different story from that of the picture prior to its cropping.

If, as the saying goes, the camera never lies, then it is clear that with modern technology it can be made to mislead. While it may be true to say that the image used on the cover of *The Economist* misleads, it is not uncommon for covers to remove other people or a background, or to otherwise manipulate images in order to shift focus or enhance the meaning.

■ Outline the arguments both for and against the manipulation of images in media texts. Remember that as an AS student, your responses to issues such as these will benefit from you adopting a balanced point of view when weighing up the arguments. After you have looked at the pros and cons, then you can express your opinion on the basis of the evidence you have given.

■ Have a go yourself! Take a picture of yourself and manipulate your image. You can crop, remove 'red-eye' or change the tone and colour (from colour to black and white or sepia, for example) with a basic software package such as Microsoft Office Picture Manager, which is standard on most home PCs. With a more advanced software package such as Adobe Photoshop, you will be able to remove people from the picture you have.

Yet there exists a safeguard against such practices being extensively used in the UK by magazines and newspapers, since the code of practice as laid down by the Press Complaints Commission states that:

> **The Press must take care not to publish inaccurate, misleading or distorted information, including pictures.**
>
> (Press Complaints Commission, article 1, section i)

What is clear with the Obama cover of *The Economist* is that there exists a kind of common-sense approach and the cover does not seem to have breached the code of practice sufficiently to have attracted the kind of criticism which would lead to action being taken. If this is the case, then we are likely to continue to see images being cropped or manipulated in order to modify or adjust the message being given out.

LIGHTING

Good lighting in a media text largely goes unnoticed yet poor lighting is immediately obvious and can be the difference between success and failure. In film and television, lighting is usually regarded together with camerawork as the components which make up cinematography, although the term is sometimes taken to mean camerawork by itself. However, the camera operators and the lighting riggers (if these are not the same person) will certainly work very closely with each other. In photography, if you have ever had a portrait taken, an official photograph as opposed to a holiday snap, the photographer will also be very much concerned with ensuring that the light is correct and will employ the use of a number of different lights and reflectors in order to achieve the desired result. In the days before automatic flashes and digital cameras, it was common to receive a picture back from development only to find that it was dark, and yet at the time of taking the photograph it seemed bright enough. In fact, cameras do not see things in the same way that the human eye does and while our eyes adjust to different light conditions, cameras can only do this up to a point and, in the making of a TV show or a film and in the case of photography, the artificial manipulation of light is needed.

The 'texture' or feel of the lighting in photography or moving images can be achieved by making the light 'hard' or 'soft'. In the case of hard lighting, deep and sharp shadows are created by shining the light directly at the subject as happens with a spotlight; soft lighting that creates only slight shadows and is less noticeable is achieved by reflecting the light off a white reflective screen, or white wall.

INFORMATION BOX *i*

In the photograph in Figure 1.22, boxer Joe Frazier is under a spotlight, an example of hard lighting in which he casts a clear, deep shadow whereas soft lighting as used in the photograph in Figure 1.23 of Robert Pattinson has more subtle light with a softer shadow.

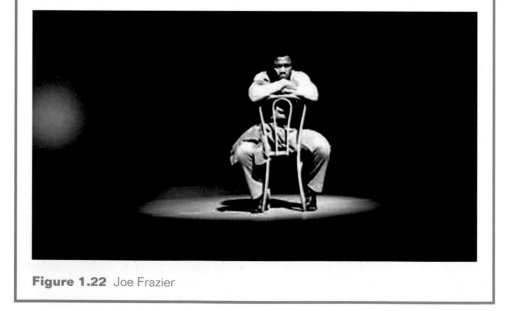

Figure 1.22 Joe Frazier

Figure 1.23 Robert Pattinson

ACTIVITY

What is the effect of these two uses of lighting on the images? What messages do you get from how the subjects are lit, and by the fact that they are both black and white images?

Light can also be used to create superb effects in media products. You can see for yourself how this happens at home by taking a torch and lighting your face in front of a mirror in a darkened room from a number of different angles. Holding the torch above your face gives a spotlight effect while holding it behind your head gives you a lit profile with your features much darker. If you hold the torch to either side, naturally only half your face will be lit and holding it under your chin with the light pointing upwards will give the kind of spooky effect typically found in horror film texts in which facial contours are emphasised as there is a contrast between the dark and light areas of the face. This is sometimes known as the **chiaroscuro effect** after the artistic style characterised by strong contrast between light and dark.

In Figure 1.24, the still from *The Godfather Part II* shows how back-lighting, here provided by the natural light from outside the windows, creates a silhouette effect for the actors in the scene. In the scene from *The Shining* in Figure 1.25, the use of side lighting which leaves half of Jack Nicholson's face in darkness reflects the dual personality of the character he is playing. The tension is heightened by the use of back-lighting to create a partial silhouette.

Figure 1.24
The Godfather Part II
screenshot (1974)

Figure 1.25
The Shining
screenshot (1980)

In terms of light positioning, the basic lighting approach in studio work in film, television and photography is the three-point lighting set up as shown in Figure 1.26.

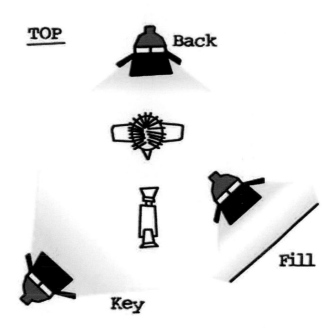

Figure 1.26 Light positioning diagram

The key light is the main light in the set-up and it points to the subject. It is usually above and at an angle so that it can throw a shadow to give depth to the shot. The fill light, which in this example faces away from the subject and has its light reflected, fills the shadows created by the key light with softer light while the back-light helps to create depth and separates the subject from the background.

FONTS AND PAGE LAYOUT

If we consider the verbal elements of a printed image, we are limited to what is written. As we have seen, a large part of the communication comes from the use of images and the non-verbal communication inherent in these, but what of the *way* things are written?

Designers of media texts which have writing on them such as printed adverts, DVD packaging, computer games or websites have a choice of hundreds of writing styles or fonts available to choose from. Generally, the term *text* describes the written aspects of something, text that is as opposed to images, but the word *text* in Media Studies refers more broadly to a media product, and for this reason we shall refer to the written elements of a media text as the *copy*, a word which in journalism is in standard usage for referring to writing.

Copy can, in media texts, be presented in a number of ways. The main distinction between the commonest forms of typing comes by using, or not using, a serif in the fonts. Those fonts which have a serif have a small bar at the end of the extremities of a letter, while those without a serif, called 'sans serif' (*sans* is the French word for 'without'), are plainer fonts and do not have the bar. Although there is no hard-and-fast rule, serif fonts tend to be used in copy for sustained or prolonged reading such as in a newspaper and can be regarded as more formal, while sans serif fonts are ideal for headlines and are regarded as less formal.

INFORMATION BOX *i*

Examples of serif fonts	Examples of sans serif fonts
Times New Roman	Arial
Baskerville Old Face	Helvetica
Palatino Linotype	Gill Sans
Rockwell	Papyrus
Bembo	Verdana

In addition to the distinction between serif and sans serif fonts, there are also script fonts which are designed to look like handwriting or calligraphy and quirky fonts. These tend to be used on displays and advertisements rather than for a prolonged piece of copy and are attention-grabbing and may be appropriate for the subject.

INFORMATION BOX *i*

Examples of script fonts	Examples of quirky fonts
Mistral	Chalkboard
Brush Script MT	Bauhaus 93
Freestyle Script	CASTELLAR
Lucida Handwriting	Haettenschweiler
Freehand	Impact

When producing an analysis, students ought to be able to comment on the formality or informality of the font used. Certainly when producing your own media text, any fonts used should be appropriate. Times New Roman is a very established formal font and is used in *The Times* newspaper but it would be totally out of place on a poster advertising a theme park or a holiday, both of which have connotations of leisure and fun.

ACTIVITY

Take a look at the following three media texts. Why do you think these fonts have been chosen? What non-verbal communication takes place through the use of the font and the colour?

Figure 1.27 *Into the Woods* theatre poster

Figure 1.28 *The Times*, 'Top banker won't budge over £17m pension pot'

Figure 1.29 First Direct advert

In the examples given above, the newspaper follows the standard conventions for newspaper layout. There is a title box or masthead towards the top of the page upon which is written the name of the newspaper and the article has a headline followed by the written copy. The serif font chosen for *The Times* says something about the formality of the publication. You can also see that it follows the conventional approach for newspapers by arranging the copy into columns.

The *Into the Woods* poster and the First Direct banking advertisement adopt different approaches to those of *The Times*. Naturally, since there is far less copy on an advert compared to a newspaper and it must be easy to read quickly by passers-by, the writing is much bigger and less detailed. A detailed analysis of the use of fonts should include not only reference to the type of font (serif, sans serif, script, etc.) and the colours but should also look at the layout and the justification of the copy. Justification, or ranging, refers to the alignment of the copy on the page. Left-justified copy has a smooth left-hand side and right-justified copy has a smooth right-hand side. Flushed text is smooth on both left and right and is typical of copy written in columns, and centre-justified text is symmetrical from the centre of the page. The adverts in the previous images each adopt different approaches to how the copy is justified. The *Into the Woods* advert centre-justifies the lower text, which gives the copy a symmetrical look, while the First Direct advert presents the bank's name on its side in keeping with the company's corporate image, but the rest of the copy is right-justified starting in the middle of the page.

INFORMATION BOX ⓘ

Examples of justification. Below, an O2/NatWest advert with centre-justification; opposite, a Canadian Toyota Touch advertisement with right-justified copy, and an article from the *Guardian* newspaper which is presented with flushed copy and typical of newspapers, text in columns.

Figure 1.30 O2/NatWest advert

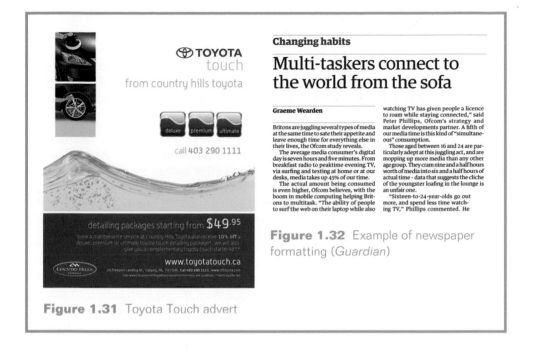

Figure 1.31 Toyota Touch advert

Changing habits

Multi-taskers connect to the world from the sofa

Graeme Wearden

Britons are juggling several types of media at the same time to sate their appetite and leave enough time for everything else in their lives, the Ofcom study reveals.

The average media consumer's digital day is seven hours and five minutes. From breakfast radio to peaktime evening TV, via surfing and texting at home or at our desks, media takes up 45% of our time.

The actual amount being consumed is even higher, Ofcom believes, with the boom in mobile computing helping Britons to multitask. "The ability of people to surf the web on their laptop while also watching TV has given people a licence to roam while staying connected," said Peter Phillips, Ofcom's strategy and market developments partner. A fifth of our media time is this kind of "simultaneous" consumption.

Those aged between 16 and 24 are particularly adept at this juggling act, and are mopping up more media than any other age group. They cram nine and a half hours worth of media into six and a half hours of actual time - data that suggests the cliche of the youngster loafing in the lounge is an unfair one.

"Sixteen-to-24-year-olds go out more, and spend less time watching TV," Phillips commented. He

Figure 1.32 Example of newspaper formatting (*Guardian*)

There is of course no all-encompassing rule for the presentation of copy in most media texts, although in many cases conventional wisdom is not to stray too far from the accepted norms and so columns, headlines in larger writing, etc. are the established presentational devices. However, as the *Into the Woods* and Toyota adverts show, some texts use a variety of sizes, fonts and colours. Given that these are adverts whose purpose is to present their message in a memorable, simple and eye-catching way, then it not surprising that they are more colourful and varied in their presentation.

Audio codes

If you have ever made your own media text, you may know just how frustrating sound can be. Just as the camera does not see things in the same way that the human eye does, then microphones do not hear in the same way that the human ear does. The 'silence' you thought was there when you filmed outside is replaced by the apparent thunderous whistling of the wind or the general hum of background noise upon playback. Microphones have a funny habit of picking up every noise and amplifying it many times.

It may seem an obvious thing to say, but sound is an integral part of the communication which takes place in media. It has been said by media teachers so many times now that it has almost become something of a cliché, but if you watch a horror film with the sound turned down, the effect is quite different from when there is sound. It simply is not scary! Once you remove the incidental music (which usually begins suddenly so that you jump) and render the horrified scream silent, then the scene loses its effect. If we are being honest, most of us will at one point or another in our lives have turned the sound on the TV down in order to reduce the intended effect of a horror scene. Of course you cannot simply turn the sound down in the cinema, so instead, people have a habit of looking away because sound without vision is equally less scary than having them both. It is the marriage of the visual images and the accompanying sound that makes horror so effective in scaring audiences.

The same can be said of many other types of text too. The film *Titanic* had audiences choking back the tears at its conclusion as Rose lets Jack's lifeless hand go and watches him sink below the icy sea after he has saved her (hopefully nobody reading this, unaware of the *Titanic*'s narrative, is planning on watching it for the first time tonight!), yet without the score – an orchestral version of the film's theme 'My Heart Will Go On' – the scene loses its intended effect.

Most fictional media create an artificial soundtrack and if you have ever watched the 'making of' documentaries which accompany DVD releases, then you will have noticed that the soundtrack you hear as the scenes are being shot consists mostly of the director's voice, often through a loudspeaker, giving instruction to actors, the guns you see fired tend to 'pop' rather than 'bang' and there is no music or voiceover at the time of filming. In fact, the sounds heard at the time of shooting a film, often including the actors' voices, are removed and re-recorded later in a much more controlled sound studio setting. In a famous example of artificial sound being used, the sound recordist on Alfred Hitchcock's classic film *Psycho* repeatedly stabbed a cabbage with a kitchen knife to achieve the sound of Marion Crane, played by Janet Leigh, being stabbed in the shower scene. The verisimilitude, a term which means the creation of the illusion of reality in a media product, of the scene was further heightened by Hitchcock's use of chocolate sauce to emulate the blood in the bathtub; he could get away with this of course since the film was made in black and white.

INFORMATION BOX ℹ

Most of the sound of a film is recorded later artificially. In Figure 1.33, a foley artist records the sounds for a film as he watches the action. Note the different surfaces on the floor so that a variety of footsteps can be recorded. In Figure 1.34, an Additional Dialogue Recording (ADR) stage is shown, where an actor re-records the dialogue from the film in sync with the footage shown on the screen. Very little of what you hear in a fictional piece of TV or a film is the result of sounds taken from the time of filming. The exception to this is soap operas which are recorded in very controlled environments so there is little by way of background sound to interfere and which by virtue of being shown so often have such tight production schedules as not to allow this kind of post-production work.

Figure 1.33 Foley artist recording sound for a film

Figure 1.34 Additional Dialogue Recording stage

Of course in live television and radio, producers do not have the luxury of being able to re-record the soundtrack and so, on occasions, there are errors such as microphones not working properly or unwanted 'rogue' sounds such as sirens or dog barks interfering with live broadcasts.

When you are deconstructing a media text, you should be aware of the two main tools of analysis for sound: diegetic and non-diegetic sound. These terms stem from the concept of diegesis, rather a cumbersome word perhaps but a useful one in textual analysis. It means the environment, or the world created by the narrative. The diegesis therefore of a TV show such as *Holby City* will be the hospital ward and the area of Bristol in which the programme is set. This is an immediately recognisable diegesis as the show deliberately sets out to create a realistic environment which the audience can identify with and which is already part of our consciousness, whereas a science fiction programme such as *Battlestar Galactica* creates an alternative environment, a verisimilitude in which space travel, alien life and technology far in advance of that which we have on Earth in the twenty-first century are part of the diegesis.

Diegetic sound therefore refers to all the sound which is part of the diegesis or the environment in the text. Perhaps a simpler way to refer to diegetic sound is the sound which both we as audience members and the characters in the film can potentially hear even though the characters may actually not hear the sound if, for example, the sound of a phone ringing in an empty room is part of the scene. These sounds include dialogue, vehicle engines, environmental sounds such as crickets chirping or birdsong, gunshots, creatures roaring, doors closing, footsteps and so on, sounds which are actually part of the diegesis. Non-diegetic sound refers to the sounds which only the audience can hear – for example, the musical score, incidental music and voiceovers or narration.

In addition to the evident use of diegesis and sound as an analytical tool to TV and film, the idea is equally useful in the relatively new computer and video game medium. Here, just as is the case with fictional TV and film, a diegesis is created in which the characters, often controlled and operated by the player, exist.

Radio is of course an entirely auditory medium which constructs its diegesis through music, voices, sound effects and silence. Radio drama operates in much the same way as visual drama in the way sound is constructed, with one major difference. Silence doesn't translate well in the world of radio and so a character's actions which are not accompanied by dialogue such as reading a newspaper alone in a room will either occur at the start or end of a scene or will be accompanied by a voiceover or the slightly unrealistic situation in which the character reads aloud. Producers of radio drama have an obligation to their audience to ensure that the programme is full of sound so that even everyday or mundane tasks such as walking, boiling a kettle or dressing will usually have exaggerated sounds.

TV sitcom presents another interesting dimension to our examination of audio codes: the use of canned laughter, that is, the artificial laughter and clapping track which is heard on many comedy shows and some game and quiz shows. Originating in the 1950s in the USA, and invented by Charles Douglass, canned laughter became an accepted feature of American comedy and is still used in many shows in the modern era. American comedy shows such as *Happy Days*, *The Fresh Prince of Bel Air* and *Friends* claimed to have been recorded in front of a studio audience. Certainly much of these shows were recorded in front of an audience but, as is the case with many fictional shows, there were several takes of some scenes, actor errors (sometimes known as bloopers), some location work and special effects which were added later and so what the studio audience saw was not necessarily exactly what the finished episode actually looked like. In any case, the laughter and clapping track would be added later to ensure it sounded as the producers desired.

The laughter track has been used in many British comedy shows: *Only Fools and Horses*, *Fawlty Towers*, the *Blackadder* series, *Father Ted*, *The Vicar of Dibley* and so on. The use of artificial audience response has been controversial since it was first used, with many critics arguing that it falsified the product. However, as Paul Iverson (1994) writes, the canned laughter track became regarded as a necessary evil in American TV; without it a comedy show was almost certainly doomed to fail.

Nevertheless, some notable, and successful, American comedy shows have eschewed the use of the laughter track. *The Simpsons* and *Family Guy* use a laughter track very rarely and only ironically to spoof traditional sitcom conventions. In Britain, comedy shows such as *The Office*, *The Royle Family*, *Extras* and *Outnumbered* do not use a laughter track but each of these has a common feature for which an artificial audience response would be misplaced – they are all deliberately structured in such a way as to lend a sense of realism. This is overtly done in *The Office*, the premise of which is that the show is a fly-on-the-wall documentary, but all of these shows are made in the style of *cinéma vérité* (literally 'truthful cinema') – a documentary form which combines realism and a naturalistic approach with a cinematic style of camerawork and editing.

ACTIVITY

Watch an episode of a comedy show with a canned laughter track and one without.

- What reasons are there for using or not using a laughter track in a comedy show?
- Consider which you find funnier. Is this in any way as a result of the laughter track?
- Do you think that the use of the laughter track suggests anything about the target audience for the shows?

So here we have an introduction to some of the technical codes frequently used by media producers in their work and while this is a good starting point, entire books have been written about the use of each of the areas of sound, cameras and lighting, which emphasises how much there is to each of these codes. As AS level students, you are not expected to know absolutely everything about the technical codes in a product however, not least because when you are analysing a media text, you must be conscious of time, and the technical codes used in the text you are analysing are only part of what you need to be writing about. Yet as we come to the end of this section on technical codes, it's worth reiterating that being able to identify a certain technique in the camerawork, lighting or sound in a media text or the use of an unusual special effect is really only half the story.

Your answers will be worth more marks if, when you identify a certain camera shot, edit, use of sound or lighting, you can also add your personal response by saying why it is there and what the effect is. Remember, and this is true with the overwhelming majority of texts, that what is there in the text is there for a reason. When a director chooses a close-up, or a crash zoom or a tracking shot, it is at the expense of every other shot which might have been chosen; a certain sound or noise is heard in the text because of what that sound specifically brings to the text and the lighting used can 'speak' to an audience just as much as the dialogue can. This is why all that we have looked at in this chapter belongs to the concept of media language – how media texts communicate meaning to those who receive them. In the next chapter, we take a look at two further codes which also belong in the concept of language: narrative and genre.

CHECKPOINTS

When you are analysing a media text:

- Deconstruct! That is, take it apart and account for each of the main elements both as individual items, such as sound, the use of colour, camerawork, etc. and how they all interact with each other to create the text as a whole. And remember that independent thought and your own critical understanding is as important as theory and concepts.

- Don't simply denote (describe) the text, make sure you connote it (explain the denotations) too. When you make a point about a text, say why it is important and what messages the producers are trying to get across to you. Remember that things are there for a reason. If the background is white, it is white for a reason. This reason is *not* because paper is naturally white or because they couldn't think of a colour to use, it is white because the producers want it to be white.

- Try to use technical vocabulary without overdoing it. Certainly you should be familiar with the main shot types, types of sound, edits and so on and use them when you can, but remember that the awarding body are interested in your personal responses and your well-thought-out points of view.

- Try to make your answers flow. Do not make them read simply like a list; rather try to make each point flow on to the next. One of the best ways you can prepare for this is to plan your answers.

- Relax and try to enjoy your work. You are very lucky to be a student of media!

References

Bordwell, D. and Thompson, K. (1996) *Film Art: An Introduction* (5th edn). McGraw-Hill.

Iverson, P. (1994) *The Advent Of the Laugh Track*. Hofstra University Archives.

Nguyan, L. (2005) *The Last Temptation of Thelma*. www.ivillage.com. 15 March.

2 TEXTUAL ANALYSIS: GENRE AND NARRATIVE CODES

In this chapter we will look at:

- What the concept of genre is and how it is used to classify media products
- The usefulness of the concept of genre to media audiences and producers
- How narratives are used in a range of media texts
- A checklist of general points for genre and narrative.

Responding to the media: genre codes

The term *genre* is used to classify media products into groups or categories and, as such, is an important means by which we understand media texts. The term is perhaps most commonly associated with film and television texts, but in fact it can be used to categorise almost any media product available for consumption. It is tempting to think of a genre simply as a group of media products which belong to the same category – for example, rock and jazz in music, or horror and gangster for film – and this is a reasonable starting point, but at GCE level the study of genre is more than simply the categorisation of media products.

However, that is a fair starting point to the topic and in classifying media products as belonging to a genre, it is necessary to identify features which that product shares with other products in the genre. These features may be very obvious, such as the Southern and Western desert states which are the setting of western films or the use of sharp weapons in horror, or they may require a little more consideration and analysis, such as the themes of violence, street life and crime which often form the central feature of the lyrics, and therefore the genre, of rap music.

ACTIVITY

Take a look at the image from the film *Pale Rider* (1985) in Figure 2.1.

It should be clear immediately that the film is a western, but what features can you see which tell you this?

Figure 2.1 *Pale Rider* screenshot (1985)

In this activity, you probably found yourself considering a number of factors in working out how you could see that the image is taken from a western film; these might include the character, the setting, the costumes and the methods of transportation shown: the horse and the cart. These features, which we might expect to see in a media product of a given genre, are often called *icons*, *signifiers* or *generic elements*.

ACTIVITY

Having established that in the case of film, the simplest way to classify the genre of a product is to look at the generic elements, see if you can produce a list of the most common examples of these for the following genres of film.

continued

You should have found some of these easier to do than others. The gangster genre is famous for typically having men of Italian heritage dressed in pinstriped suits and Trilby hats in a city setting engaging in criminal activity and violence. This covers the setting, costumes, types of weapons used and some of the typical actions which might occur, but if we look at romantic comedy, there is less of a formula to follow. If we can say that the cowboy hero in a western wears leather chaps, a Stetson hat, spurs and a waistcoat, what does the hero in a romantic comedy wear? Invariably this will be jeans and a T-shirt or perhaps a business suit, but the costumes by themselves are not sufficient to inform us of the genre, whereas a character dressed in the manner described for the cowboy will almost certainly be part of a western film.

In addition to these signifiers, films can often have another key indicator as to the genre: the people involved. Actors such as Jim Carrey or Eddie Murphy are closely associated with comedy, as are directors such as John Hughes and the Farrelly Brothers.

ACTIVITY

Which film genres are the following people closely associated with? If you need to you can consult the internet. www.imdb.com is a good place to find out about actors and directors.

Actors

■ Harold Lloyd
■ Gary Cooper
■ Ginger Rogers
■ Will Smith
■ Lon Chaney
■ Jennifer Aniston
■ Sarah Michelle Gellar
■ Hugh Grant

- James Cagney
- Jason Statham
- Sylvester Stallone
- Robert DeNiro

Directors

- John Ford
- Wes Craven
- James Cameron
- Martin Scorsese
- John Carpenter
- John Woo
- Tony Scott

ACTIVITY

Conduct some research into the films that are currently being shown at your local cinema.

- Categorise them into different genres.
- What signifiers can you identify in the films? (If you haven't seen them, look on the internet at the trailers, still images from the film or the film posters.)
- Are there any actors or directors who you can identify as frequently being associated with these kinds of film?
- How popular are the genres of the films? Suggest reasons why you think this might be.

These signifiers or icons form a pattern which is repeated in products of a genre over time. However, this approach looks at how a genre can be identified when the repetition of features is found across a range of products. An examination of a single product can often reveal that it has features of more than one genre.

These products, known as *hybrids* due to the fact that they exhibit features of more than one genre, are becoming more popular in modern media as producers seek out new ways of adapting genres and providing a balance in their products between repetition of tried-and-tested (and therefore potentially predictable) formulas and the difference the audiences that consume the products demand.

Examples of this are found across many media types. Films such as *The Terminator* series could be said to have elements of at least three genres in them – action, science fiction and horror – while the *Lord of the Rings* trilogy combines elements of fantasy, historical epic and action.

In music, too, products can often be a blend of musical styles or genres – for example, bhangra is a genre which merges traditional Indian music with a modern dance beat – and an examination of reality TV shows such as *Big Brother* would reveal that it has features of at least three genres.

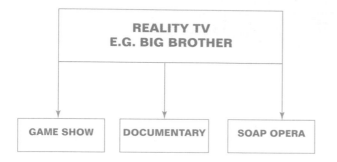

Figure 2.2 Reality television diagram

As a competition, *Big Brother* has the features of a game show and of a fly-on-the-wall documentary since hidden cameras are used to record the activities of the participants in the house. However, given the nature of the relationships within the house and the scandal and gossip the show has generated, it could also be said to have common features with British soap operas, although these are far more scripted than *Big Brother*. Nevertheless, some of the things you find in a soap opera are there in an episode of *Big Brother*.

While there are some features which remain constant in most genres, on the whole, genres tend to develop and change over time. A look at a modern fantasy or science-fiction film compared to their historical predecessors would reveal that thanks to improvements in technology which have allowed computer-generated imagery (CGI) and special effects to become more sophisticated, there are many visual differences but closer inspection might also reveal differences in terms of style, theme and content, so much so that some films from the same genre seem to have more differences than areas of commonality. *Blade Runner* visually shares little in common with *Star Trek* yet both can broadly be labelled as science fiction. These differences in media products which, nominally at least, belong to the same genre have led to a recognition that some genres are made up of many smaller sub-genres which broadly belong to the same 'parent' genre but which establish their own sets of conventions.

Blade Runner and *Star Trek* share little in common visually but both belong to the genre of science fiction.

Figure 2.3 *Blade Runner* screenshot (1982)

Figure 2.4 *Star Trek* screenshot (2009)

Blade Runner with its over-industrialised, ravaged and desolate vision of the future could be said to fall into a dystopian and bleak sub-genre, a warning perhaps of what lies ahead if we continue to plunder the Earth's resources, whereas *Star Trek* falls more into the conventional space adventure sub-genre. The area of commonality which binds the two films together as sci-fi is the presence of technology or science which makes the impossible (to us at least) happen.

Dividing a genre into smaller sub-genres with as many differences as areas of common ground is perhaps nowhere better illustrated than with the genre of horror.

Sub-genres

If you were to say that you were going to watch a horror film at the cinema or on DVD, then the only thing which is certain about the film you are going to see is that there will be violence and death and that it is intended to unnerve or frighten you – whether it actually does or not is another matter. In terms of the visual signifiers and characters you see, there may be knives, axes, haunted houses and castles, ghosts, vampires, serial killers, etc. – there could be some of these, none of these, or perhaps even all of these. However, if you say that you are going to see a certain type of horror film, say, a slasher film such as *Scream* or *Halloween*, then it becomes clearer what you can expect to see – a masked killer, teenage victims at school or a summer camp, for example, stabbing instruments and so on. Visually, however, a film such as *Halloween* has little in common with a film such as *Dracula*, and even less in common with the British horror film *The Wicker Man*, yet all are labelled as 'horror'.

ACTIVITY

Watch two films from the same genre but from different sub-genres and outline their similarities and differences. This comparison should include visual signifiers such as costume, weaponry, transport, the setting and also the stories the films tell and the theme within. Here are some examples you could choose:

- Gangster (*Goodfellas* and *Menace II Society*, or *The Untouchables* and *Lock, Stock and Two Smoking Barrels*)
- Science fiction (*Blade Runner* and *Back To The Future*, or *The Matrix* and *Star Trek*)
- War (*The Longest Day* and *Apocalypse Now*, or *Saving Private Ryan* and *All Quiet on the Western Front*)
- Police crime drama (*Dirty Harry* and *Witness*, or *Heat* and *Lethal Weapon*)

You could do a similar exercise for TV shows:

- Game show (*Deal Or No Deal* and *The Weakest Link*, or *Mastermind* and *Total Wipeout*)
- Drama (*Coronation Street* and *Waterloo Road*, or *Casualty* and *Lost*)
- Comedy (*Friends* and *QI*, or *The Royle Family* and *Little Britain*)

A genre is therefore often not a closed shop which has generic elements that are only found in that genre, but rather any media text that can demonstrate features from a number of genres. Nor is a genre a single set of texts, but something which is made up of smaller sub-genres which can move in and out of vogue. The 1970s and 1980s were regarded as the golden age for the slasher sub-genre with the *Halloween*, *Friday the 13th* and *Nightmare on Elm Street* series of films, while the *Twilight Saga* and even *Buffy the Vampire Slayer* have helped to revitalise the vampire sub-genre in more recent times.

ACTIVITY

Study the following DVD covers for recent films.

- Identify the generic signifiers or icons present in each one.
- How easy is it to identify the genres of the films through looking at the covers?
- A DVD cover must attract the attention of potential consumers and so they communicate important messages about the film. How important do you think the genre of these films is as a message compared to other considerations such as the actors, awards, the special effects, the director or suggestions about the narrative?

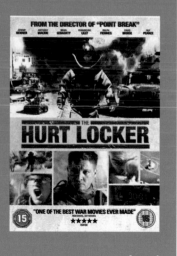

Figure 2.5 *The Hurt Locker* DVD cover (2008)

continued

Figure 2.6
The Departed DVD cover
(2006)

Figure 2.7 *The Bounty
Hunter* DVD cover (2010)

Figure 2.8 *The
Descent, Part 2* DVD
cover (2009)

Genre and audiences

As a concept, genre is very useful to media audiences although many members of an audience may not realise that they are in fact using genre as an analytical tool when they ponder one of the most important decisions they make as consumers – what to consume and what not to consume. For many of us, the decisions about our consumption are simply based upon the genres we like. People know, for example, whether they will venture into the thrash metal section or the jazz section in a music shop before they even enter, because they have already formed an opinion about those genres. The same can be said for visits to the cinema and generally for TV consumption – although, for many of us, TV consumption frequently happens more passively and can result in the thoughtless watching of a TV show without really realising that we are watching it. However, we are unlikely to consciously watch a TV show of a genre we know we dislike.

Genre, or more specifically the audience's knowledge of genre, satisfies the audience's expectations by promising the familiar generic patterns we discussed earlier. Audiences are reassured by this and enjoy having their expectations fulfilled; Patrick Phillips (1996) calls this 'comfortable reassurance' (p. 128), a kind of satisfaction when consuming a media product. High viewing figures for soap operas, the continued popularity of the James Bond franchise and sales of R&B and pop music are all evidence of this; audiences must like something if they are to consume it in such volumes. Audiences also become very familiar with the conventions of a genre and so this saves both them and the producers time and effort when a media product is consumed: a new set of conventions do not need to be established and learned; rather, audiences understand the generic conventions through their prior consumption of the genre.

It can be argued therefore that a genre acts as a means by which audiences are directed towards certain media products. Producers of a new docu-soap on TV, for example, will know that audiences who are attracted to both documentary and soap opera should find pleasure in their consumption of the new product. It is generally accepted that genres can be gendered in their appeal to sections of the audience. Sport, documentary and current affairs are generally seen as appealing more to the male audience, while fiction, fantasy and reality and makeover programmes appeal more to females. Of course this is a generalisation and it is certainly false to say that all the viewers of soap operas are female and that all the viewers of *Newsnight* are male, but these shows are constructed in such a way as to appeal to male or female sensitivities. Targeting a certain section of the potential audience such as a gender, age group, ethnic group or even simply enthusiasts of a certain genre with a product rather than trying to make it appeal to as many people in the mass audience as possible is very common practice. The reasons for this are looked at in the next section on genre and producers.

In his book *Television, Audiences and Cultural Studies* (1992), David Morley lends weight to this argument by suggesting that males are more inclined towards non-fiction, citing what he calls 'men's recurrent expressions of a strong preference for "realistic/factual" programmes' which acts as a 'mode of defence against fiction, fantasy or emotionality, all of which would constitute . . . femininity' (p. 162).

Genre and producers

Genre as a concept is also incredibly useful to media producers, perhaps even more so than for audiences. It is always worth keeping in mind when studying media from the industry point of view just how competitive and expensive the media business is. Budgets for films can run into hundreds of millions of dollars. Likewise producing episodes of TV shows, recording CDs, launching a new magazine or developing new computer games require huge creative and technological input, and therefore financial input, and yet in most cases all of the investment in the product has to be made before a single ticket or copy has been sold. All the financial requirements for the development, production and marketing of many media products have to be met 'up front' and a producer cannot make the first half an hour of a film or the first five pages of a magazine and then make the rest if the audience indicate approval, nor can they develop part of a new Xbox or Playstation game and then continue the game through to the later stages if the first part is successful. On the whole, media requires a huge investment before revenue is received and as such, media, and film especially, is a very financially risky and unpredictable industry to be involved in.

Genre helps producers to cope in this unfavourable business environment. Branston and Stafford (1999) suggest that organising media products into genres helps to 'minimise risk and predict expenditure' in an industry which is 'costly and volatile' (p. 106). There are a number of ways in which this happens.

■ Genre helps producers to focus their marketing and publicity work for their products. With a genre comes a ready-made target audience, fans of, for example, soaps, horror, documentary, rock music, quiz shows, etc. This helps with a type of marketing known as segmented marketing whereby the mass audience is divided into groups with similar interests and desires, and each group is targeted with marketing for products they are most likely to want to consume. This is a more cost-effective and efficient way to market a product than a more blanket marketing approach in which the entire audience is targeted.

■ Second, genre provides a blueprint for producers, a kind of checklist which they can refer to when producing a text of a certain genre. When developing a new point-of-view action and shooting game such as those in the *Call of Duty* or *Halo* catalogues, the producers know that there are certain elements present in all other games of this type which precede the new one they have to include. Getting the balance right in a product between repetition of the tried-and-tested formula while providing sufficient difference so the audience do not feel that they have paid for something which offers nothing new is seen as one of the keys to success for new products. Audiences like similarity and predictability yet they also like difference and surprise. Furthermore, as we have already seen in the opening part of this section, media products have a tendency to mix generic signifiers and to demonstrate features from more than one genre, a trend known as *hybridity*. The concept of genre is therefore useful in hybridity as it allows media producers to see how their products can consist of any number of generic features. This is another way in which products become less predictable and difference is achieved for the audience. However, media products combine generic features with different results. Few would argue that the hybridisation of documentary and game show in TV shows such as *Big Brother* or *I'm A Celebrity, Get Me Out Of Here* is a commercial success. Although opinion among commentators and media writers as to the critical success of these shows is more divided, the hybridisation of science fiction and the western in the film *Wild, Wild West* was met with less success both commercially and critically.

■ A further use of genre to producers comes simply in terms of deciding which products to make and which to avoid. It is knowledge of genre which tells the film producers to avoid making westerns and to make fantasy, comedy and horror films instead. The simple fact is that people do not show the same interest in westerns as they do for these other genres. Any study into the popularity of the western genre would reveal that while in the 1950s and 1960s (the heyday of the cinematic western film) it was the most popular of film genres with up to ten films being made in Hollywood each month, by the 1990s the popularity of the genre with the mass audience had all but gone, notwithstanding the critical success of *Dances With Wolves* and *Unforgiven*, both of which bucked the trend in the overall decline of the genre by winning Oscars for Best Picture and Best Director and yielding good financial returns. The finite financial resources of the media companies are better channelled towards the genres which are popular with the public at any given time even if this leads, as many claim it does, to a repetitive and uninspiring media output of limited innovation and creativity in some quarters.

Responding to the media: narrative codes

The term *narrative* is usually taken as referring to the story in a media text. This definition will inevitably suggest that it refers primarily to fictional film and television but it applies equally to factual film and television such as in news articles and documentaries as well as completely different media types. Songs, for example, often tell stories through their lyrics, as do articles in magazines, comic books and newspapers, and many modern computer games are designed around a central scenario or narrative.

The building of a narrative is something which we have been familiar with for most of our lives. The nursery rhymes we heard and the stories we were told as youngsters were of course built around a narrative and the fact that most started with the words 'Once upon a time . . .' and ended with '. . . they all lived happily ever after' implies that they tend to follow a regular pattern or a structure.

Our response to a media text is shaped partly through our reaction to the narrative. If we watch a TV news report, especially one in which a point of view is expressed by someone being interviewed with which we disagree, we are likely to reject the narrative on the grounds that we take an alternative point of view. Sometimes, a text may present a complex narrative or one which we do not find particularly engaging and so our natural reaction is to dismiss the film irrespective of its other merits such as the cast, use of special effects or music.

INFORMATION BOX

i

The actions of the former prime minister Tony Blair over the invasion of Iraq form a narrative which many people disagreed with; quite literally the 'story' he constructed as a justification for war was rejected by these protesters. This image acts as a frozen moment in the ongoing narrative which began with Saddam Hussein's refusal to allow UN weapons inspection and continued with the invasion of Iraq, the absence of weapons of mass destruction which were believed to be there, the protests over the invasion and culminated in the publication of Tony Blair's memoirs in which he reaffirmed his belief in the justification of the war. This particular narrative has an unpredictable outcome. The way in which the narrative of news items may be structured is examined later in this chapter.

continued

Figure 2.9 Anti-Blair/anti-war demonstration

What is important, however, is that before we can form an opinion of a narrative or react to it we first understand how it communicates its messages to us. A good starting point here is to consider the structuralist concept of binary oppositions. This suggests that our understanding of the world we inhabit comes not from actually understanding what we see or experience in itself, but rather through recognising that what we experience has an opposing quality or force through which we make sense of all our experiences. For example: day only has meaning when it is seen in the context of night; if you won a £10 million prize, you would only be classed as wealthy so long as there was poverty and people with far less money; and people are only classed as tall because the opposite quality of short also exists.

In the same way, narratives in media are often constructed around this presence of opposing forces or qualities, as the following list of common binary opposites and examples of the media in which they may be found shows.

Binary opposite	Examples found in
Police and criminal	News Crime and gangster film Police TV drama
Good and evil	Horror film
Hero and villain	Action film
Relationship and loneliness	Romance film and TV Pop music
Wealth and poverty	Game/quiz show with cash prizes Rap music

INFORMATION BOX

The *Star Wars* films are striking in their use of binary opposites to help tell the narrative. From the presence of the 'good' Rebellion against the 'evil' Empire to the costume of the black-clad and masked villain Darth Vader and the white-clad, blond-haired, blue-eyed hero Luke Skywalker the film is replete with binary images.

Figure 2.10 Darth Vader

Figure 2.11 Luke Skywalker

Another way of approaching narrative is by looking for a structure in the way in which the narrative unfolds. At its simplest, a narrative structure can be identified when there is a pattern which occurs in many texts. In film and most fictional TV that structure can be something quite basic such as a beginning, a middle and an end. Of course this needs a little more detail: in the beginning, the scene is usually set and the main premise of the story is established; various complications and plot twists follow in the middle section before the conclusion when, typically, to refer back to binary opposites again, the forces of good triumph over the forces of evil.

The Bulgarian theorist Tvetzn Todorov offers a more detailed approach to defining the typical structure in a narrative, one in which each of five stages present in a narrative has a relationship with normality or peace, a state which he terms *equilibrium*.

INFORMATION BOX – TODOROV'S NARRATIVE THEORY

Stage 1

Equilibrium (there is a state of peace in which opposing forces are balanced)

Stage 2

Disruption of equilibrium (something happens to disrupt the peace)

Stage 3

Recognition of disruption of equilibrium (key characters in the narrative realise that disruption has taken place)

Stage 4

Repair of disruption of equilibrium (this often accounts for a very large part of the narrative as the main characters struggle to restore the peace)

Stage 5

Return to equilibrium (a better peace is restored, one in which the source of the disruption has been eliminated)

This may appear to be rather a simple theory but when analysing the narrative of episodes of TV drama shows such as *Midsomer Murders*, *Spooks*, *A Touch of Frost* or *Waking The Dead* or a film narrative, it is surprising just how many times this structure is there in the text. However, like many theories we encounter in Media Studies, it is by no means universal. There are other slightly different theories such as that offered by the American screen writer Robert McKee and some fictional TV such as soap operas that do not have such linear narratives with beginnings, middles or ends; rather, they have more continuous narratives in which characters move in and out of the centre of the action, the overall narrative is made up of a series of smaller narratives reflecting the nature of the lives of the characters and like the characters whose lives overlap, so too do these narratives.

INFORMATION BOX – ROBERT MCKEE'S CLASSIC FIVE-PART NARRATIVE THEORY

Stage 1

Inciting incident (an event happens to set the story going)

Stage 2

Progressive complications (for a key character, things get worse)

Stage 3

Crisis (things get even worse)

Stage 4

Climax (things get so bad that drastic action is required)

Stage 5

Resolution (whatever the problem was is sorted out and all is well again)

A final way in which the structured approach to narrative is subverted is when we consider the trend among some film and TV programme makers to dispense with the chronological approach to narrative and adopt a non-linear more complex approach in which action does not take place chronologically but is presented in a more random way. Examples of this are found in the TV show *Lost* and in films such as *The Usual Suspects* and *Pulp Fiction*.

ACTIVITY

Watch a film of your choice and see if you can apply Todorov's narrative theory to the narrative of your chosen film.

Now watch a film such as *Pulp Fiction*, a film from the *Kill Bill* series or *The Usual Suspects* and try to produce an analysis of the structure of the narrative.

ACTIVITY

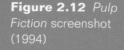

Figure 2.12 *Pulp Fiction* screenshot (1994)

Figure 2.13 *Kill Bill: Volume 1* screenshot (2003)

Pulp Fiction and *Kill Bill: Volume 1*. To what extent could these films be said to subvert the established rules of narrative structure?

A further important aspect of narrative is character. We come to expect certain characters when we consume certain media products, so much so that often these characters have become stereotypes; yet through their presence in the product, we have our understanding of the narrative enhanced. For example, there are certain characters which we come to expect in a James Bond film: the twisted, occasionally deformed and psychotic villain and the attractive and athletic heroine are among the stock characters. Nosey older people and angst-ridden teenagers are commonly found in soap operas.

Through an examination of the narratives of fairy tales, the Russian structuralist Vladimir Propp established the regular presence of certain character types and functions associated with them. Propp's theories of character have been adapted to apply to a range of media products, especially films. His main character types and their functions in the narrative are as follows:

- The hero
- The villain
- The donor (who offers a gift with magical properties)
- The dispatcher (sends the hero on a mission)
- The helper (aids the hero)
- The princess (hero's reward).

When we look at the function of other characters in the Bond films such as Q, M, the unfortunate helper usually assigned to assist him on the mission and who is killed at some point in the film and the leading lady with whom Bond liaises at the end of the film, then we can see how relevant Propp's characterisations and functions are to this particular film franchise.

Narrative is a concept which is not confined to fictional dramatic media however, and the telling of a story is something found in other perhaps less obvious media types. Songs often tell stories and in the ever-expanding world of computer and video games, narratives also operate but with the added refinement of interactivity in which the participant can affect the course of the narratives as the games are being played.

The way news items are presented in newspapers and on television also tends to follow a narrative structure. Typically, a news story will be structured with a summary of the news item first followed by more detail such as the background to the people involved or a brief outline of the events leading up to the story. The opinions or views of other people may follow; this could be from eyewitnesses, family members, friends or experts who are used to give more detail. Television, which is bound by broadcasting codes of practice to be balanced in its news casting, will usually offer a more impartial and neutral stance in the way it presents the news than will newspapers, and so the opinions and backgrounds given on one side will usually be balanced by alternative opinions offered by others. Equal weight should be given to political stories in which the political parties adopt different positions. However, newspapers are much freer to adopt a partisan stance and so the narratives in newspapers are much more biased towards the point of view or the ideology adopted by the newspaper itself.

The final part of the narrative of a news story will be to look to the future. Phrases such as 'the case continues' or 'there will be a statement issued later in the week' are used to provide continuity to the narrative; this works in the opposite way to closure or resolution in the fictional narratives and are the news media's way of keeping the narrative live in the future.

ACTIVITY

Conduct some research into the way news is presented in a selection of newspapers. What do you notice about the structures of the narratives? Why do you think the news in print media is presented in this way?

To conclude this section, most of this chapter seems to have been written in such a way as to inspire you to search for accepted structures and approaches to media texts which are set in stone. The fact is that media texts do not work in this way at all and it is likely that for every text which follows the codes and conventions of a narrative or adopts a regular narrative structure, there is one which doesn't follow these established codes as closely, if at all. In the genre of science fiction, for example, a study of the generic signifiers may reveal that spaceships, laser guns and alien creatures are commonly part of the repertoire, but the film *Back to the Future* contains none of these and yet with its time-travelling car one of the genres it demonstrates features of is sci-fi. Likewise, there is no hard-and-fast rule which dictates that a film, TV show or comic book must follow an established structure. A useful point to bear in mind when analysing a media text from any structural or theoretical point of view is that once the conventional approach has developed and the rules have been established, the rules can be subverted and an unconventional approach can be, and frequently is, adopted by producers.

CHECKPOINTS ✔

When you are analysing a media text:

- Try to classify the text as belonging to a genre and provide reasons for your conclusion. Often, media texts have features of more than one genre in them, in which case the text can be said to be cross-generic.

- Remember that as a concept, genre is very useful to both audiences and producers.

- Examine the narrative and see if it follows a pattern which is typical of those kinds of texts. It is equally likely that your text doesn't follow a structure perfectly, in which case you can argue that rather than obeying the conventions of the type of text, it challenges the conventions.

References

Branston, G. and Stafford, R. (1999) *The Media Student's Book*. (2nd edn). Routledge.
Morley, D. (1992) *Television, Audiences and Cultural Studies*. Routledge.
Phillips, P. (1996) 'Genre, Star and Auteur' in Nelmes, J. (ed.) *An Introduction To Film Studies*. Routledge.

3 APPROACHES TO REPRESENTATION

In this chapter we will look at:

- the role of selection, construction, focus and anchorage in constructing representations
- how the media uses representations
- the points of view, messages and values (ideology) underlying those representations.

Representation is the way in which any form (literature, art, the media) takes aspects of reality (people, groups, places, objects, ideas) and recreates or constructs these in writing, paintings, TV programmes, etc.

The key concept – or theory – of representation is central to an understanding of how media texts are constructed by producers and how they are received by a range of different audiences. In Media Studies representation is understood to be important because of the belief that the image of the world found in media texts shapes the way in which audiences think about specific people and places. In turn this might have repercussions for how particular groups and places are treated.

The study of representation involves all three stages of creating, distributing and exhibiting a media text; therefore representation is relevant across all areas of the course and is something you will need to consider when you produce your practical work.

You will look at specific representations across a range of media texts:

- gender
- ethnicity
- age

- issues
- events
- national and regional identities.

You will find case studies of each of these areas in Part 2.

Key terms

Representation is a form of **mediation** – the process by which the media selects, constructs and anchors a particular view of the world.

Whatever ends up on screen, in a magazine or newspaper, etc. will have gone through a process of **selection** – the media can't include everything and therefore decisions are made about what will and won't be covered. Once these decisions have been made, then the text will be **constructed** through media language – composition, layout, shots, editing, *mise en scène*, etc. – in a way that real life isn't. This **construction** means that media producers can force the audience to **focus** on some things – a headline, a close up, etc. – more than others and attempt to control the way they react. Another way that producers shape audience response is through **anchorage**. As we will see, images are often open to a range of interpretations – they are **open** texts. Adding a caption, slogan or headline to an image **closes** its meaning by making the producer's intentions clear.

Anchorage in practice

The attempt to anchor the meaning of images can be seen in political campaigns with official party political advertising being altered by opponents to change the meaning of the message. This has become increasingly prevalent with the opportunities provided by new technology to alter images and then distribute them via the internet.

The Conservative Party poster campaign 'We can't go on like this' (2010) (Figure 3.1) attracted graffiti when it was posted on billboards and digitally manipulated versions were common on the internet.

Figure 3.1 Conservative election campaign 2010 poster: 'We can't go on like this' attracted a lot of graffiti

 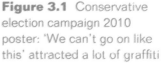

The original campaign poster (with graffiti) is shown in Figure 3.1, while Figure 3.2 provides one of a series of 're-anchored' examples from the internet (many more on mydavidcameron.com).

Figure 3.2 Edited version of original Conservative poster: 'Airbrushing you can believe in'

How effective is anchorage?

It tends to be accepted that an image is closed by providing an anchor but this isn't necessarily the case. During the same 2010 election campaign, the Labour Party produced a poster which used a reference to the TV detective Gene Hunt (*Ashes to Ashes*) to link the current Conservative Party to the previous recession of the 1980s. It had to be dropped when audiences responded positively to the association with the popular character, rejecting the anchored message.

What is representation?

1. Representation refers to the process through which producers, journalists, writers, editors, directors, etc. translate events, ideas and stories into a media text. This might be an item on the TV news, a celebrity profile in a magazine, a soap opera, a video game, etc. It might be fiction or non-fiction; the theory of representation argues that all texts are representations however real they may seem.
2. The media text cannot show the whole event, celebrity's life, etc. and therefore the finished text is the result of a process of selection and construction by media producers. This selection might be based on the most exciting, dramatic, shocking items of a news event, or it might be shaped by the need to show a celebrity in a positive light.

   There are a range of reasons for the different selections which occur, but all the reasons lead to a 're-presentation' of the event.
3. The 're-presentation' is received by a range of audiences who will interpret the representation in a variety of ways.

Representation is a process

In the definition above it is clear that representation as a term doesn't only refer to the finished text but to the processes involved in constructing and receiving the representations. At each stage of the process, key factors of identity – age, gender, race, class, etc. – are likely to have an influence.

The key questions in analysing representations are:

■ How has the representation been constructed (textual analysis)?
■ What reasons are there for the nature of specific representations? (e.g representations of youth, gender, ethnicity, etc.)
■ What effect might these representations have on:

 – The audience which receives them?
 – The group being represented (there may or may not be an overlap between the two)?

ACTIVITY

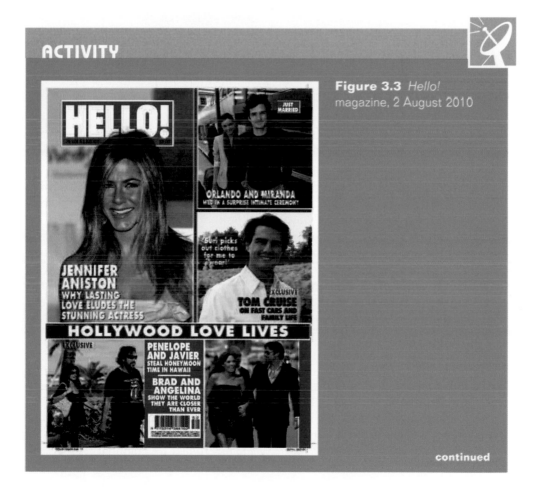

Figure 3.3 *Hello!* magazine, 2 August 2010

continued

This activity is a foundation to build on, to develop your ideas about representation and could be used as a framework to analyse the representation of any media text.

Study the front cover of *Hello!* magazine and make notes on the following questions:

Part 1: Genre, style and content

1. What/who is being represented?
2. What is the media? Refer to form and genre.
3. Provide a brief overview of the technical codes used in the text.
4. What characteristics of the group being represented are foregrounded in the text?
5. Are there any notable absences from the text?
6. Give examples of other representations of celebrities in magazines – are they similar or different?

Part 2: Producers and audiences

7. Who produced the representation? Which institutions are involved? What reasons might they have for producing this specific representation?
8. Who do you think this representation is aimed at? How do you know?
9. How do you respond to this representation?

The last two questions in the above activity suggest that different audiences may read the same representations differently. Even though the producers may have an intended meaning, it is not always the case that this is the one which will be accepted by the reader. Therefore representation is a relationship between the messages the producers want the text to convey and the meanings the audience takes from these representations. To help understand this process we can approach the analysis of representations in different ways; Stuart Hall (1997), a media and cultural studies academic, developed the following model which identifies three different approaches to analysing representation.

THE REFLECTIVE APPROACH

This is the most straightforward approach to analysing representation – it suggests that representations are a direct reflection of reality, holding a mirror up to the world in an attempt to show the world as it is. This approach would suggest that there is very little mediation – the media text simply captures the world as it is. This approach is easier to apply to texts which use realist techniques – which look like the world they're referring to.

Application to Hello! *magazine cover*: Hollywood celebrities are beautiful and glamorous.

THE INTENTIONAL APPROACH

This approach is in direct contrast to the reflective approach. The intentional approach emphasises the way in which producers shape reality through representation and suggests that an audience's understanding of the world is directed by those representations. This approach could be applied to advertising where producers intend an audience to believe that, for example, driving a particular type of car will make you more attractive and successful.

Application to Hello! *magazine cover:* celebrities, although richer, more glamorous and just better than the rest of us, share our experiences of life, good and bad; they are 'just like us'. Therefore despite being 'stunning' Jennifer Aniston cannot find love, despite being a huge star. Tom Cruise is not vain (his daughter picks out his clothes) and his role as father is most important. These narratives are reinforced by the technical codes – all the main stars on the cover look directly at us, establishing a connection with the audience but the level of grooming apparent (white teeth, shiny hair, expensive clothes) in these images again emphasises their distance from the reader of *Hello!* These examples provide evidence that the dominant or intended meaning of the representation of celebrity in *Hello!* magazine can be summarised as: they are like us; money doesn't always buy happiness; family and love are more important than money.

THE CONSTRUCTIONIST APPROACH

This approach is central to the study of representation in Media Studies and can be seen as a mix of the previous two – as well as addressing what can be seen as weaknesses in those approaches. The constructionist approach argues that representations create – or construct – meaning (the intentional approach) but that this meaning is understood through reference to reality (reflective) and the audience's own ability to analyse, accept and reject. Here the audience's response is shaped by its own experience, background and knowledge of the world. It is this process which is the constructionist approach.

Application to Hello! *magazine cover:* Your reaction to this representation is likely to depend on a variety of factors: other information about the stars from other media forms such as gossip sites; whether you like or are interested in these celebrities – if you're a fan of *Friends*, then you may be more sympathetic to this account of Jennifer Aniston's love life; your level of cynicism – is it really likely that Hollywood A-list stars have their children (rather than a member of their entourage) dress them? Your political and moral views will also contribute to your analysis – is the celebrity lifestyle one to aspire to or evidence of an unequal society? As a Media Studies student you could also draw on your knowledge of how *Hello!* magazine is produced – its deals with stars, competition with other celebrity magazines, etc.

The constructionist approach states that a representation is a mixture of:

- *The actual individual, group, place, country, object.* Jennifer Aniston, Tom Cruise, Orlando Bloom, etc., Hollywood.
- *The values and interests of the people and institutions constructing the representation.* This is not always straightforward – individual writers, photographers, editors, etc. may question some of the celebrity stories in *Hello!* but the institution's interest (profit) relies on the representation of celebrities as being glittering but accessible.
- *The reaction of the individual to the representation.* A combination of different factors – age, gender, religion, education as well as psychographic variables such as being part of the mainstream or alternative culture – are likely to determine, or shape, the way you react to celebrity culture.
- The context of the society in which the representation is taking place. In Britain celebrity culture is widespread, with film (and other media) stars seen as important with their lives covered across the media; therefore the front cover of *Hello!* looks quite normal – or natural – to its audience.

ACTIVITY

Figure 3.4 Armani Code advert

Why does representation matter?

The concept of representation reveals that media texts are constructions; they represent the world to the audience. Any media text is mediation, an interpretation of the world, produced for a variety of artistic, economic and social reasons. In the process of mediation and re-presentation, media texts, it is argued, can carry and convey ideological messages.

Key term: ideology

Ideology is a system of ideas, values and beliefs promoted by dominant groups (governments, state institutions, corporations, etc.) to reinforce their power.

The concept of ideology was developed by Karl Marx (economist and revolutionary, 1818–1883) who analysed the way in which the property-owning, richest class protected their interests by representing their privileged position as being natural, even 'god given'. Ideological processes can be found throughout society in religion, the family, education and the mass media. A popular narrative in Hollywood film is the American Dream – the belief that if you work hard and/or are persistent, there is no barrier to success in the US (see *The Pursuit of Happyness* (Muccino, 2006), *The Blind Side* (John Lee Hancock, 2009), *Cinderella Man* (Ron Howard, 2005), *Dragon: The Bruce Lee Story* (Rob Cohen 1993), etc.). This narrative is represented as a direct reflection of an ideal society where opportunity is available to all. It can also be read as an ideological construction: the rich and successful deserve their position while the poor are poor because they do not work hard and lack ambition.

Ideology extends beyond class to other social groups. For example:

Gender

■ Patriarchal ideology (patriarchal society is one which is organised around the principle that the male is superior) makes the woman's role as housewife and mother appear natural; therefore a man who stays at home and looks after children would appear unnatural.
■ As part of the campaign for gender equality, feminist ideology revealed that this 'natural' female role was a construction.

In your analysis of representation you will need to consider ideology in a variety of ways:

- How ideology affects the ways in which we interpret the world – ideologies as values, attitudes and beliefs
- How ideologies are conveyed through texts
- How ideologies have affected the production of the texts
- How dominant ideologies are reinforced and/or challenged by texts.

This final bullet point relates to another key area of representation in Media Studies – the concept of positive and negative representations.

What do we mean by positive and negative representations?

Representations rely on the shared recognition of ideas, groups and places. However, there can certainly be disagreement in the interpretation of representations – whether, for example, they are read as negative, positive, inaccurate or partial images – and it is the analysis of how and why these representations are constructed and received that is important. The concept of positive and negative representations is not a simple one, as can be seen through the discussion of representation as process; audiences are likely to interpret and respond to representations differently.

In considering the question of negative and positive representations we need to consider:

- Are 'negative' representations responsible for the prejudicial treatment of a particular group (perhaps defined by sexuality, class, gender, race, etc.)?
- Can 'negative' representations be challenged by 'positive' ones, which will in turn change people's attitudes and behaviour?
- If representations do affect the way in which we think about particular groups, what does that suggest about the media audience?

Central to analysing this area is the study of stereotyping. Stereotypes are constructed with reference to some or all of the following:

- Appearance: physical appearance (weight, height, hair colour, etc.), clothes, accent and pitch of voice, etc.
- Behaviour: the typical things that people in the group might do.
- Media codes and conventions: in the media the stereotype is constructed in a way that is appropriate to the codes and conventions of a specific media form. This means that a sitcom will use a stereotype in a different way to a news programme – although they will be used in both.

- Ideology: stereotypes are created within the context of what is seen as normal and/or abnormal in society.

It is easy to identify these categories in familiar stereotypes, such as the gay man:

- Attention to appearance, expensive clothes, meticulous grooming, high-pitched voice, exaggerated mannerisms, theatrical.
- Works in the arts, fashion, cares about interior design.
- In romcom and sitcom the gay best friend (GBF) has a specific role of support and nurturing to the female central character, rather than having their own story line.
- The stereotype of the gay man is constructed in contrast to the heterosexual male with more reference to female gender characteristics.

What is more complicated is whether this is a positive or negative representation; the following examples from recent US TV and film all use aspects of the gay male stereotype.

The US TV series *Queer Eye for the Straight Guy* played on the stereotypes of gay and straight men, with a team of gay men 'rescuing' the clueless heterosexual and helping to improve their life.

Looking at the advert for the series in Figure 3.5, consider how stereotypical characteristics are used.

Figure 3.5 *Queer Eye for the Straight Guy*

Sex and the City 2 opens with the 'gay wedding' of supporting characters Stanford Blatch and Antony Marantino (see Figure 3.6). How does the *mise en scène* use stereotypical characteristics?

In addition to defining stereotypes it is also important to consider who is being stereotyped and who does the stereotyping. Tess Perkins (1997) argued that there are six groups which are more stereotyped than others:

Figure 3.6 *Sex and the City 2* screenshot (2010)

1. Major structural groups: these are defined by colour, gender, class and age.
2. Structurally significant groups: ethnicity, artists, scientists, mothers-in-law, etc.
3. Isolated groups: this can refer to social and/or geographic isolation: gays, American Indians, gypsies, etc.
4. Pariah groups: gays, black people, communists in the US, etc. (these groups will also belong to another group in 1 to 3).
5. Opponent groups: upper-class twit, male chauvinist pig, fascists, etc.
6. Socially/ideologically insignificant groups: milkmen, redheads, etc.

Do you think this list is still an accurate reflection (if it ever was) of which groups are stereotyped? Are there new categories which you could add to these groups?

This approach is further complicated if we think about who is representing these groups, as those constructing the representation will often also belong to one or more of these categories.

Negative and positive stereotypes

How many negative stereotypes can you think of?

It's probably quite a long list ranging from seemingly mild or humorous stereotypes such as women drivers, dumb blondes/Essex girls to more explicitly offensive examples such as linking black men and criminality, the Irish and stupidity, Muslims and terrorism.

Choose two examples from your list of negative stereotypes and consider the following:

■ Where have you come across this stereotype? Is it one which is still in use? (It may have developed, been updated, etc.)

- What was the purpose of the use of the stereotype in your examples? (Was it to sell something, create humour, illustrate an argument, etc.?)
- What would be the ideological reading of the stereotype?

Are positive stereotypes prejudiced too?

Now list all the examples of positive stereotypes you can think of. This is likely to be a shorter list and are probably more difficult to come up with than negative ones.

Here are some suggestions:

- Asian children are good at maths and science
- The mentally strong black woman
- African American men are physically strong and good at sport.

Can you think of examples of these stereotypes in the media?

These types of positive stereotypes have been referred to as 'countertypes' which are a deliberate attempt to counter, or go against, the characteristics of negative stereotyping. It is important to consider whether stereotypes can ever be positive or if they always restrict the way in which a particular group is seen. For example:

- How did the positive stereotype emerge?

The examples of racial stereotyping above came about through the effects of racism and inequality – black women had to be mentally strong to raise a family without access to the same resources as white families; the tough black male stereotype emerges from images of slaves doing hard, physical work. Critics of countertypes argue that those problems in society – such as racial inequality – are still there but are hidden by these representations.

- What effect does the positive stereotype have on the group being represented?

As with any form of stereotyping it may limit the choices available to the particular group through pigeonholing them. For example, Asian Americans may find it harder to work in non-scientific fields; black women may be seen as weak if they need help – and somehow not 'properly' black.

- What effect does the positive stereotype have on groups not included?

There may be negative implications for other groups. If Asians are intellectual, then does that mean that other racial and ethnic groups are not?

Linked to the concept of countertypes is the idea of over-representation. This is where one group is repeatedly represented in a particular way – whether positive or negative – distorting the way in which they are seen and understood. Another way to consider this is the effect of under-representation, when a particular group is never represented as clever, funny, fast, beautiful, etc.

Positive stereotypes and countertypes: BBC athletics coverage

Figure 3.7 European Championships 2010 athletics coverage, BBC

Many of these issues can be discussed through the example of sports coverage in the media. Figure 3.7 is from the BBC coverage of the European Athletics championships in Barcelona 2010 and shows the BBC presenter John Inverdale on the left interviewing three successful athletes – Christian Malcolm, Michael Johnson and Colin Jackson. Michael Johnson is from the US, Christian Malcolm and Colin Jackson are Welsh.

ACTIVITY

Looking at Figure 3.7 (it was typical of the BBC coverage), consider the following:

■ What stereotypes are evident?
■ Are these positive or negative?
■ How might this type of representation reinforce and/or challenge existing views about the groups represented? Consider the concept of over-representation.

Summary of representation

■ The media is not a direct reflection of reality but a process of selection, construction and focus.
■ All media texts are a form of representation.
■ Representations are affected by genre and form.

- Representation is a process which occurs between media producers and audiences.
- Different audiences will interpret representations differently.
- The definition of positive and negative representations is subjective.

References and further reading

Baker, S., Allison, D. and Wallace, S. (2007) *Representation*. http://www.media support.org.uk/PDF/Representation%20booklet.pdf.

Dyer, R. (1993) *The Matter of Images: Essays on Representation*. Routledge.

Hall, S. (1997) 'The Work of Representation' in *Representation: Cultural Representations and Signifying Practices*. Sage.

Lacey, N. (2009) *Image and Representation: Key Concepts in Media Studies*. Macmillan.

Perkins, T. (1997) 'Rethinking Stereotypes' in T. O'Sullivan and Y. Jewkes (eds) *The Media Studies Reader*. Hodder.

4 APPROACHES TO AUDIENCE RESPONSE

Audiences are examined in a variety of ways in Media Studies:

1. How the media industry uses audience:

- As evidence of the success of a product through the number of viewers, listeners, readers, etc. for a media text (ratings, box office, sales, etc.).
- To predict and target the market for a media text or product, perhaps through the use of advertising to increase sales or to launch a new product.

2. Media academics are interested in theories of audience:

- To analyse the effects of the media on a specific audience – and the wider society.
- To understand the relationship between the audience and the media.

ACTIVITY

- Do you think of yourself as an audience member?
- List the different audiences you are part of on a regular basis – e.g. for a TV programme, radio programme, website, video game, etc.
- Do you consume these texts alone or as part of a group? How typical do you think this is for other members of the audience?
- Do you think of yourself as experiencing these texts as an individual or as part of a wider audience?
- How much do you know about the audience for these texts (this might refer to audience size, age, gender, etc.)? Are you part of the target audience for these texts?

As an AS student you will need to understand the following concepts of audience:

- The different ways in which audiences can be described
- How texts position audiences
- How different audiences respond to, use and interpret texts, through the application of relevant audience theories and models.

Target audience and mode of address

No single media text is designed to target, or address, everyone. The producers will have a specific audience that they want to address and therefore design the style and content of the text to best attract that audience. This process of construction includes:

- Style and content; use of codes and conventions, genre, narrative, etc.
- A view of the world which the target audience can relate to; this is often conveyed through representation.

In addition to targeting an audience, media texts are constructed to try to position the audience, to make them respond in a particular way:

- Texts make assumptions about the lifestyles and interests of the audience
- Each text has a particular discourse: a set of ideas which shape the way in which we understand the world.

ACTIVITY

Different media texts address audiences in different ways; analysing the mode of address can help to define the target audience.

Use the definitions above to compare and contrast the mode of address of the two magazine covers in Figures 4.1 and 4.2.

You will need to analyse:

■ Visual and technical codes
■ Target audience.

Figure 4.1 *Company Magazine*, September 2009

Figure 4.2 *Harper's Bazaar*, October 2010

Ways of categorising the audience: demographics and psychographics

Some of the most influential ways of categorising audiences have been developed in marketing where it has been driven by a commercial need to be able to accurately predict the behaviour of audiences. In defining their target audiences, media producers consider a range of ways of grouping together the potential audience members. This process has become increasingly complex and combines categories which are objective and measurable and those which are much more subjective.

Demographic data

Demographics are a breakdown of the audience based on a range of easily identifiable, quantifiable factors (data which can be measured). Demographic data was traditionally the main tool used to identify a target audience in media industries. In the last 30 years a related approach, psychographics, has been used in conjunction with statistical data to try to produce a fuller, more detailed description of the target audience. The main elements of demographic data are:

- Age
- Gender
- Income
- Education
- Family relationships
- Geographical location.

INFORMATION BOX – SOCIAL GRADE

Social grade is a demographic classification system based on the occupation of the 'chief income earner' of a household. It was introduced in the 1950s and has remained influential in identifying target audiences.

The classifications are as follows:

		% of population (NRS 2008)
A	Higher managerial, administrative and professional	4
B	Intermediate managerial, administrative and professional	23
C1	Supervisory, clerical and junior managerial, administrative and professional	29
C2	Skilled manual workers	21
D	Semi-skilled and unskilled manual workers	15
E	State pensioners, casual and lowest grade workers, unemployed with state benefits only	8

(Table from the National Readership Survey website which contains many other population surveys used in marketing as well as the readership statistics for magazines and newspapers: http://www.nrs.co.uk/)

ACTIVITY

- How useful do you think a person's social grade is in predicting what media they might consume?
- Why do you think that media industries still use this type of information?
- What information isn't included in the above form of classification?
- How do you think changes in society (gender roles, changing job patterns, increased diversity, etc.) might affect this form of classification?

Classification by neighbourhood

A more recent form of demographic analysis is based on the belief that people who live in similar types of areas (e.g. suburbs, city, country, etc.) will share certain values and characteristics. This method combines a traditional approach to audience segmentation (objective data of where people live) with newer ideas about how personality and aspirations influence consumer choice.

Marketing companies collect information about different segments of the population through the use of census data, consumer surveys, electoral rolls, loyalty card schemes, etc. New digital technology allows an even more detailed record of consumer habits: for example, a PS3 will store information on games played and films watched (DVDs and downloads).

The information generated from these sources is studied for indicators about lifestyle, consumer and leisure habits, education and attitudes, age, employment and ethnicity. This type of audience profiling is a competitive business (ACORN and MOSAIC are two of the most well-known systems) with a whole range of organisations – not just the media – paying for their findings.

INFORMATION BOX – ACORN CONSUMER CLASSIFICATION

This system divides neighbourhoods by postcode into categories and groups (the groups are then further subdivided – for a full list see the companion website). Although based on geographic and demographic data, this form of classification also makes reference to psychographic factors: 'settled', 'prudent', 'aspiring', etc.

Category	Group
Wealthy achievers	Wealthy executives Affluent greys Flourishing families
Urban prosperity	Prosperous professionals Educated urbanites Aspiring singles
Comfortably-off	Starting out Secure families Settled suburbia Prudent pensioners
Moderate means	Asian communities Post-industrial families Blue-collar roots
Hard-pressed	Struggling families Burdened singles High-rise hardship Inner-city adversity

Psychographics

Psychographics is a way of categorising audiences by their different values and characteristics based on the belief that this influences their consumption. Unlike the demographic approach, this is a subjective analysis and focuses on a consumer's personality, beliefs and aspirations. These characteristics may or may not relate to demographic similarities: people of quite different ages, social groupings or life stages might share an 'adventurous' approach to fashion, for example.

One of the most influential psychographics models is VALs (Values, Attitudes and Lifestyle) which categorises the population into eight lifestyle groups. Each of these groups is then measured in terms of their 'resources' (education, income, intelligence, health, energy, eagerness to purchase), ideals and achievements.

The eight lifestyle groups are:

- Innovators
- Thinkers
- Believers
- Achievers
- Strivers

- Experiencers
- Makers
- Survivors.

There is a hierarchy to these lifestyle groups: innovators are defined as having the most resources and motivation while survivors have the least. (More detailed information on lifestyle groups is available on the companion website.)

INFORMATION BOX – EARLY ADOPTERS AND MAINSTREAMERS

Early adopters are an example of a psychographic segment. As the name suggests, they are a segment of the target audience who will buy new innovations in technology when they are first released. For this group the thrill of owning the new product overcomes the high price and relatively poor performance often associated with early models. Early adopters tolerate risk, unlike 'mainstreamers' (a much larger segment of the target audience) who would rather be safe and wait for the tried-and-tested model. Early adopters are ideal consumers in the current technology market where companies need to launch continually updated models to maximise profit; the problem is that they are only a small percentage of the target audience.

The following article identifies how the Apple company has developed a specific strategy to increase the number of 'early adopters':

Whether the object in question is a phone, social networking website or electric car, these consumers have a common psychology: they want the status of being first and they're willing to pay for that privilege. They also have a higher tolerance for risk, as early adoption often means dealing with glitches and investing significant sums in technology that will inevitably be upgraded and cheaper within a short time frame.

'The iPhone's popularity is partly driven by mainstream consumers Apple has converted into early adopters', said Michael Gartenberg, a partner at emerging technology consulting firm Altimeter Group.

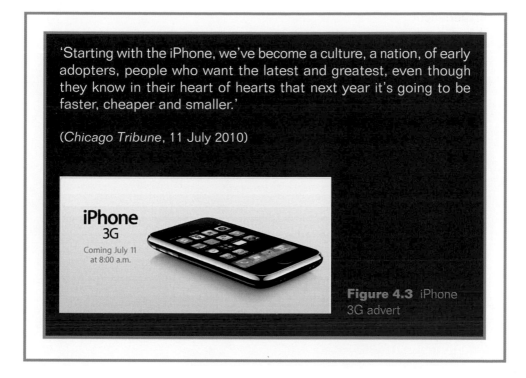

'Starting with the iPhone, we've become a culture, a nation, of early adopters, people who want the latest and greatest, even though they know in their heart of hearts that next year it's going to be faster, cheaper and smaller.'

(*Chicago Tribune*, 11 July 2010)

iPhone
3G

Coming July 11
at 8:00 a.m.

Figure 4.3 iPhone 3G advert

How does this advert for the iPhone 3G attempt to persuade mainstreamers to become early adopters?

Psychographic audience research is becoming more and more detailed with the audience categories broken down into smaller segments for more precise targeting. The following is a summary of recent research into teen buying habits in the US and uses psychographics to break down a demographic group and link it to actual consumer behaviour.

Teen consumers can be segmented into four attitudinal groups:

- *Socially driven:* they have the highest disposable incomes, are the most brand conscious, and spend heavily on personal grooming and clothing to give them status.
- *Diversely motivated:* they are the most energetic, adventurous and cultured, and are equally as comfortable in solitary activities as in group ones.
- *Socio-economically introverted:* they like solitary activities and spend money on products and services for use in these pursuits.
- *Sports-oriented:* they represent the biggest market for sports and home video equipment.

(Research by Young and Rubicon advertising agency, 2010)

- How would knowledge of these segments of the teen market help a media institution to:

  a) Launch a new teen magazine about film?
  b) Increase sales of a video game?

- Choose the segment that you think would be most receptive to the products above and:

  a) Explain why they are the target market
  b) Identify existing products/brands they would be likely to consume
  c) Identify where you would advertise your products to reach the chosen segment of the audience.

- What information don't you have about the target audience which you think would be helpful? How would you be able to find out this information?

Case study

ADVERTISING

A study of the advertising industry demonstrates how audience categories are used in practice.

Olivia Johnson, Planning Partner at the advertising agency McCann Erickson, describes the process of identifying and selling to target audiences.

Researching the audience

In advertising we start off defining the marketing target audience – for example, those people we hope to influence who will deliver the commercial objectives. Commercial objectives differ from project to project, but some examples are as follows. We may want to increase brand share, which in turn means we need to get more people to buy the brand. We may want to get people to pay more for a brand, which often means strengthening the sense that it is a high-quality brand. For service brands, where the 'path to purchase' is more complex than for a grocery brand, we may want to increase the number of people who phone a call centre or go on online to get more information.

Regardless of the commercial objective, we use a number of approaches to define the target group – definitely demographic, still social class (although less so), sometimes psychographic (although this is falling out of favour a bit as people's overall attitudes often don't correlate with brand purchase or a given brand will have lots of different psychographic types buying it).

We also use MOSAIC/ACORN classifications which are postcode-based and group people together according to where they live. The classification is based on the belief that people in neighbourhoods share lots of characteristics (for example, living in Hampstead, North London is categorised as Urban Intelligence – broadsheet-reading, interested in the arts, liberal views on drugs and sexuality, affluent, like to go to interesting, off-the-beaten-track places on holiday. This audience is of interest to you if you're an Arts organisation or an up-market travel company, for example).

Plus, we spend a lot of time looking at brand and category behaviour and explore as best we can the attitudes that lie behind that behaviour. So, an audience is likely to be defined in part by being a buyer of competitive brands, or people who don't yet buy in the category but easily could, etc.

So, the VW Passat target audience was defined as 'road warriors' – middle-ranking business executives who spend a lot of time driving up and down Britain's motorways. They want to drive a BMW or Audi but their company car budget often won't stretch to that. They worry that cars they can afford seem a bit standardised and unimaginative. This is not how they see themselves so they don't want their car to project that image. Hence the Passat message that the cars are 'designed rather than merely manufactured'. In contrast, the VW Polo audience was defined as empty nesters approaching retirement. The children have left home and it makes sense to trade down from a family estate to a hatchback. However, small cars feel a bit vulnerable and scary after a big car. Hence the Polo message of 'solid build and a sense of protection' (source: IPA and APG papers).

TGI and IPA Touchpoints are two huge, industry-wide databases that we all use to define audiences from a brand/category behaviour and attitudinal point of view. We also use qualitative research to understand how people feel about our client's brand, the competitors' brands, the whole category and, indeed, about their lives in general. All of this information is pooled and

continued

sifted to give us as robust an understanding of the target audience as possible.

Buying media space for advertising

When it comes to buying media to reach these people it often gets a bit blunter. Media still tends to be sold via quite broad-brush demographic groups – for example, you can buy 25–40, AB women, or 55–65-year-old, C2DE men. And the main TV audience measurement is BARB data which until recently was still quite crude demo/income type data. So media buyers try to marry the more nuanced audience defined at stage 1 with the blunter audiences offered by media owners.

What helps is that most media owners will measure their audiences in terms of MOSAIC/ACORN profile and both TGI and IPA Touchpoints ask people about their claimed media behaviour as well as brand and category behaviour. So, the media buyer can put together a media schedule of channels, websites, programmes and magazines, etc. that is likely to deliver more rather than less of the audience defined at stage 1.

ACTIVITY

Study the adverts in Figures 4.4 and 4.5.

■ How are the target audiences (as defined above) being addressed?
■ Make reference to codes and conventions, mode of address and link to demographic and psychographic factors.

The safest place to be. Polo.

Figure 4.4
Volkswagen Polo advert

Figure 4.5 Volkswagen Passat advert

INFORMATION BOX – MEASURING MEDIA USE: BARB AND OFCOM

i

BARB (Broadcasters' Audience Research Board) is the organisation responsible for providing the official measurement of UK television audiences. BARB provides estimates of the number of people watching television. This includes which channels and programmes are being watched, when they are watched and the types of people who are viewing at any one time. Viewing data is collected second-by-second and delivered on a minute-by-minute basis for channels received within the UK. Viewing at anything other than normal speed (fast forwarding/ rewinding live or recorded content) is not reported. The data is available for reporting nationally and at ITV and BBC regional level.

Viewing estimates are obtained from a panel of television-owning private homes representing the viewing behaviour of the 26 million TV households within the UK. The panel is selected to be representative of each ITV and BBC region, with pre-determined sample sizes. Each home represents, on average, about 5,000 of the UK population.

Lifestyle Insights classifications have been available for the new BARB panel since the first week of January 2010. In addition to the standard demographic classifications available for analysis, Lifestyle Insights categories allow viewing habits to be analysed according to viewers'

continued

interests and activities. The classifications are collected via a self-completion questionnaire sent to adult panel members. The areas covered are:

- Holidays and travel
- Spare time activities
- Cars
- Grocery shopping
- Newspapers and TV listings readership
- Radio stations listened to
- Computers, communications, internet use, mobiles
- General interests, lifestyle and attitudes
- Mobile phones.

For more information, viewing figures, analysis, etc. go to: http://www.barb.co.uk/.

Ofcom is the communications regulator. From their website www.ofcom.org.uk:

We regulate the TV and radio sectors, fixed line telecoms and mobiles, plus the airwaves over which wireless devices operate. Ofcom is funded by fees from industry for regulating broadcasting and communications networks, and grant-in-aid from the Government.

What we do

Our main legal duties are to ensure:

- the UK has a wide range of electronic communications services, including high-speed services such as broadband;
- a wide range of high-quality television and radio programmes are provided, appealing to a range of tastes and interests;
- television and radio services are provided by a range of different organisations;
- people who watch television and listen to the radio are protected from harmful or offensive material;
- people are protected from being treated unfairly in television and radio programmes, and from having their privacy invaded.

Key term: pick and mix media

The need for detailed information about audience segments is partly driven by the increased variety of media available to the audience today compared to ten years ago. This means that there is increased competition for the audience's attention. The term 'pick and mix' refers to the way in which the audience has much more freedom in choosing what type of media to receive and when and where to consume it.

In 2010 Ofcom published a report on the use of communication media in Britain, and the following article summarises the findings:

Multi-tasking media consumption on rise among Britons, says Ofcom study

Graeme Wearden, the *Guardian*, Thursday 19 August 2010 (full article with links at: http://www.guardian.co.uk/media/2010/aug/19/multi-tasking-media-ofcom-study/print)

Britons are juggling several types of media at the same time to sate their appetite and leave enough time for everything else in their lives, the Ofcom study reveals.

The average media consumer's digital day is seven hours and five minutes. From breakfast radio to peaktime evening TV, via surfing and texting at home or at our desks, media takes up 45% of our time.

The actual amount being consumed is even higher, Ofcom believes, with the boom in mobile computing helping Britons to multitask. 'The ability of people to surf the web on their laptop while also watching TV has given people a licence to roam while staying connected', said Peter Phillips, Ofcom's strategy and market developments partner. A fifth of our media time is this kind of 'simultaneous' consumption.

Those aged between 16 and 24 are particularly adept at this juggling act, and are mopping up more media than any other age group. They cram nine and a half hours' worth of media into six and a half hours' of actual time – data that suggests the cliche of the youngster loafing in the lounge is an unfair one.

'Sixteen-to-24-year-olds go out more, and spend less time watching TV', Phillips commented. He also acknowledged that this multitasking can

continued

mean we devote less attention to any one media source, although this was more pronounced when using new technology. It appears we are simply better at combining reading, landline-calls or TV-watching with another activity without our attention drifting.

Discovering that teenagers are happier than their parents to combine web surfing, phone calls, tweeting and TV is not exactly a revelation, and Ofcom's research does show that some other truisms also still apply. The over-55s are still wedded to their TVs and radios (67% of all the media they consume), while computers, mobile phones and handheld gadgets make-up 58% of 16- to 24-year olds' media diet.

But there are also plenty of surprises in this latest snapshot of the UK marketplace. The gap between the way different generations use old and new media is closing fast. For the first time, more than 50% of over-55s have broadband at home, and a third are sending and reading emails each day.

'Television still has a central role in our lives. We are watching more TV than at any time in the last five years', said James Thickett, Ofcom's research director.

While TV appears to have maintained its ability to hold our attention, 17% of viewing is still taking place alongside another media format – typically a computer or mobile phone.

Smartphone sales have risen rapidly in the UK in recent years, up 81% in the 12 months to May. The research shows this led to much more media consumption 'on the go', although in many cases people appear to be heading straight for Facebook and staying there.

'The average user spent around six hours and 30 minutes on Facebook in May 2010, compared with nearly one hour 30 minutes for users of Google, and nearly two hours for users of MSN [Microsoft] services', said the regulator. Twitter holds second place on the social networking ladder ahead of MySpace and LinkedIn, with traffic to its website up 56% in the past year.

ACTIVITY

Read the article above and summarise the key findings with reference to audience, range of media referred to and changes in media use.

- Are you a typical member of the 16–24 audience segment as described by Ofcom?
- What are the main differences in media use between younger and older audiences?

Summary of psychographic and demographic audience classification

- Demographic data gives objective information about income, age, gender, etc.
- Demographic analysis is less widely used in identifying audiences but is still used for selling and buying advertising space.
- Psychographics are subjective and don't always provide an accurate reflection of a consumer's actual choices.
- Advertisers target audiences through access to databases which collate information about what products we buy and which brands we like.
- Media institutions need to understand who their audience is in order to sell advertising space.

Audience theory

The central part of your study of audience will be to apply and evaluate the range of audience theories which have emerged alongside developments in the mass media. Audience theories and research are concerned with exploring two areas:

- What effect the media has on audiences
- How the audience affects the media.

In turn these areas raise further questions:

- What is meant by an effect and how can it be measured? Is it an immediate effect or one which occurs over a long period of time?
- Is the audience a mass – responding to the media in the same way – or a group of individuals who may respond differently to the same media?

Academic theories of audience can be split between models which see the audience as passive and those which see it as active. The move from viewing the audience as passive to active is also chronological: the earliest audience theories characterised the audience as passive.

The passive audience

THE HYPODERMIC SYRINGE MODEL

This is one of the first (developed in the 1930s) theories of the relationship between the media and the audience. The theory states that the media transmits immediate, powerful messages to the audience and the audience is powerless to resist these messages. In this model the media is received in the same way by all audience members – a mass audience behaving as one unit. This idea was influenced by the contemporary theory of human behaviour: behavioural psychology, which argued that humans were only a more sophisticated type of animal and that their behaviour and responses could be shaped in the same way as an animal's could be. The hypodermic model was also developed at a time of rapid increases in mass media such as film, radio and television as well as the emergence of advertising and marketing. These changes in society provoked a great deal of debate and anxiety about how people would be affected by the new media.

EVALUATING THE HYPODERMIC MODEL

The accuracy of the hypodermic model was increasingly questioned as researchers began to gather more evidence about how real audiences behaved. Audience research became more sophisticated through the use of questionnaires and focus groups; the audience became more 'visible' through participation in the media such as radio phone-in shows, TV game shows, etc. This greater knowledge of the audience made it difficult to argue that all members of the audience reacted in the same way or that they were a gullible mass accepting everything the media told them.

The hypodermic model is the foundation for the concept of media effects – the theory that not only does the media affect the way an audience thinks, but it can also alter behaviour. This theory has most commonly been used to discuss the effect of films on a mass (usually young) audience but now it is often used to analyse the use of video games.

Cultivation analysis

Cultivation analysis is also a model which sees the audience as passive but is more interested in how the media – specifically TV – shapes attitudes and understanding of the world rather than specific behaviour. The central argument in cultivation theory is that repeated viewing of TV programmes which reinforce messages about, for example, crime, violence, gender roles, age, etc. will affect the way people think about these things in the 'real' world. Therefore people who watched a lot of TV were more likely to believe in the truthfulness of that representation rather than the reality. These findings (over a 20-year period) led the researchers to name the effect the 'mean world syndrome' as people who watched a lot of TV overestimated levels of crime and violence in society, had more traditional views of gender roles and more negative views of older people. More generally, researchers identified a 'mainstreaming' effect among high TV viewers – they tended to believe the same things with little difference in their views.

Cultivation theory argues that the media is able to 'cultivate' a particular view of the world over a long period of time; it creates a form of storytelling about the world which the audience accepts.

The most influential research in cultivation analysis had been into the representation of violence. Work has also been carried out into how the media affects the way audiences think about politics and politicians, arguing that the media cultivates a message of cynicism, a response to politicians which has become mainstream.

EVALUATING CULTIVATION ANALYSIS

One of the strengths of cultivation analysis research is its long-term approach, carrying out surveys over – in some cases – a 20-year period. These surveys are based on content analysis of the TV programmes watched and audience responses to questions about their world view. Audience members were not aware of the nature of the research but understood they were taking part in market research.

Criticisms of this approach point out that there is a limited distinction between light and heavy viewers of TV and that there can be no control group because only a tiny percentage of the population doesn't watch TV. The main criticism of this approach though is that it focuses on media consumption without taking into account other factors which would affect the audience's reaction to TV and to the 'real world'.

Key term: situated culture

In addition to demographic categories other influences can shape the way an audience interprets texts. This includes our daily lives, routines, relationships with family and friends, and our upbringing. These factors are referred to as situated culture and critics of cultivation analysis argue that this culture will affect our views about the world: the audience doesn't just get information from the media.

Closely related to cultivation theory is the theory of desensitisation which argues that repeated viewing of violent screen images means that audiences become less affected by them: they become desensitised to violence.

ACTIVITY

Read the report *Violent games 'affect behaviour'* (9 January 2006) from the BBC News website (use the link http://news.bbc.co.uk/1/hi/health/4594376.stm) and identify the following:

■ What points conform to the hypodermic theory?
■ What arguments are made against this theory?
■ What references are there to cultivation theory and desensitisation?
■ How are these theories evaluated?

The active audience

The active audience has become the dominant, or most accepted, model of audience theory in Media Studies with the concept of the passive audience almost totally rejected.

The first development in theories of active audience was the 'Two-step model' in the 1940s which was based on research into the effect of the media during political campaigns in the US. The findings of this research by Katz and Lazarsfeld suggested that:

■ The media alone wasn't that influential in affecting an audience's attitudes but was part of a system made up of other influences including the opinions of friends, family, colleagues, etc.
■ The audience often received the media's message through 'opinion leaders', individuals who paid attention to the media and filtered the information to a wider circle of friends, family and colleagues who would trust their views. Therefore people were receiving the media message even if they hadn't consumed the original text.

This two-step model demonstrated that the relationship between the audience and the mass media wasn't the straightforward, passive one that the hypodermic model suggested. This development was the basis for more theories of the active audience with the uses and gratifications model being one of the most influential.

Uses and gratifications theory

This model, introduced in the 1970s, argues that the audience is active and exerts choice in its use of the media. Uses and gratifications theory suggests that the audience uses media in a variety of different ways to fulfil different needs and motivations. The central uses and gratifications were identified as:

- Diversion:

  - An entertainment, something to do, a relaxation.

- Personal relationships and social interaction:

  - Audiences can become involved in the social lives of the people presented in media texts, perhaps through interviews, gossip or the storylines in fiction texts.
  - Audiences can observe a range of relationships with others and understand the behaviour and dynamics involved.
  - Audiences can learn empathy.

- Personal identity:

  - Audiences can identify with characters represented by the media.
  - Audiences can make comparisons between characters and their own behaviour.

- Surveillance:

  - The media provides information and education, helping the audience to stay informed and to know what's happening in the world.

It is clear from this brief outline that the uses and gratifications model has a very positive view of the relationship between the audience and the media. Here the media is a force for good in the audience's life; it is there to respond to their needs and desires. In this model the audience uses the media and controls how the messages from it are received. This is a complete reversal of the hypodermic model; here the audience is in control and decides what effect – if any – the media will have on them.

ACTIVITY

This activity is based on a survey of media consumption which can then be used to evaluate – or test – the uses and gratifications model.

1. Make a note of the different media you encounter throughout a day. You could use a table like the one below to keep your account.
2. Compile the same information for another audience member – it would be useful to choose someone from a different demographic from yourself so that you are more likely to get a range of media use

continued

Media form	Title/ institution/time	Context of reception	Use and gratification?
Radio	Chris Evans/BBC Radio 2/8.30 am	Car radio/on way to college/compromise choice	I didn't choose this programme – but quite enjoyed the phone-in and quiz

Entertainment |
| Magazine | *Heat* magazine, latest issue | Read at lunchtime with friend | Seems to fulfil all the uses and gratifications above – also provides social interaction |

and response. You could collect the information through interview or by asking them to fill in the table.

3. Once you've completed your research, use the information to write a report which considers the following:

■ The range of uses and gratifications available in contemporary media – give specific examples.
■ How useful you find the uses and gratifications model in analysing the relationship between the media and the audience.

EVALUATING THE USES AND GRATIFICATIONS MODEL

■ Does the model apply when the audience hasn't chosen to receive the media? For example, cinema trailers and adverts, pop-ups on websites, music in shops and restaurants, etc.
■ How much choice does the audience have in selecting media?
■ Are the uses and gratifications available for everyone? How much of this model relies on the ability to access a range of media products – which may not be possible for all the audience?
■ Some parts of the audience (older people, ethnic groups, people with disabilities, etc.) may not be able to use the media for social identity as they are not represented enough in the media to allow this to happen.
■ Some parts of the audience may not find anything in the media to interest – or divert – them.
■ Uses and gratifications theory argues that the audience uses the media to fulfil needs – is it possible that sometimes those needs have been created by the media in the first place?

- Uses and gratifications theory ignores demographic, social and cultural factors which influence audience response.
- Is this model affected by developments in new technology? Do we need to add to the list of uses and gratifications?

Reception theory: encoding and decoding

Early audience theory suggested that the media transmitted messages and meanings to the audience. This assumed that there was a clear message in the media text which had been put there by media producers and which would be received as intended by the audience. With the acceptance of the active audience, this analysis shifted to consider the different ways in which the audience received messages. One of the most useful of these approaches is the theory developed by Stuart Hall in the 1970s, known as encoding and decoding.

This model is based on semiotic (see Chapters 1 and 2) analysis which argues that all signs – or texts – have meanings; the audience's job is to interpret these meanings.

- Texts are encoded with meaning.
- Different audiences respond to media texts in different ways; they receive the meaning – or decode them – differently.
- Both the encoded and decoded meaning will be understood in the context of the social and cultural background of the producer and audience

The different ways of 'decoding' the media text are referred to as readings:

- *Dominant reading*: the audience uncritically accepts the preferred – or intended – meaning of the text.
- *Negotiated reading*: this is the most common reading and describes the audience position of partly accepting the message and partly rejecting it. This could be where the audience member has specific knowledge of a topic covered in the media text and is able to compare their own experiences to the representation. If a documentary is about the reduction in waiting list times in the NHS but the member of the audience has just had a very long wait for treatment, they may accept what the text is saying and see their own experience as unusual.
- *Oppositional reading*: here the audience rejects the message of the text and outlines their reasons for opposition.

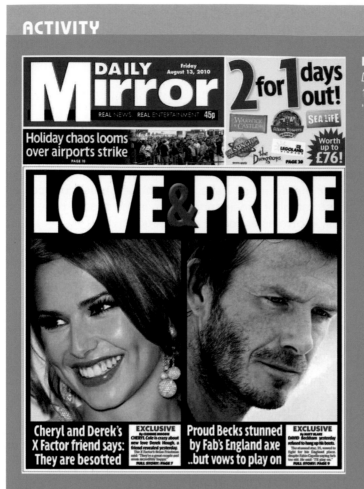

Figure 4.6
Daily Mirror, Friday
13 August 2010,
'Love & Pride'

Study the front page of the *Daily Mirror* in Figure 4.6 and make notes on the following questions about encoding:

1. Identify the codes and conventions of layout and content used.
2. Is the mode of address typical for a tabloid newspaper?

Using this analysis as context, answer the following on decoding:

3. Identify the preferred, negotiated and oppositional readings which are encoded in the front page.

If you found answering question 3 difficult it might highlight some of the problems with this model of audience theory.

- Is there one single message in a text which has been deliberately encoded by producers?
- Would all audiences agree on the intended meaning?
- How do we know if we've found the preferred meaning? It might be that we've brought our own meaning to the text.
- If there isn't a single preferred meaning, then does that mean there is a range of oppositional readings?

Below are some possible responses.

Dominant reading. If we read the front page literally then the preferred meaning is very straightforward: Cheryl Cole is besotted with her new friend; David Beckham is stunned at being told his career is over but remains strong. These preferred meanings are reinforced by the images – Cheryl Cole looking pretty and happy, David Beckham represented as handsome and determined – and also because the *Daily Mirror* is a trusted source.

Oppositional reading. In an oppositional response, the reader may reject the stories on the grounds that they are 'gossip' from unreliable sources or because of the implied value of celebrity in society. In the context of the news, the reader may reject the concept of 'celebrity news' when there are far more important stories to be covered.

Negotiated reading. In this response the reader may believe the story about Beckham because they have read other coverage in the sports press, but they don't think it should be front page news. Similarly, the reader may agree that celebrities are newsworthy – but the story about Cheryl Cole isn't very interesting or dramatic.

In the encoding and decoding model, dominant readings are ideological – not just descriptive. To understand this it is useful to consider the context of the message and reading. For example, a national newspaper with a large circulation has selected these stories as the most important for that day (news values), constructing a dominant reading about the importance of celebrity in society. (For more about the ideological analysis of celebrity see chapters on Representation.)

In evaluating this audience model it is also important to consider how these readings might be affected by audience context – for example, whether you're a member of the target audience, a regular tabloid or broadsheet reader, previous knowledge of Cheryl Cole, etc.

Do you think a regular reader of the paper is more or less likely to accept the preferred reading?

ACTIVITY

The most recent of the audience models referred to in this section was developed 30 years ago when the media landscape was quite different from today.

In the UK in the mid-1980s the available mainstream media was:

- Terrestrial TV: four free to air channels – BBC 1 and 2, ITV 1, Channel Four (launched in 1982). Channel Five didn't broadcast until 1997
- Analogue radio: BBC and commercial stations
- Press and magazines
- Film: cinemas, home video (mass take-up by the late 1980s)
- Home video games consoles (limited market until late 1990s).

1. Make a list which reflects the available media today.
2. How do these changes in technology and in the introduction of new media forms affect the relationship between the audience and the media?

You should consider:

- Reception

  - Where and how do you receive media texts?
  - Are there times when you receive more than one media simultaneously?
  - What are the different platforms (e.g. computer, TV, phone, etc.) you use to receive media?

- Existing audience models

  - Does the increased range of media forms affect the theory of encoding and decoding?
  - Does the emphasis on interactive technology make the audience more or less likely to be active or passive?
  - Do new media technologies provide alternative uses and gratifications?

ACTIVITY

This activity uses the different audience models to construct an analysis of the advert in Figure 4.7.

Figure 4.7 Australia.com advert

1. What assumptions are being made about the VALs of the target audience?
2. How might someone outside of the target audience respond to the advert?
3. What are some of the uses and gratifications available to the audience?
4. Provide a dominant, negotiated and oppositional reading for the advert.
5. How might the theory of desensitisation be applied to advertising?
6. How might you use the example of advertising to argue for and against the effects model?

References and further reading

Blumler, J.G. and Katz, E. (1974) *The Uses of Mass Communication*. Sage.

Hall, S. (1980) 'Encoding/Decoding' in S. Hall *et al.* (eds) *Culture, Media, Language*. Unwin.

Lacey, N. (2002) *Media Institutions and Audiences: Key Concepts in Media Studies*. Palgrave Macmillan.

Lazarsfeld, P., Berelson, B. and Gaudet, H. (1968) *The People's Choice*. Columbia University Press.

part 2

PREPARING FOR MS1: REPRESENTATION AND AUDIENCE – CASE STUDIES

REPRESENTATIONS OF GENDER

5

In this chapter we will look at:

- The distinction between gender and sex
- Concepts of masculinity
- Male representations in the media
- Concepts of femininity
- Female representations in the media
- Feminism, sex-positive feminism and post-feminism
- Queer theory
- Gender and the media industry.

Key terms: sex and gender

Sociologists use the term *sex* to differentiate between males and females, whereas *gender* refers to the distinction between masculinity and femininity. The former is biological and the latter is affected by social and cultural influences. In Media Studies, we are concerned with both of these definitions to some extent and, in particular, how the media represents men and women, the biological groupings, masculinity and femininity, and the cultural or social groupings.

Men and masculinity

Masculinity in the media

Media representations of anything are, to say the least, broad, and pinning down a definitive version of a representation or even a narrow selection of representations of males is always going to be difficult. Or is it? In terms of sex, the biological distinction; that is, men are always represented as men. This may seem an obvious thing to say and indeed since there is a biological measure in operation here, all males, even when they are engaged in stereotypically non-male activities, such as wearing women's clothing, are still males and are represented as such albeit as in this case as males masquerading as females. Of course, the real area of interest for media students which will be examined later in this section is the nature of these representations and what they say to the viewing audience.

When in character, males such as Paul O'Grady, Danny LaRue (Figure 5.1), Boy George and Dustin Hoffman in the film *Tootsie* (1982) did not *become* female; they were always men but were assuming female identities in their acts.

Figure 5.1
Danny LaRue

What is masculinity?

So in the matter of their representations in media, men are quite simply always men and even when they are not appearing as men, they are men pretending to be or acting as women. In contrast to this rather simple and obvious suggestion, however, the representation in the media of masculinity – the social, cultural and psychological state – is a little more complex. We are left initially to consider exactly what it means to be masculine. For some this will conjure up images of the macho or manly character common in 1970s and 1980s TV shows such as *Starsky and Hutch* or *Magnum*. It may also be associated with the gentlemanly demeanour exhibited by British army officers in old war films or by suave and sophisticated characters such as James Bond who make females melt into submission before them. In the modern era, masculinity is perhaps less to do with these traditional stereotypes and is indeed much harder to define.

ACTIVITY

- What is your interpretation of the term *masculinity*?
- Find examples of male representations from magazines; these might include covers, adverts or articles about people.
- What do these representations say about masculinity?

Whatever your thoughts on masculinity, whether it is the tough and manly approach or the more modern perspective which sees men as willing to show emotions, not afraid to wear make-up, taking more pride in their appearance and more in touch with their feminine side, one thing that is certain is that, as a quality, masculinity changes and is not one single thing.

ACTIVITY

Building upon your findings from the previous activity, look at these two magazine covers (Figures 5.2 and 5.3), both featuring males. How do these offer different representations of masculinity? Do you consider one of the representations to be more masculine than the other? Give a reason for your answer.

continued

Figure 5.2 *Men's Fitness*, May 2010

Figure 5.3 *Kerrang*, 9 October 2010

One more recent development in the representations of masculinity came with the emergence in the mid-1990s of the metrosexual male. This was defined by Mark Simpson (1994) in an article titled 'Here Come the Mirror Men' in the *Independent* as a young, single man with high disposable income, living in the city because that is where all the best shops are. Simpson describes him as representing the most promising consumer market of the decade. Arguably, Simpson's prediction was true not just of the 1990s but has also continued into the new millennium as well.

The metrosexual male is not gay but he is often 'confused with homosexuality' (Coad, 2008, p. 13) since the metrosexual and the homosexual male share many stereotypical features such as pride in appearance, both physically and sartorially, this often leading to high consumption of hair care and other cosmetic products, a high regard for women and the refusal, often at odds with more traditional concepts of masculinity, to objectify or overly sexualise them and a nod towards femininity as shown by the occasional use of make-up, wearing of tight jeans (often which are actually women's jeans) and jewellery.

INFORMATION BOX – THE METROSEXUAL MALE

It is argued that metrosexual males are increasing in number and offer huge potential as consumers. From left to right: David Beckham, Cristiano Ronaldo and Zac Efron have all at some time been labelled as metrosexual.

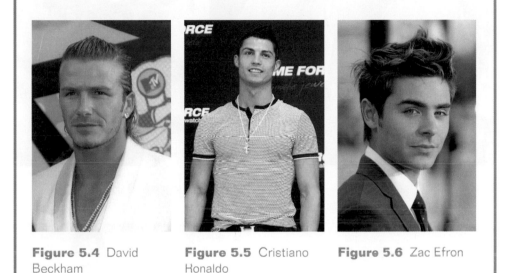

Figure 5.4 David Beckham

Figure 5.5 Cristiano Ronaldo

Figure 5.6 Zac Efron

Media is a powerful means by which messages are transmitted to the public and so how masculinity or 'maleness' is shown in texts can have the power to help define what masculinity or 'maleness' actually is. Let us look back at the representations of masculinity in the 1970s and 1980s, quite at odds with metrosexuality, when it could broadly be identified as shown in Figure 5.7–9.

These images, typical of the earlier and (to be honest) rather dated brand of masculinity, contrast sharply with the modern images of masculinity. What this demonstrates in terms of the messages transmitted to audiences about masculinity is that it is something which has many aspects and that it, like most representations, has the tendency to change over time. We are left therefore with rather a mixed bag of the features of masculinity in the media. Masculinity has at various times in the media been synonymous, perhaps even stereotypically so, with a traditional conception of masculinity as defined by:

- rugged features
- moustaches and stubble
- long hair (the mullet in the early 1980s!)

Figure 5.7 Tom Selleck

Figure 5.8 Phil Parkes

- denim
- open shirts and medallions
- being rough and ready
- action, violence and a general 'toughness'.

And by contrast, a more modern concept of masculinity is:

- smooth features
- short hair
- thoughtfulness
- use of cosmetic and hair care products
- concern for appearance
- designer fashion wear
- a caring and gentle approach.

Figure 5.9 Starsky and Hutch

Naturally, masculinity also has a close association with the biological state of being male but, with the exception of facial hair, these other facets of masculinity are largely cultural and refer more to what society sees as masculine rather than to any biological consideration and therefore are characteristics not confined to men. Women too are more than capable of demonstrating masculinity in how they are represented in the media, an idea which is examined in more detail in the section on femininity.

How men are represented in the media

The main consideration, however, when you are analysing the representations of men and masculinity, or indeed when analysing any representation, will be regarding issues of fairness and accuracy and what the representation is actually saying to the audience. One area which has been the focus of much study is the relationship between males and violence in the media. Earp and Katz (1999) in their study into male representations in the media reveal 'a widespread and disturbing equation of masculinity with pathological control and violence' (p. 5) and they argue that the media is responsible for a 'steady stream of images which define manhood as connected with dominance, violence and control' (p. 6).

Certainly an examination of many examples of fictional TV and film and news articles in newspapers and on TV would reveal this to be the case, but concern is raised by Earp and Katz at how the tendency for males to be represented in this way appears to be normal and an accepted part of masculinity.

> **The media help construct violent masculinity as a cultural norm. Even a cursory survey of media imagery and discourse reveals quite strikingly the repeated and unquestioned assumption that violence is not so much a deviation as it is an accepted part of masculinity.**

(Earp and Katz, 1999, p. 6)

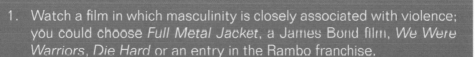

ACTIVITY

1. Watch a film in which masculinity is closely associated with violence; you could choose *Full Metal Jacket*, a James Bond film, *We Were Warriors*, *Die Hard* or an entry in the Rambo franchise.

- How important to the main character's identity is the violence that they exhibit throughout the film?
- What does this say about the character?
- What other characteristics does the character have besides the tendency for violence?

continued

- What effect do you think these representations of males have on the watching audience?

2. Watch an episode of the hit Sky TV show *24*.

- How many times throughout the course of an episode, which equates to an hour of real time in the show, is violence used by males to achieve an end?

Nevertheless, despite the reasonable association with masculinity and violence, the report 'Boys to Men: Media Messages About Masculinity' (1999) published by the pressure group Children Now found that there were six common stereotypical representations found in media of masculine characters, not all of whom are necessarily associated with violence. The table below shows these representations.

Common masculine representations in the media (Source: www.media-awareness.ca)
The Joker is a very popular character with boys, perhaps because laughter is part of their own 'mask of masculinity'. A potential negative consequence of this stereotype is the assumption that boys and men should not be serious or emotional. However, researchers have also argued that humorous roles can be used to expand definitions of masculinity.
The Jock is always willing to 'compromise his own long-term health; he must fight other men when necessary; he must avoid being soft; and he must be aggressive'. By demonstrating his power and strength, the jock wins the approval of other men and the adoration of women.
The Strong Silent Type focuses on 'being in charge, acting decisively, containing emotion, and succeeding with women'. This stereotype reinforces the assumption that men and boys should always be in control, and that talking about one's feelings is a sign of weakness.
The Big Shot is defined by his professional status. He is the 'epitome of success, embodying the characteristics and acquiring the possessions that society deems valuable'. This stereotype suggests that a real man must be economically powerful and socially successful.
The Action Hero is 'strong, but not necessarily silent. He is often angry. Above all, he is aggressive in the extreme and, increasingly over the past several decades, he engages in violent behaviour.'

The Buffoon commonly appears as a bungling father figure in TV ads and sitcoms. Usually well-intentioned and light-hearted, these characters range from slightly inept to completely hopeless when it comes to parenting their children or dealing with domestic (or workplace) issues.

Women and femininity

Femininity in media

Women have always tended to suffer from a rather narrow set of representations in media and usually these relate to a domestic situation which sees women as housewives or mothers, or a sexual objectification in which they are represented as entertainment for males. In fictional media, women's roles have tended to be smaller and fewer than those of their male counterparts and, given the patriarchal nature of wider society, women are less likely to be the source of the leading news articles which relate to politics, business, the law, religion or the media itself, since their roles in these areas tend to be less obvious and again fewer in number.

The narrow representations which exist in the way women are represented in media are found nowhere more evidently than in the area of advertising and in magazines, where women are frequently shown as young, slim, overwhelmingly white and conforming to a very narrow stereotype of beauty with perfect hair, skin and an alluring gaze.

Many theorists, among them Laura Mulvey and Janice Winship, are critical of the way in which the representation of women as sex objects feeds the demand of male audiences. A further consequence which has become of increasing concern in recent years is what such a narrow representation says to young girls who regard the perfect and unblemished models in adverts, on magazine covers and in films as role models and as people to be looked up to.

INFORMATION BOX *i*

The narrow representation of women in adverts and magazines has been highlighted as a major contributor to the rise in ill-health among young girls as they strive to achieve the perfect body. Can the use of women such as these in adverts for male products such as aftershave, men's clothes or on the cover of men's magazines such as *Zoo* be seen as blatant sexual exploitation?

continued

Figure 5.10 Zoo, 5–11 March 2010   **Figure 5.11** IX RocaWear advert

Figure 5.12 Dolce & Gabbana advert

What is femininity?

Femininity, like masculinity, is a cultural rather than a biological state and, as such, differs from culture to culture. In Western societies, some aspects of feminine representations in media have changed considerably in recent years while others have remained fairly unchanged. The representation of the maternal and domestic woman has been a representation which has remained more constant, and when you are looking at an advert for a domestic or household product, you are just as likely to see a female in the advert as at any point in the past. An interesting point to consider here is whether the media by associating cleaning products, washing machines and cookers with women is reflecting society or whether it is helping to shape it by suggesting through the over-representation of women in these adverts that it is the norm for women to assume the chief role in these domestic scenarios.

The other femininity which has changed considerably in nature over the past twenty or so years is that of women when associated with sex. One of the most common representations of people of both genders is a sexual representation where the subject is made to look alluring and appealing so as to be attractive to a section of audience and also to help define the meaning of sexuality; to be a role model for the consumer. Naturally in this last function, as fashions change, so too will the nature of 'sexiness' and sex appeal. Much of the study of how sexual femininity in the media differs from sexual masculinity has led to a conclusion that representing women as sex objects has become the defining representation in the media.

ACTIVITY

- What is your interpretation of the term *femininity*?
- Find examples of female representations from a range of media texts. What do you notice about the way women tend to be represented in the media?

In the following advertisements from the 1960s and 1970s, there is a clear representation of women in a sexualised way but there is an element of exploitation since, in both cases, the products the two texts refer to are aimed at the male market: aftershave and men's jumpers.

More recently, however, femininity has also become associated with a stronger, more independent and confident woman. While still often stereotypically represented as sexy and therefore heavily criticised by the feminist movement which speaks out against the narrow representation of women in this way, the modern brand of femininity owes much to The Spice Girls with their culture of 'Girl Power' and the emergence of successful women in business and the arts.

Figure 5.13 Jade East aftershave advert

Figure 5.14 Drummond sweaters advert

INFORMATION BOX *i*

The modern concept of femininity is quite different from how it used to be. The modern woman is likely to be represented as confident, self-assured and independent in addition to retaining the stereotypical sex appeal.

Figure 5.15
Evangeline Lilly in *Lost*

Figure 5.16
Natasha Kaplinsky

Figure 5.17
J.K. Rowling

How women are represented in the media

As we have seen, there is a tendency for women to be represented predominantly in domestic situations which sees them as housewives or mothers, or alternatively in terms of their sex appeal, albeit in a more confident and independent way in modern media. In the world of TV soap operas, female characters tend to fulfil fairly routine roles in the narratives, either as housewives often in frustrating relationships, bar workers, mothers, nosy pensioners or as the dangerous and rather promiscuous woman who is never far from trouble. These 'stock' characters who appear frequently in a range of soap operas reflect the trend for this particular genre to remain largely unchanged over time, although of course new characters will appear from time to time.

However, one area in which representations of women have changed considerably is in the genre of action in films and on television in which women have been recast as the action hero(ine). Prior to the release of Ridley Scott's *Alien* in 1979, most female roles in action films were largely secondary and passive and not usually directly involved with the main thrust of the narrative; as Laura Mulvey (1975) argues, the male character was the 'active one forwarding the story, making things happen'. In fact the whole dynamic of cinema was seen in terms of, as Jean-Luc Comolli and Jean Narboni (1977) suggest, a natural position of the film viewer as masculine and women's roles in films were primarily for the enjoyment of men. In *Alien*, however, while it is perhaps true to suggest that the patriarchal audience remained, the representation of women changed as Ripley, played by Sigourney Weaver, outlived her male colleagues as her spacecraft was attacked by the hostile alien, killed the intruder and survived, thus ensuring the reconsideration of females in action films.

Later examples of this female action hero are found in films such as *GI Jane*, *Terminator 2* and the *Lara Croft Tomb Raider* franchise. On TV, characters such as Renee Walker in *24* and *Lost*'s Ana Lucia have also helped to present an alternative representation of women. These women are fierce, tough and resourceful and have rejected the violence shown towards women by men by becoming equally violent and adopting many of the tough characteristics usually attributed to male characters. Hilary Radner (2000) refers to these women as the 'psychofemme' and asks if they are the 'sane response to the . . . lunacy of men'. What is clear, however, is that there has been a convergence in these characters between femininity – often these female characters retain sex appeal and in the case of films such as *Tomb Raider*, many of the traditional narrow sexual stereotypes – and masculinity which sees them adept at handing weapons, using them and of an indifference to violence. Rather than redefining femininity, it has been argued that such characters are simply demonstrating 'feminine masculinity'.

Characters such as Agent Renee Walker from *24* and Ana Lucia from *Lost* are the modern female action characters on television, while Lara Croft, Sarah Connor and Ripley (*Tomb Raider*, *The Terminator* films and *Aliens*) represent the feminine action character in cinema. Later, we look at how these characters may be seen to be products of 'post-femininity'.

Figure 5.18 Agent Renee Walker, *24*

Figure 5.19 Ana Lucia, *Lost*

Figure 5.20 Angelina Jolie as Lara Croft in *Lara Croft: Tomb Raider* (2001)

Figure 5.21 Ripley, *Aliens* (1986)

Figure 5.22 Sarah Connor, *Terminator 2* (1991)

ACTIVITY

Consider the following question:

■ To what extent do you think these characters are redefining femininity or are they, as has been suggested, simply becoming 'masculine feminine', that is, women who adopt masculine traits of action, violence and a willingness to use a gun?

Feminism, sex-positive feminism and post-feminism

The feminist movement is synonymous with the idea of gender and sexual equality in a society, in particular the pursuit of equality for women. You are probably familiar with the feminist movements to secure equal pay and conditions of work for women stretching back to the suffragette movement in the early twentieth century. The feminist movement has also spoken out against pornography, the stereotypical representations of women and the male domination of the main social structures in society. As media representations are one of the main ways in which such messages are transmitted, the media and feminist activists and sympathisers have often found themselves at odds with each other.

INFORMATION BOX

i

This image shows how the message within this 1979 Fiat advertisement, which is a typical example of how women were frequently represented in advertising during this era, was met with anger by some who felt that

Figure 5.23
Fiat billboard advert (with graffiti)

continued

REPRESENTATIONS OF GENDER 121

Some of the stereotypical roles attributed to women in media, including those of the housewife, the dumb blonde and the sex object, have been criticised by feminists as helping to maintain the position of women in wider society and as contributing to the continued dominance of men. Recently, however, movements from within feminism and without it have led to an emerging complexity within the movement, which means that equality for women in terms of pay, opportunity and reputation is no longer the sole result.

Sex-positive feminism offers an alternative viewpoint to many of those held by traditional feminists, in that some of the representations of women in a sexual context symbolise not the exploitation of women but an example of the liberty and freedom enjoyed by women to express themselves and explore their sexuality. Stereotypically, according to Wendy McElroy (1995), feminists are represented as lesbians and so many who sympathise with feminist ideologies are afraid to openly support feminist aims for fear of being associated with homosexuality. Sex-positive feminism embraced all sexual orientations and argued that true liberty for women cannot be achieved without promoting freedom for all, regardless of sexual preferences.

Post-feminism, literally a movement 'after' feminism, or as it is sometimes called third-wave feminism, argues that the struggle for gender equality as it is in the traditional feminist ideology has been replaced with a more 'fun' or ironic type of femininity in which lifestyle choices, pleasure and individuality are encouraged. This is of course hugely significant in the way in which women are represented in the media. The representations of women as action heroes, albeit possibly in a feminine masculinity setting, are very much the product of post-femininity. Freedom to wear lipstick and extravagant make-up, designer and often revealing clothes, to party and enjoy themselves, to 'try on' identities and to have fun in the process are qualities totally at odds with those of the traditional, and even sex-positive, feminism, but they are the features connected with feminism in the third wave – a feminism which sees women exploring pleasure and enjoyment as a means of redressing the imbalance rather than engaging in direct attack or confrontation with those opposed to the feminist ideology.

INFORMATION BOX

The Spice Girls and the characters from the film *Charlie's Angels* express their (post-)feminism in ways totally removed from the traditional feminist movement.

Figure 5.24 The Spice Girls

Figure 5.25 Charlie's Angels

continued

Figure 5.26 Women for Equality march, 1970s

ACTIVITY

- Conduct some research into representations of women in media. To what extent do you feel that the post-feminist or third-wave feminist movement is evident in modern representations?
- Is traditional feminism dead in modern media?

Queer theory

Despite the connotations of the name, queer theory is not synonymous with homo-sexuality; although its origins can be traced back to studies into gay culture, it is also connected to gender and feminine studies. Queer theory is of interest to us here in our case study into gender representations as one of its features is a rejection of the simple notion of the importance of gender and sexuality, arguing that as an audience, we do not simply fall into the category of male or female, hetero- or homosexual and so on, and that representations in the media likewise do not always conform to these simple binary opposites.

Chiefly, queer theory, which traces its origins back to the medium of film, is concerned with the notion of characters occupying space outside the mainstream, as outsiders or minorities. The key, however, to a text being seen as a queer rather than gay is the characters' attitude to this sense of difference. Consider, for example, Tom Hanks playing a homosexual character as he does in the film *Philadelphia*. In the verisimilitude of the film, we know his character, Andrew Beckett, to be both gay and dying of AIDS, yet in reality we know Tom Hanks to be neither, but because the film deals with issues of homosexuality and has a homosexual main character, should the film be regarded as a 'gay film' or a queer film?

A film in which the character is queer, as in unusual or non-normative as opposed to gay, is regarded as a queer film. From this point of view, the central issue which is the source of that 'unusual-ness' may be racial (mixed race, for example, in a predominantly single race setting), it may be to do with gender (a cross-dresser), class (working class in an upper-class environment) or disability. It may of course also be a sexual difference but a queer text is one in which these differences are celebrated and encouraged, so that *Philadelphia* which sees the main character striving for equality and justice is less a queer text than a gay text, whereas the film *Edward Scissorhands*, which incidentally does not have an openly gay character, could be seen as a queer film since its main character is a non-conformist, an outsider and non-normative.

A man dressing as a woman and celebrating this non-normative or maybe even deviant behaviour, as Eddie Izzard frequently does in his stand-up routines, could be seen as an example of queer theory in action. So too could the examples of men dressed as women in the opening section of this case study, as, irrespective of their sexuality, they are straying from the mainstream, whereas a character such as Syed Massood (Marc Elliot) in *Eastenders* who struggles with his sexuality and tries to hide within the mainstream is ironically (perhaps despite his sexuality) not an example of a 'queer' character. Queer theory allows us to apply another perspective to our analyses in addition to the conventional representational approaches of masculinity, femininity or sexuality which you may be familiar with and thereby offer another strand of analysis in this more challenging advanced level of study.

Gender and the media industry

Finally, it would be remiss in looking at issues of gender not to spend a moment considering the role of men and women in the positions of power and influence in the media industries. Despite the ground won by the feminist movement and the greater freedom for women, at least relative to previous eras, it is generally accepted that we live in a male-dominated, or patriarchal society in which much of the power and authority in the most prominent areas of life is held by men. These include politics, the judiciary, business and the media itself. This is especially so in terms of the ownership and control of the media.

If asked to consider who are the most influential people in the management, ownership and control of the media, you might come up with the following people: Rupert Murdoch, CEO of News Corporation; Archie Norman, Chairman of ITV; Mark Thompson, Director General of the BBC; Robert Iger, President and CEO of The Walt Disney Company; and George Lucas, Chairman and CEO of Lucasfilm Ltd. Your research might just extend to Jay Hunt, the controller of BBC1 (and as such, junior to Mark Thompson) who according to the *Guardian*'s media supplement is placed at number 13 – making her the highest-placed female on the list of the 100 most influential people in the media in 2010.

The entire MediaGuardian 100 list for 2010 (which can be accessed at www.guardian.co.uk/media/mediaguardian-100-2010) contains only 18 women.

Few would doubt that the media, like most other institutions, is male-dominated in that overwhelmingly the people in positions of power and authority are men. Perhaps this could be at least partially responsible for the nature of both masculine and feminine representations which we see in our consumption of media on a daily basis.

References

Coad, D. (2008) *The Metrosexual, Gender, Sexuality and Sport*. State University of New York Press.

Comolli, J.-L. and Narboni, J. (1977) 'Cinema/Ideology/Criticism' in J. Ellis (ed.) *Screen Reader 1*. London Society for Education in Film & Television.

Children Now (1999) 'Boys to Men: Media Messages About Masculinity'.

Earp, J. and Katz, J. (1999) *Tough Guise: Violence, Media and the Crisis in Masculinity*. Media Education Foundation.

McElroy, W. (1995) 'From a Sexually Incorrect Feminism', *Penthouse* magazine, July.

Mulvey, L. (1975) 'Visual Pleasure and Narrative Cinema', *Screen*, Autumn.

Radner, H. (2000) 'New Hollywood's New Women' in Neale, S. and Smith, M. (eds) *Contemporary Hollywood Cinema*. Routledge.

Simpson, M. (1994) 'Here Come the Mirror Men', *Independent*, 15 November.

6 REPRESENTATIONS OF ETHNICITY

In this chapter we will look at:

■ What is meant by ethnicity
■ Key contemporary issues around ethnicity
■ Ethnic stereotypes
■ Three case studies.

Richard Dyer (1997) argued that 'racial imagery' is central to the 'organization of the modern world', in his book *White: Essays on Race and Culture*, when considering how images of race and ethnicity are important within the media and wider culture.

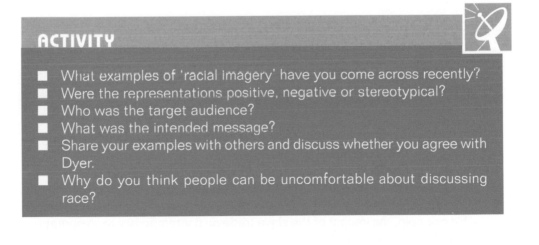

ACTIVITY

■ What examples of 'racial imagery' have you come across recently?
■ Were the representations positive, negative or stereotypical?
■ Who was the target audience?
■ What was the intended message?
■ Share your examples with others and discuss whether you agree with Dyer.
■ Why do you think people can be uncomfortable about discussing race?

Ethnicity is a problematic term, being often understood to be synonymous with race. In fact it is rather more complex, referring to:

■ heritage
■ culture
■ religion
■ ancestry,

whereas 'race' can be defined as referring to the grouping of humans on the basis of heritable characteristics.

ACTIVITY

■ Define your ethnic identity under the bullet points above.
■ Do you feel that you are part of an ethnic group with a strong sense of identity?
■ What media texts target your ethnic group?

Members of an ethnic group tend to identify themselves as having particular characteristics, as distinct from the rest of the population. The labelling of an ethnic group can be the source of controversy, being bound up with assumptions regarding race, identity and prejudice. The Channel 4 report, *Race, Representation and the Media* (2007), observed that 'White British respondents found it hardest to articulate their identity and they worried about using terminology which could be interpreted as racist. Ethnic minorities were more comfortable defining their ethnicity.'

Why study representation of ethnicity?

Our ethnic identity is an intrinsic aspect of who we are and how we see ourselves. To some of us our ethnic identity may not be an issue, especially if we belong to the dominant ethnic group within society (see below). In examining the representations of ethnicity we need to consider:

■ Who is represented, and who isn't represented – for example, certain ethnic groups are more commonly represented than others.
■ The impact of stereotypes on different sectors of the audience.
■ How our understanding of other ethnicities is formed by media representations.
■ How representations evolve over time, but are based on historical background – for example, the impact of the slave trade on contemporary representations of black African characters.

The suggested ethnic groups for the 2011 national census were updated to try to reflect the diversity of ethnicity in the UK (see Figure 6.1). This was an attempt not only to reflect the broad ethnic make-up of the country but also to counteract criticism that broad racial groupings such as black African are too generalised, as members of this group see themselves as belonging to more specific ethnic identities.

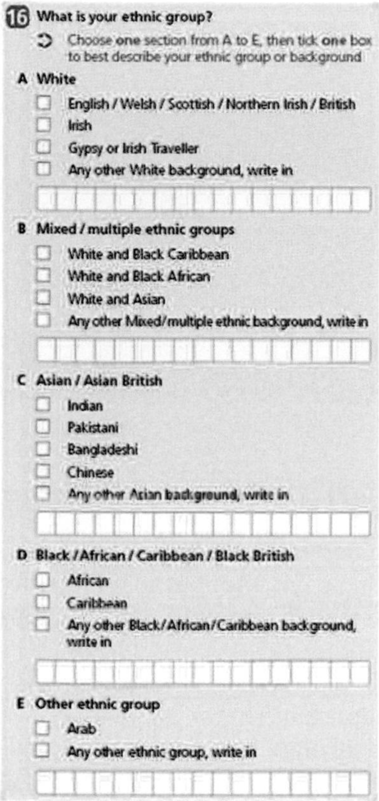

16 What is your ethnic group?

↻ Choose one section from A to E, then tick one box to best describe your ethnic group or background

A White

☐ English / Welsh / Scottish / Northern Irish / British
☐ Irish
☐ Gypsy or Irish Traveller
☐ Any other White background, write in

B Mixed / multiple ethnic groups

☐ White and Black Caribbean
☐ White and Black African
☐ White and Asian
☐ Any other Mixed/multiple ethnic background, write in

C Asian / Asian British

☐ Indian
☐ Pakistani
☐ Bangladeshi
☐ Chinese
☐ Any other Asian background, write in

D Black / African / Caribbean / Black British

☐ African
☐ Caribbean
☐ Any other Black/African/Caribbean background, write in

E Other ethnic group

☐ Arab
☐ Any other ethnic group, write in

Figure 6.1 National census 2011 – ethnicity

Ethnic minorities were estimated to be 8% of the UK population in 2001, projected to grow to 20% by 2050. Global upheaval caused by war, labour shortages, natural disasters and poverty has resulted in waves of immigration having an impact on the ethnic mix of the country. In recent years there has been an influx of Eastern Europeans with the expansion of the EU, and refugees from wars in the Middle East and Africa. These ethnic groups have not been featured widely in contemporary media, except in news reporting which often represents them as being problematic and disruptive:

THEY'VE STOLEN ALL OUR JOBS

(Daily Star)

BOMBERS ARE ALL SPONGEING ASYLUM SEEKERS

(Daily Express)

ACTIVITY

Consider the headlines above from the *Daily Express* and the *Daily Star*.

- How do the headlines represent ethnicity?
- What do the headlines assume about the readership and their attitude to the issue?

British broadcasting and ethnicity

Britain's broadcasting industry still has a strong commitment to public service broadcasting, even though some commercial channels have sought to reduce this commitment. The BBC's equal opportunity policy makes its public service ethos clear, stating that:

- The BBC is committed to promoting equal opportunities for all, irrespective of colour, race, religion or belief, ethnic or national origins, gender, marital/civil partnership status, sexuality, disability or age.
- The BBC is committed to reflecting the diversity of the UK and to making its services accessible to all. This applies both to our output and to the people who work here.
- The BBC aims to create and sustain an inclusive work environment which provides equality of opportunity for everyone.

Source: http://www.bbc.co.uk/aboutthebbc/policies/diversity.shtml

Figure 6.2 All-black *Eastenders* episode (screenshot)

The BBC's first ever all-black episode of popular soap *Eastenders* was broadcast in 2009. The programme included references to civil rights leader Martin Luther King and racism. Ratings revealed an increase of over one million viewers in comparison to the usual audience size for the soap opera.

Prior to this one off, specials of the soap had included episodes featuring all-female and all-Asian casts.

It could be argued that there are now more positive role models within the media such as Krishnan Guru-Murthy and George Alagiah, news presenters on Channel 4 and the BBC respectively, a role which connotes authority and leadership. Meanwhile there has been a growth in the number of media texts which target ethnic minorities – for example, the newspaper *The Voice*, and the magazines *Pride* and *Asian Woman*.

ACTIVITY

■ Research examples of other texts that target a specific ethnic group.
■ Research the websites for some of these publications. Consider how ethnicity is represented in terms of the target audience.
■ What is the purpose of such texts?
■ What factors have led to the increase in the number of texts targeting different ethnic groups?

Figure 6.3 *Asian Woman*, Summer 2010

The digital era has resulted in TV and radio stations specifically targeting ethnic minorities, recognising their value to advertisers but also the needs of communities – for example, BBC's 1Xtra, Prime TV (a British Pakistani channel) and Sunrise Radio. The internet also allows access to websites which cater for a range of niche interests, providing a forum for ethnic communities, with websites such as asiansinmedia.org and blackcommentator.com.

Commentators have argued that we are entering a new era as regards the representation of ethnicity, following on from the election of Barack Obama in 2008 as President of the United States, being the most successful African American in the history of the country (the media tends to largely ignore the fact that he is actually mixed race, his mother being white American).

Post-9/11

Despite many positive developments within the media as regards representation of ethnicity, there have been recent challenges to the more liberal climate. One example of this was the emergence of powerful negative stereotypes of Muslims in the wake of the terrorist attacks on the Twin Towers in New York in 2001. This signalled a new era of xenophobia within Western society, specifically a fear of Islam.

The ensuing conflict in the Middle East and subsequent terrorist attacks has led to the media often equating Islam with violence and fear, with Muslim women being represented as oppressed and victimised. Islamophobia has dominated certain areas of the popular media, specifically tabloid newspapers, with Muslims represented as being outsiders within British culture. These representations are clearly created by a largely white, Christian, Western media, with little opportunity for a Muslim voice.

Media texts exist which seek to represent the viewpoint of the Muslim population – for example, the digital television channel, Al-Jazeera. These texts typically target a Muslim audience on the whole, and therefore have a negligible impact on the outlook and attitudes of other ethnicities.

ACTIVITY

Al-Jazeera English states its mission on its website as 'Building on Al-Jazeera Arabic channel's ground breaking developments in the Arab and Muslim world that have changed the face of news within the Middle East, Al-Jazeera English is part of a growing network that is now extending this fresh perspective from regional to global through accurate, impartial and objective reporting.'

Research Al-Jazeera by visiting its website (http://english.aljazeera.net). Consider how the organisation represents ethnicity in comparison to the British media.

White

The largest ethnic group in Britain would inevitably tick the first box under Section A of the census above, categorising themselves as 'White: English/Welsh/Scottish/Northern Irish/British'. The census breaks down the category of 'white' into subgroups, recognising that 'white' covers a number of different ethnic identities, ranging from English to Irish traveller. Students may be more accustomed to discussing representations of minority ethnic groups than the dominant ethnic group.

The media is dominated by images of the white majority, and as a result it can be difficult to analyse the representations of ethnic identity associated with 'whiteness'.

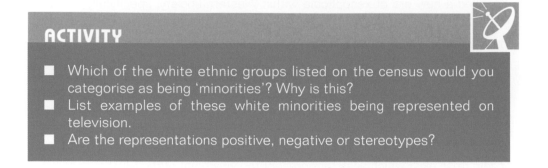

ACTIVITY

- Which of the white ethnic groups listed on the census would you categorise as being 'minorities'? Why is this?
- List examples of these white minorities being represented on television.
- Are the representations positive, negative or stereotypes?

Richard Dyer examines what is meant by 'white' in his book of the same title (1997). His central argument is that white culture has so established itself in Western society that it is seen as the 'norm'. He argues that:

- Whiteness defines normality: anyone who isn't white is therefore seen as 'being different'
- Power and privilege is the domain of the white population
- White people create the dominant images and define how we all see ourselves, having control of the media
- White Westerners do not term themselves as 'white'; for them their race is not an issue – it is normal.

The predominance of media imagery that supports this position is very much taken for granted by many of us. When analysing representations of ethnicity you need to consider the relationship between ethnic groups, and how ideas about normality, difference and power might be implicit in the representations. An example of this can be seen in the following case study on *The IT Crowd*.

Visibility

To what extent is an ethnic minority visible in the media? To what extent do the representations of that group reflect the reality of their cultural identity and position within society? We live in a multicultural society, but the media is often criticised for failing to reflect this and for stereotyping ethnic minorities. In past years the media tended to represent members of ethnic minorities as:

- being subservient to white characters
- problematic – for example, disobedient or even disruptive

- a source of racial tension (typically as victims of racism)
- a threat
- exotic.

When analysing media representations of ethnic minorities it is important to consider the extent to which they have been tailored to suit the ethnicity of the target audience. For example, is there pressure on ethnic minorities to 'whiten' their identities to become acceptable to a Western audience? (See the case study on L'Oreal and Beyonce for an example of this.)

Stereotyping ethnic groups

Minority groups will tend to be stereotyped by the dominant ethnic group in any society. These stereotypes tend to be negative, often growing out of historical attitudes and prejudice, reflecting the balance of power between the social groups. Stuart Hall (1995) identifies three base images recurring in the early years of Hollywood cinema. These types can be traced to the prejudices and fears dating back to the time of slavery in the United States:

- The noble, long-suffering slave-mentality character, who passively allows whites to walk all over him; their devotion to their masters removes any guilt from the white audiences.
- The harmless clown, who is ignorant and fearful, but who has an innate ability to entertain.
- The 'native', who has a primitive nature and thus cheats, is savage and uncivilised; liable to turn nasty.

Figure 6.4 Haven Foods advert

These representations are rarely explicitly used within the media, but can often be seen to be implicitly present in terms of how race is represented. For example:

■ Proliferation of imagery that racial minorities are a problem e.g. gangsta rappers, race tension, connections between Islam and violence, wearing of burqas
■ Popular acceptance of black actors in comedy as opposed to more serious roles, with global success of sitcoms such as *The Cosby Show, My Wife and Kids* and *Everybody Hates Chris*
■ Marginalisation of black characters when featured in film and television drama – rarely taking leading roles.

INFORMATION BOX *i*

Figure 6.5 Morgan Freeman in *Bruce Almighty* (2003)

Morgan Freeman plays a leading role as God in *Bruce Almighty* (2003). This could be argued to show the growing influence and popularity of ethnic minorities in Hollywood. Nevertheless, US website blackcommentator. com noted 'Freeman's God can walk on water. But when He first appears, God is mopping the floors. Yes, He humbles Himself to teach the title character, Bruce, about humility. He then hands his powers over to him, popping in from time to time to save the world from Bruce's bumbling . . .' Is this just a modern update of Hall's servant type?

Contemporary issues

The main accusation faced by the media is that ethnic minorities have been generally invisible, with some ethnic groups being more visible than others. Commentators have criticised the lack of positive role models for members of ethnic minorities, as well as noting how the reality of our multicultural population is not reflected in media texts. Research for Channel 4 in 2007 revealed that 'White British and ethnic minority viewers differed greatly in their assessment of how well broadcasters reflect multicultural Britain.' Generally, white viewers thought they were doing a satisfactory job. Yet other racial groups felt that broadcasters' performance was 'very poor'. The research concluded that in order to better serve their needs, ethnic minority viewers desire:

- More ethnic minority characters/actors in the mainstream in leading roles, not as token representatives of their group
- Realistic storylines
- Mainstream programming with ensemble, multi-ethnic casts (not just one black or Asian character in isolation)
- Ethnic minority programmes shown in prime time
- More ethnic minorities recruited into the industry and promoted to positions of power within it, to facilitate better writing, producing and casting of multicultural programmes (http://www.channel4.com/about4/pdf/race-representation-media.pdf).

Case study 1
L'OREAL – ADVERTISING AND ETHNICITY

L'Oreal recruited actor Freida Pinto, fresh from her success in *Slumdog Millionaire*, to be the new face of the beauty company in 2009. She was featured in international advertising campaigns.

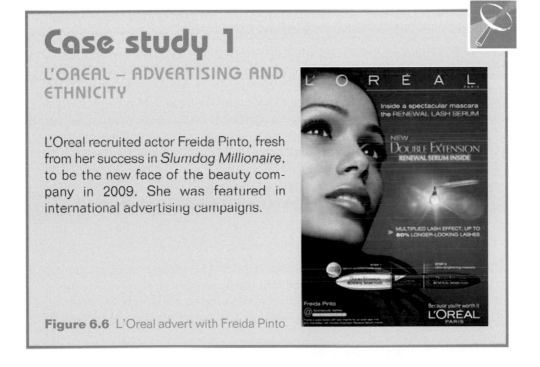

Figure 6.6 L'Oreal advert with Freida Pinto

- How is media language used to create a representation of Freida Pinto? Consider camera shot and framing, use of colour, composition of the advert, facial expression and use of lighting.
- What connotations are suggested by this image?
- What do the image and connotations suggest about the product?
- How does this help market the product to the target audience?
- Who is the target audience?
- How important is Freida Pinto's ethnicity in this advert?

This advert is dominated by a blue/gold colour palette, with connotations of heat and exoticism. Gold signifies wealth, and the contrasting deep blue of the surrounding sky suggests a tropical setting. The droplet (of serum) is intensely golden, forming the image of the sun against the blue sky. The exotic setting is further enhanced by the tropical foliage which frames the image of the mascara. Against this backdrop, Freida Pinto gazes intensely into the distance, perhaps suggesting wistfulness and yearning. She appears sensual, with her lips parted and glossy, lighting being used to accentuate this and to heighten the sense of heat.

The advert clearly constructs an image of exoticism, using *intertextuality* in appealing to the audience's knowledge of the actor's role in *Slumdog Millionaire*, with the tropical setting and evocative sense of longing. This is a romantic image which draws on the narrative of the film in suggesting a woman in need, whether it is to be rescued, or for a man (or even for L'Oreal's mascara). This echoes the stereotype of Asian women as being victims and needing to be rescued from their plight (whether it be poverty, arranged marriages or from the hands of men). Nevertheless, it can also be seen as a positive move that companies such as L'Oreal are seeking to use models from various ethnic groups to appeal to their target audience.

Mode of address

This advert draws on the audience's prior knowledge in constructing an evocative image of desire and the exotic. A low-angle shot positions the reader to look up to Pinto's face, yet she looks away from us, creating an image of mystique and remoteness. The audience are positioned to simultaneously recognise the narrative implicit in this mysterious image, but also to aspire to this image of exotic beauty, being literally positioned below Pinto's gaze. The familiar slogan 'Because you're worth it' addresses the audience directly, reflecting this promise of riches and reward implicit in 'worth' reflected in the golden imagery.

Race controversy

It is clearly in the interests of multinational businesses such as L'Oreal to use a wide range of ethnic representations, given the multicultural nature of key markets in the West, and the emergence of new markets in the East, including India. Nevertheless, the French company has had a bumpy ride in coming to terms with the multicultural global market, having lost a long-running court case in 2009 when it was revealed that they had specifically recruited an all-white sales promotion team, barring anyone of colour from taking part.

Beyonce was the subject of controversy when featured in an advertising campaign for L'Oreal in 2008 (see Figure 6.7). The advert for a hair high-lighting product depicted her with strawberry blonde hair and pale skin. The company were attacked for digitally lightening her skin, although they denied the allegations. Gossip website TMZ launched an online poll asking if the whitening is 'a slap to blacks' while the *New York Post* attacked the advert with the headline 'Beyonce The Pale'. *The Voice*, a newspaper for the British Afro-Caribbean community, noted that the most recent L'Oreal advert features a much darker Beyonce. L'Oreal have also placed a short film on Youtube giving a behind-the-scenes look at the making of a lip gloss advert, creating an image of transparency to counteract claims that they photoshopped her skin colour.

ACTIVITY

- Why would L'Oreal choose to use this representation of Beyonce?
- Why do you think the advert was so controversial?
- Look through a range of women's magazines and identify other examples of adverts using non-white models.
- Is their ethnicity of significance given the brand and target audience? Are you surprised by the number of adverts that feature ethnic minorities?

continued

Beyoncé Knowles: L'Oreal accused of 'whitening' singer in cosmetics ad

Mark Sweney
guardian.co.uk, Friday 8 August 2008 09.09 BST
Article history

Beyoncé Knowles: in person (left) and in the L'Oreal ad (right)

Cosmetics company L'Oreal has been accused of "whitening" singer Beyoncé Knowles' skin colour in a series of press ads in women's magazines in the US.

The ads, for L'Oreal Paris' Feria hair colour product, feature in the September editions of Elle, Allure and Essence magazines in the US.

In the ads the 26-year-old star, who is married to rapper Jay Z, appears to be much whiter than typical pictures of the singer-cum-actress.

There has been a backlash in the US over the images. The New York post said that the "digital lightening" made her "virtually unrecognisable".

Gossip website TMZ described the Beyoncé images as "bleached out" and "Photoshopped", launching an online poll to ask if the whitening was "a slap to blacks?".

However, L'Oreal maintained there has been no lightening of the singer's complexion in the ads.

"We highly value our relationship with Ms Knowles. It is categorically untrue that L'Oreal Paris altered Ms Knowles' features or skin tone in the campaign for Feria hair color," the company said in a statement.

Knowles has worked with the cosmetics company since 2001.

This 2008 advert caused controversy, as shown by this article in the *Guardian*.

Figure 6.7 Press coverage of backlash over L'Oreal advert with Beyonce

Case study 2
THE IT CROWD

Figure 6.8 *The IT Crowd* screenshot

The IT Crowd is a long-running sitcom broadcast on Channel 4 (episodes available on 4OD), first broadcast in 2006. Channel 4 as a public service broadcaster has always had a strong policy commitment to diversity, and being a 'platform for voices outside the establishment' (http://www. channel4.com/corporate/4producers/commissioning/commissioning_4. html). The narrative revolves around the IT department of Reynholm Industries, centring on three characters: Roy, Jen and Moss. Roy and Moss are both IT technicians while Jen is their manager, despite the fact that she knows nothing about IT. The head of Reynholm Industries is the unhinged Douglas Reynholm.

continued

At a first glance the text seems unproblematic in terms of representation of ethnicity. What is easy to overlook is that the central characters represent a range of minority groups: Roy is Irish, Moss is mixed-race black British and Jen is female. Gender is a key source of comedy within the sitcom, but issues regarding ethnicity are absent. In this respect *The IT Crowd* is typical of contemporary comedy and sitcoms, as ethnicity is no longer the source of humour, reinforcing prejudice and often racist attitudes as in sitcoms from the 1970s such as *Mind Your Language* and *Love Thy Neighbour*. The casting of *The IT Crowd* reflects more progressive times, as the central characters represent diverse social groups.

The IT Crowd can actually to be seen to be an ironic critique on the power structures of our society in its representation of the workplace. In the sequence it is made clear that the head of Reynholm Industries is irrational, incompetent and unpredictable; yet he is in charge and has all the power. He clearly has no idea about IT and yet appoints Jen as manager of the IT department. This situation subverts the dominant representation of whiteness in Western society, representing the powerful white English male as incompetent.

Jen is exiled from the glamour of the 34th floor of the building to the basement, which is represented as a hell, dilapidated and threatening, far from the centre of power. It is here that we find Moss and Roy, literally at the bottom of the power structure, exiled and disgruntled, in a chaotic office. The three characters are outcasts, and the programme follows their efforts to be accepted and integrated with the rest of society. The programme does not explicitly link this to their minority status, yet perpetually represents power in the hands of the white boss, mismanaging the company, while Jen, Moss and Roy can never escape from their 'ghetto'.

Audience positioning is important in terms of how ethnicity is represented in the text. We are aligned with Moss and Roy, the ethnic minority characters, as they reveal their insecurities and anxieties to us in contrast to the distancing techniques which are used in positioning us regarding Reynholm. Reynholm is presented unsympathetically, indeed as a caricature of a white, middle-aged, power-crazed boss.

He shouts rather than talks, and looks very unprepossessing with his pin-striped suit and slicked-back hair, lacking any humanising characteristics and taking up very little screen time. Moss and Roy are given most of the screen time, along with Jen, displaying characteristics which enable the audience to identify with them, as well as feeling sorry for them. Roy is desperate to impress Jen on first meeting, applying antiperspirant to his T-shirt and face, as he struggles with his social skills. Moss is childlike and means well, but undermines Roy's efforts to impress as he fails to understand why Roy is talking in such a strange voice about Tolstoy. Moss and Roy are essentially childlike in much of their appearance and behaviour, Moss particularly so, living at home with his mother, who packs his lunch and dresses him.

Sitcoms have been an area of the media that has featured characters from ethnic minorities more extensively than many other broadcasting genres. One point of view questions why ethnic minorities are more acceptable in comedies than serious programming, suggesting that humour helps us acknowledge other ethnicities in a non-threatening way. Social tensions can be defused as we laugh at and with characters such as Moss and Roy.

We could approach the text from a more critical point of view and suggest that it actually works to reinforce certain enduring stereotypes. For example, the Irish have been stereotyped as being lazy, devious, stupid and hopeless by the English. Roy does little to dispel this stereotype in the sequence, as he can barely be bothered to answer the phone and resents having to do any work. He is a slob with his messy hair and T-shirt, and lacks social skills. Moss is a more ambiguous representation: he is freakishly intelligent and a misfit, seemingly suffering from arrested development as far as his social

continued

skills are concerned. Both characters are misfits within the company, in terms of their status, ethnicity and social skills. Yet the sitcom subverts our view of normality, as we learn that their co-workers range from the unpleasant to the deranged, making the IT department seem an innocent and benign part of the workplace.

Sitcoms rely on stereotypes to create much of their humour. In his book *Television: A Media Student's Guide*, David McQueen (1998) observes:

> **Sitcoms tend to provide familiar settings, situations and character types as a recognizable background to the comic excess of exaggerated plotting and performance . . . the use of stereotypes should be set against the comic requirement of transgressing expectations that is fundamental to the success of the genre.**

With *The IT Crowd* the power relations and representations can be argued to satirise our society, while the audience are encouraged to laugh with, and at, the central characters, whose ethnic identity plays no overt role in the narrative.

ACTIVITY

- List other examples of sitcoms featuring characters from ethnic minorities.
- How are these characters represented?
- How is the audience positioned to feel about the characters?

Case study 3

50 CENT

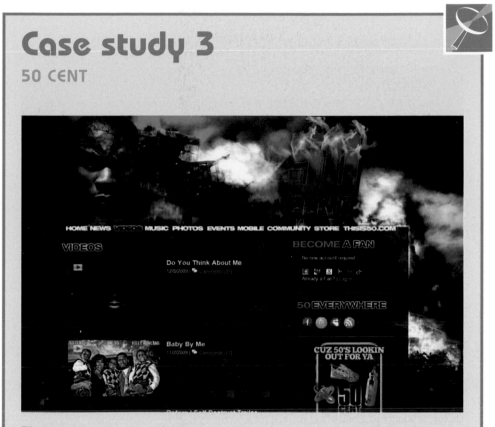

Figure 6.9 50cent.com homepage

50 Cent's website:

> 50 Cent is one of the most successful recording artists of the past decade, having sold millions of albums around the world, and having built an extensive business empire. His name has evolved into a brand responsible for clothing lines, video games, toiletries and even 50 Cent branded platinum! 50 Cent is now a respected business man having diversified away from the music industry in an era which has witnessed a substantial decline in income from record sales. 50 Cent has control over his image, and hence over how he is represented in the media texts he produces.

continued

ACTIVITY

Look closely at the homepage for 50 Cent's website and make notes on the following:

- Make notes about the use of *mise en scène*, camerawork and lighting in the main images.
- What representation is created of 50 Cent?
- How is this representation typical of the star?
- Who would be the target audience for the site?

At a first glance the page is dominated by a contrast between a dark, gloomy palette and the explosive oranges which stand out. The overall scene of the main image is that of destruction, with the backdrop of buildings bursting into flames and collapsed into piles of rubble, perhaps signifying conflict. The urban setting has become a hell with no signs of life, just billowing clouds of smoke rising into the night sky. The artist's logo stands out boldly against this dramatic backdrop, flames rising from the orange letters to further develop a sense of danger and heat. 50's face is superimposed in close-up on the opposite side of the page, looking impassively at the audience. Half of his head is clearly burnt, glowing orange as if he is superhuman, a disturbing and menacing image which pays homage to the *Terminator* films, the science fiction action films in which apocalypse is narrowly averted.

This disaster scenario is promoting 50's latest album *Before I Self-Destruct*, the title of which suggests that the star is dangerous, under pressure and in a state of crisis. The CD cover repeats the image of his half-burnt head, echoing this sense of him being divided between destruction and normality, and also represents him as a hero as he coolly looks at us, despite his disfigurement and the destruction going on around him.

The title of the album suggests that 50 Cent is responsible for this destruction, that he is the source of danger and hence has immense power. This is crucial to 50's image; his music repeats themes of violence, crime and machismo, often creating controversy. In this respect 50 Cent can be argued to reinforce a negative stereotype of young black men – that of being a threat to society, a criminal and a danger. This image is reinforced in the headshot in the bottom left-hand corner of the frame which again represents 50 as menacing, as he is largely hidden in the chiaroscuro, underlighting being used to highlight his mouth area. Again he is looking confrontationally at the audience, signifying self-assurance. The dress codes are typical of this stereotype, wearing a dark-coloured hoody and peaked hat, signifying urban street wear. The images and messages within this text are central to the media image of 50 Cent, with the deliberate courting of controversy caused by his aggressive masculinity. His torrid life forms the subject matter for his music, videos and films; he was involved in drug dealing at an early age, served time, survived attempts on his life and has been involved in lawsuits. His musical persona is that of the outlaw, who is not afraid of anyone or anything, with song titles such as 'Death To My Enemies', 'Guns Come Out', and 'I'm Supposed To Die Tonight'.

Audience issues

Hip hop and rap are forms of contemporary black music which reflect the experiences of and give voice to an ethnic minority who are largely unrepresented in politics and mainstream media. Tricia Rose in her book *Black Noise* (1994) writes that 'Black music has always been a means of cultural expression for African Americans, especially during particularly difficult social periods and transitions . . . it articulates many of the facets of life in urban America for African Americans situated at the bottom of a highly technological capitalist society.' It is clear that a primary target audience for 50 Cent and the hip hop/rap genre is young black men, providing powerful images of success and confidence in the face of the realities of the black urban existence.

50 Cent and other rap stars have a global appeal that clearly goes beyond ethnic divides, appealing to young men who have not necessarily grown up in the ghettos of black America. Rap and hip hop share a similar appeal to youth audiences with other musical genres in perpetuating images of rebellion and non-conformity, which may be offensive to older generations but reflect the issues experienced in younger life: you may live in a small sleepy Suffolk town, but you may still feel disaffected and rebellious.

Cynically it may be argued that the likes of 50 Cent need to create controversy in order to sell product, and that they need to evoke the oppositional readings that many older people would form in response to their music. The oppositional reading formed by older audiences may well be that 50 Cent is a harmful role model to vulnerable younger people, particularly among the black community.

continued

Moral panic

A moral panic is when a media text or genre is blamed for problems within society. The media itself is largely responsible for fostering the panic, with news coverage of the issue which builds a sense of panic among society.

Rap and hip hop have been blamed for the rise in violent crime among the black community. David Lammy, a black British politician, commented on the 50 Cent album *Get Rich Or Die Tryin'*: 'Get rich or die trying is a language of fast cars and faster lives, a language that replaces the social values that once knitted communities together with a destructive law of the jungle, in which honour codes create the justification for pointless spirals of killing and revenge' (http://www.guardian.co.uk/commentisfree/2009/aug/09/black-teenagers-money-matthew-ryder). The panic over the impact of rap music is not just restricted to the white community, but clearly extends to the older generations of the black community.

It is paradoxical that 50 Cent has gained greater acceptance and respect among the white media for his success as a businessman, as reflected in the article in the leading business publication *Forbes Magazine*, which celebrates his business acumen: 'in the comfort of a midtown Manhattan office, just miles from the Queens, NY streets where 50 once dealt cocaine, the glowering rapper whose lyrics are often punctuated with gunshots is nowhere to be found. In his place is Curtis Jackson, businessman. Less gangster, more Gordon Gekko, he ticks through the contents of his portfolio: stocks, bonds, real estate, investment pools, all carefully monitored by brokers' (http://www.forbes.com/2008/08/15/music-50cent-hiphop-biz-media-cz_zog_0818fifty.html).

ACTIVITY

- Focus on how female black music stars are represented, by visiting their websites, watching videos and looking at CD covers. Interesting examples would be Beyonce, Rihanna and Leona Lewis.
- Investigate how black British ethnicity is represented by researching representations of stars such as Dizzee Rascal and Tinchy Stryder.
- Rio Ferdinand has developed a business empire (albeit rather smaller than 50's), diversifying into a range of media including an online magazine, *Rio*. Investigate the representations and target audiences for these texts.

Summary

■ Representation of ethnicity is tied into issues regarding power, status, culture and history.
■ Representations are evolving to reflect the nature of our multicultural society.
■ Stereotypes of ethnic identity can be seen to endure in some texts.
■ Representations can depend on the control that the subject has over the text.
■ Representations are tailored to suit the type of text and target audience.

References

Channel 4 (2007) *Race, Representation and the Media 2007: Research Report*. http://www.channel4.com/about4/pdf/race-representation-media.pdf.

Dyer, R. (1997) *White: Essays on Race and Culture*. Routledge.

Hall, S. (1995) 'The Whites of Their Eyes: Racist Ideologies and the Media' in G. Dines and J.M. Humez (eds) *Gender, Race and Class in Media: A Text Reader*. Sage.

McQueen, D. (1998) *Television: A Media Student's Guide*. Hodder Arnold.

Rose, T. (1994) *Black Noise*. Wesleyan University Press.

7 REPRESENTATIONS OF AGE

In this chapter we will look at:

- The importance of age representations
- Representing the young
- Moral panics
- Representing the old
- Age in sitcom.

The importance of age representations

This may seem an obvious thing to say, but we are all only one age at any one time in our lives. Furthermore, we will never have experienced life at an older age and we have all experienced all the younger ages than we currently are. So at any given time, we are really only able to know about the age we currently are; naturally, although we might have an idea, we don't really know what it is like to be older and although we have been younger, our later life experiences and the natural passing of time serve to blur the experiences we had as younger people, especially those from when we were very young. For example, this book is aimed at 16- and 17-year-old first-year GCE students. Now around 12 years ago you were all four or five. So your experiences as a four- or five-year-old are as a four- or five-year-old 12 years ago and not now, so 12 years have passed during which time you will have forgotten some of the experiences you had at that age and, also, the world and our society was quite different then from how it is now. Therefore, are you really well placed to know what it is like to be a four- or five-year-old now? Probably not! And given that we haven't experienced older life, again, we are not really well placed to know what life is like for older people.

So how do we know about younger or older people? Some of our knowledge will come from our first-hand experiences, from our siblings, parents, grandparents and from friends of different ages and what they tell us. In the case of younger people, some of our knowledge comes from our being that age, although, as we have just discussed, this may be clouded by the passing of time and the fact that we were that age at a different period. But much of our knowledge of various age groups, including our own incidentally, will come from the way in which different age groups are represented in the media. Our attitudes and opinions of other people are partially shaped by the media, which is a powerful, some might argue the most powerful, influence on our lives. This section will look at some of the common representations in the media of people of different age groups.

ACTIVITY

Before we get down to case studies, write down your initial thoughts about how the following age groups are represented in the media:

- Teenagers
- Middle-aged people (that's about 45–55 years old)
- Old people.

Representing the young

'What is it about the youth of today?' cry the nation's grandparents in unison, the length and breadth of the country. 'This never happened when I was young.' Well of course, much of the behaviour attributed to young people in the media didn't happen when your grandparents were young. They weren't sat in front of the TV all night because they probably never had a TV, much less an Xbox or PSP. They didn't copy violent crimes they saw in films because strict censorship at the cinema forbade the graphic violence we now see. They didn't hang around in gangs getting drunk on street corners – a popular stereotype attributed to today's youth – because there was hardly any money in the austerity of the post-war period to buy alcohol for working adults, much less for children, and they never spoke rudely to teachers! (Actually they did, it's just that they didn't get away with it because teachers could quite legally hit children with belts, canes, slippers, hands, chalk rubbers, books – anything to hand in fact – so fear of more pain usually prevented bad behaviour.)

On the whole, the way young people are represented in the media is largely negative. The common stereotypes which are frequently associated with the young include yobbish and antisocial behaviour, gang culture, disrespect for elders, drink and drug abuse, and teen pregnancies.

INFORMATION BOX

The way young people are commonly represented in the media as shown in these examples from British newspapers is generally negative. Does this leave us with a clear picture of young people or is it a narrow and biased representation?

'**Don't call us for help about yobs say police**'

'**Dad at 13**'

'**Young thugs rule in our towns**'

'**The feral gangs who rule our streets**'

'**Spared: Ex-soldier who snapped after years of torment**'

'**Cameron sets aim for thugs**'

Articles such as those in the above examples help to perpetuate an image that young people are out of control, that they are responsible for many of the ills we see in society and that they 'rule' large areas of the country, bringing anarchy and disruption – but is this an accurate picture? It is an old adage in the press that bad news helps to sell newspapers and so the newspapers, especially those with a right-leaning political slant, are quick to latch on to these negative representations, but the consequence of this is the establishment of a narrow stereotype which is applied to young people and the consequence of this is that more positive representations of young people are harder to find, especially in newspapers. However, they do exist, often in connection with examination success or when young teenagers gain entry into top universities as is shown in the two extracts from national newspaper websites in Figures 7.1–3. The competitors on the BBC's *Junior Apprentice* show, all of whom were teenagers, also suggest that teenagers are not all members of the feral gangs they are often made out to be in some news coverage.

Stereotypes are representations, usually of a group of people, where a characteristic which is seen in a few people is applied to a whole group. Certainly there are young people whose behaviour and attitude is at odds with that deemed acceptable by wider society, so there is the required minimum of a grain of truth for the creation of a stereotype, but even the most hardline disciplinarian cannot claim that this is true of all young people. Over time, however, this negative depiction of young people becomes the dominant representation – the stereotype against which all representations are measured.

Figure 7.1
Telegraph.co.uk, 'A-level results: maths prodigy is youngest to get university place'

Figure 7.2 *Mail Online*, 'Maths prodigy Arran Fernandez, 15, becomes youngest Cambridge student since 1773'

Figure 7.3 Arjun Rajyagor, Junior Apprentice winner 2010

Teenagers who gain early entry into universities and contestants on shows such as *Junior Apprentice* all challenge the stereotypes used in some of the news media about young people.

The dominant representation or the stereotype becomes the standard against which all other representations are measured.

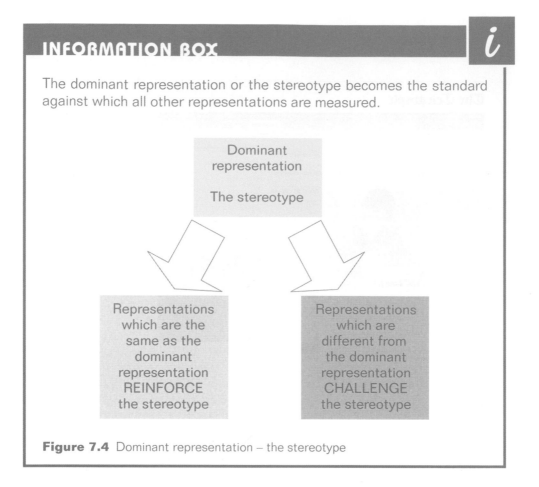

Figure 7.4 Dominant representation – the stereotype

Fictional media also contributes to the reinforcement of the negative stereotype. One of the stock characters in many soap operas is the troubled teenager whose behaviour often places them at odds with authority figures. The *Eastenders* character Martin Fowler, who as the first character to be born in the programme has had his entire life chronicled in the show, represents the stereotypical youth seen in many news stories. Having been represented as engaged in antisocial behaviour with gangs, as a teenage and unmarried father and receiving a prison sentence for manslaughter only to resume his criminal behaviour upon release, Martin's portrayal serves to reinforce many of the negative stereotypes about young people in contemporary Britain.

Figure 7.5 *This Is England* film poster (2006)

Watch the film *This Is England* (2006) and produce a commentary about young people's representations in the film. You might consider the central character, Shaun, as the only young character, but most of the other characters are in fact teenaged and as such should be considered in your analysis. Without wanting to pre-empt your response, given the contentious nature of the film it is tempting to regard all the representations as reinforcing negative stereotypes – but do they?

Moral panics

In his book *Folk Devils and Moral Panics* (2002), Stanley Cohen identifies how over time young people – mostly working-class males starting with Mods and Rockers in the 1960s (the period when he first studied the topic), and up through the 1970s with football hooligans and culminating in the more modern representation of youth as muggers, vandals and mobile phone snatchers – have constantly been labelled as responsible for many of the ills which are argued by some to have engulfed British society over this period. Identifying working-class male 'yobs' as 'the most enduring of suitable enemies' (Introduction, p. 8), Cohen sees how these negative representations of the young as 'folk devils' as he calls them lead to a heightened sense of moral panic when the collective feelings of the population are that the moral fabric of society and the social order are threatened.

Cohen points to media coverage of events such as the murders of James Bulger and Stephen Lawrence as contributing to this sense of moral panic. Events such as these, while heinous, deeply disturbing and undoubtedly shocking, are still relatively rare but the coverage in the news media and the responses offered by some politicians suggest differently. Cohen points to a speech given by the then Shadow Home Secretary Tony Blair in response to the Bulger killing in which he refers to the event as a 'hammer blow struck against the sleeping conscience of the country', and to an article in the *Sun* calling for a crusade against a sick society and in the *Independent* which stated that 'Britain was a worried country'.

In these two cases, and many others besides, the common feature is that those accused (in the Lawrence case no one was ever actually convicted) were young, working-class males. Certainly, few would argue that suitable punishment should not be forthcoming for those found guilty but the crucial question here for us is not one of guilt or innocence, but rather to what extent coverage of these issues and the general representations of young people in the media both factual and fictional add fuel to the stereotype that the youth are responsible for moral panics.

In the case of the Bulger murder, the judge in the trial of the two young boys who committed the crime added a further point of interest in terms of the role of the media by suggesting how exposure to violent video films, particularly *Child's Play 3*, may have been a contributing factor to the two accused boys' actions. Later investigations by the police in the case revealed no evidence to suggest that the two accused had seen the film in question.

Stuart Hall (1978) argues that the negative representation of young people is deliberate as it justifies social control by authority figures such as police and government. Hall identified the media as having a key role in this 'social production' of news.

ACTIVITY

■ Draw up a questionnaire aimed at finding out how adults feel about how young people are represented. Conduct your survey among some of the adults in your life – parents, uncles, aunties, friends, even your teachers will probably be willing to participate – and ask them how they feel about the way young people are represented.

Representing the old

The concept of 'young' is quite easy to define: just ask an adult; they will tell you what 'young' is because they all want to be it again! Generally, young people are seen as being 19 or less with subdivisions for teenagers, juniors, infants, toddlers and babies. Does this mean therefore that a 20-year-old is in fact old? This book is targeted at 16- and 17-year-olds so does this mean that you are only three or four years away from being called old because you are an adult? Not by most reckonings it doesn't but defining 'old' is problematic. To a 12-year-old, a person of 30, their teacher, for example, will seem old whereas to a 70-year-old, that same teacher will seem full of youth.

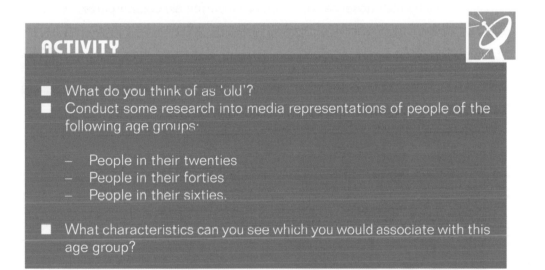

ACTIVITY

- What do you think of as 'old'?
- Conduct some research into media representations of people of the following age groups:

  - People in their twenties
  - People in their forties
  - People in their sixties.

- What characteristics can you see which you would associate with this age group?

Part of the reason why defining what it is to be old is complex is due to the mixed messages we get from the media about older people and what older people are. Let us take for a moment the classification of people as pensioners. To draw a pension in the UK, you need to be of pensionable age; that is, 65 for a male and 60 for a female. Unfortunately, by the time a 16-year-old reaches pensionable age, they are likely to be older than those retiring in 2010. However, pensionable age might be considered as one of the markers for being called old. It would seem that when gender is taken into consideration, the messages about what constitutes an old person become even less clear.

It seems that there are certain actors whose roles in films belie their real age. Take Harrison Ford, for example, an actor who played action heroes Han Solo in *Star Wars* at the age of 35 and Indiana Jones for the first time in 1981 at the age of 39; granted this is older than the teacher of the 12-year-old we mentioned earlier, but is still relatively young and he was able to hold his own and win the day against enemies of a similar or younger age. Ford's latest turn as Indiana Jones sees him in an equally active and challenging role pitting his wits, fists and legendary bullwhip against opposition which has not aged as he has from the first to the most recent film in 2008 at the age of 66 – a year after he would be eligible to draw a pension in the UK. There are, as this book goes to print, rumours of a fifth entry into the franchise with a projected release date in 2012, when Ford, should he be in the film, will be a mere 70 years old.

Sean Connery who shot to fame as James Bond in 1962, at the age of 32, was still fighting bad guys in the 1996 film *The Rock* at the age of 66. In many ways, these two representations serve to challenge one of the stereotypes commonly held about older people: inactivity, ongoing senility and a kind of 'dodderiness'. It is perhaps refreshing that these older people are able to escape the stereotypes of the slippers, cardigans and receding hairlines and punch below their ages. Conspicuous by their absence, however, are their female counterparts.

INFORMATION BOX

i

Figure 7.6 Harrison Ford in *Star Wars* (1977)

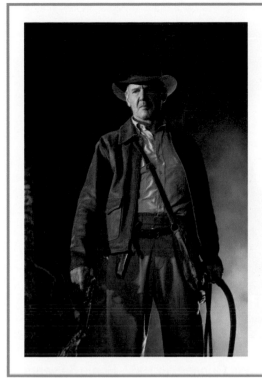

Harrison Ford as Han Solo aged 35 in 1977 and still fighting fit in 2008 as Indiana Jones, aged 66.

Figure 7.7 Harrison Ford in *Indiana Jones and the Kingdom of the Crystal Skull* (2008)

Figure 7.8 Sean Connery as James Bond in *Goldfinger* (1964)

continued

Figure 7.9
Sean Connery in
The Rock (1996)

Cinema's James Bond played by Sean Connery in 1962. Some 34 years later, Connery, still the action hero, in *The Rock*.

It would seem that where women have been represented as action characters, as discussed in the previous case study on gender, they are not as likely to retain this status into older age. Perhaps this is due to the fact that it only seems to be a recent feature that leading roles in action films have been given to females, so time will tell as to whether actors such as Angelina Jolie, Carrie-Anne Moss, Cameron Diaz, Uma Thurman and Lucy Liu who have been in action films will still be playing these roles in the future, assuming that is that they even want to.

One female movie star who seems recently to be bucking the trend and appearing as an action lead in older age is Helen Mirren. Although perhaps better known for her film roles in *The Queen* or *Calendar Girls* as well as her TV roles, Mirren takes one of the female leads opposite Bruce Willis, who through his role as John McClane in the *Die Hard* films has cemented his place in the action genre, in the 2010 film *Red* (see Figure 7.13). As the film poster shows, Mirren is not relegated to playing a role normally associated with the older female (in 2010 she was 65), but as a 'gun-toting' bona fide action character.

Figure 7.10 Angelina Jolie in *Wanted* (2008)

Figure 7.11 Carrie-Anne Moss in *The Matrix* (1999)

Figure 7.12 Uma Thurman and Lucy Liu in *Kill Bill: Volume 1* (2003)

From top: Angelina Jolie in *Wanted* (2008), Carrie-Anne Moss in *The Matrix* (1999) and Uma Thurman and Lucy Liu do battle in *Kill Bill Volume 1* (2003). Will they be playing these kinds of roles in 30 years' time?

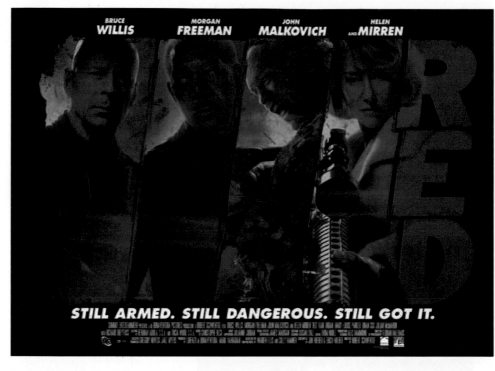

BRUCE **WILLIS** MORGAN **FREEMAN** JOHN **MALKOVICH** HELEN and **MIRREN**

STILL ARMED. STILL DANGEROUS. STILL GOT IT.

Figure 7.13 *Red* film poster (2010)

ACTIVITY

In *Red*, the four lead actors, Willis (aged 55), Freeman (aged 73), Malkovich (aged 57) and Mirren (aged 65), with a combined age at the time of the film's release of 248 years, may certainly seem to be challenging some of the stereotypes of older people in general, although as we have seen it is less unusual to see older males appearing in such films.

Take a look at the tag line however: what does this tell you about how these older people are being represented in this film?

These, however, are all examples from fictional film texts which, in terms of the business side of media, are, as texts go, just about as unpredictable, costly and liable to lead to bankruptcy among producers as it is possible for them to be. Films cost a great deal of money to make, to market and to distribute, and all the costs have to be met before a single ticket is sold for a seat in the cinema or before a single copy has been sold on DVD or Blu-ray. It perhaps therefore makes sense to give the audience what they demand. It is a buyers' market and, disappointing though it may be to consider, if audiences are not prepared to accept older women as action lead characters and yet are prepared to accept men in these roles, then the producers of films are unlikely to reconsider their casting of older women as leads in action films.

Television by contrast is less expensive and certainly lead roles for older women do seem to be a little more numerous, albeit not necessarily within the genre of action. Older women have been very positively and prominently represented in TV shows such as *Waking The Dead* in which Sue Johnson plays Dr Grace Foley, one of the show's main forensic psychologists, *Prime Suspect* again with Helen Mirren as DCI Jane Tennyson and many good roles exist for older women in regulars such as *Casualty* and *Holby City*, but the male dominance is evident in TV with many more substantial roles for men of all ages than for women.

ACTIVITY

- How do you account for the number of men such as Harrison Ford and Sean Connery who manage to remain cast as action heroes in films long after they might be classed in wider society as old? You might also consider the likes of Bruce Willis, Kurt Russell, John Travolta and Sylvester Stallone who are all approaching 60 years of age.
- Why do you think there are more opportunities for older women in fictional TV than film?

ACTIVITY

A simple way of analysing the media representations of older people would be to adopt a similar approach to that taken for representations of young people. Examine the representation in the light of commonly-held stereotypes of older people and ascertain the extent to which the representation challenges or reinforces the stereotype.

ACTIVITY

Collect some representations of old people from a range of media texts which conform to the follow stereotypes associated with the elderly:

- Impoverished (poor)
- Fussy

continued

- Senile
- Infirm
- Interfering
- Victims
- Dependent
- Kindly
- Generous
- Happy
- Engaging in stereotypical pastimes such as ballroom dancing, bingo and coffee mornings.

A further interesting area in terms of age representations comes when we consider those who look a different age from their actual age. Regularly we hear of people in the public eye who have gone to extraordinary lengths to appear younger than they really are. Cosmetic surgery and punishing fitness regimes are employed in an attempt to defy the ageing process.

INFORMATION BOX – BEFORE AND AFTER i

Madonna as she was in 1998 (left) and then in 2008 (right).

Figure 7.14 Madonna in January 1998   **Figure 7.15** Madonna in May 2008

Perhaps it is a sad reflection on the way celebrities are treated by media industries that they feel the need to try to defy the onset of age but the demands of the audience cannot be overlooked. Judging by the celebrities, music, film and TV stars and TV presenters we see in the media, it does seem that the demand is for younger people or those who, if not young in age, are young in attitude and appearance.

Older people in sitcom

One of the established characters in British situation comedy is the older person whose elderly mannerisms and characteristics form a basis for much of the humour. Idiosyncrasies such as forgetfulness, senility, grumpiness and the ability to say the wrong thing at the wrong time are among the repertoire of humorous devices frequently associated with older characters in this genre. So much has the representation of older people in sitcom been like this that it is arguable that this genre of TV has been largely responsible for reinforcing or maybe even initiating many of the stereotypes associated with older people.

Perhaps the most obvious example of an old person in a sitcom to fulfil many of these stereotypes is Victor Meldrew, the central character in *One Foot In The Grave* played by Richard Wilson. Running from 1990 to 2001, the show spawned six series and is still popular as a rerun show on some of the satellite channels. The show stands out as an example for representations of older people, as Meldrew is, rarely for the older person in a sitcom, the central character.

Meldrew is cantankerous, impatient and grouchy and he often finds himself the victim of preposterous bureaucracy and an inability to keep up with modern technological advances. The verbal onslaught to which he resorts when faced with the situations he finds himself in, often aimed at Margaret, his timid and retiring wife, including his famous 'I don't believe it' catchphrase, was a mainstay of the show. Despite his age, Meldrew became something of a representative for the 'little people' looking on incredulously as the world races by refusing to wait for those who can't or don't want to keep up.

Meldrew is, however, generally still in control of his faculties, unlike one of television's most famous senior citizens, Major Gowen from *Fawlty Towers*. Clearly suffering the onset of dementia, the Major is responsible for some of the most memorable moments of comedy from the show – some achievement given its sometimes overpowering lead character Basil, his even more overpowering wife Sybil and the famous Spanish waiter Manuel. The Major's forgetfulness goes even as far as forgetting his train of thought midway through a conversation, thus allowing him to begin talking about one thing and switch to another, as in the episodes where he is discussing his love for women and dislike for Germans. 'Still, you've got to love them I suppose' he states to his audience who still think he is talking about Germans when in fact he has switched back to women. Further examples of the foolish, but lovable nonetheless older characters from British sitcom include Del and Rodney's Granddad and Uncle Albert in *Only Fools and*

Horses, whose humour is largely based on the ineptitude and possession of odd and irritating habits frequently attributed to older people in the genre.

Older people in situation comedy have tended to conform to a narrow stereotype upon which most of the humour associated with them is based.

Figure 7.16 Victor Meldrew, *One Foot in the Grave*

Figure 7.17 Major Gowen, *Fawlty Towers*

Figure 7.18 Nora Batty, *Last of the Summer Wine*

Figure 7.19 Hyacinth Bucket, *Keeping Up Appearances*

What is clear from these examples is that for them to be funny, and this is probably true of all comedy characters, older people need to have a flaw in their character. For older women, this is often a domineering and no-nonsense attitude as seen in characters such as Hyacinth Bucket from *Keeping Up Appearances*, Nora Batty in *Last of the Summer Wine* and Reggie Perrin's mother in the 2009 revival of the 1970s sitcom *The Fall and Rise of Reginald Perrin*. In all of these cases, although for different reasons in the case of Hyacinth Bucket, the women are represented as strong to the point of domination over the weaker males whose lives they influence.

Perhaps sitcom, despite seeming to have a special place in the British viewer's heart, can be accused of portraying older people in a stereotypical way. While the setting, names, accents, wealth and appearance change between shows, the general representation of old people is as a homogeneous whole; a group of funny, fussy, forgetful and rather doddery pensioners whose prime function is to annoy, distress or otherwise antagonise the younger characters with whom the sympathy of the target audience lies. Since the placement of the audience is with the younger characters, the older characters could therefore be seen to be antagonising us as well. Such a view is at odds, however, with journalist and writer Katharine Whitehorn, who argues that there are as many differences between a 60- and an 80-year-old as there are between a 15- and a 40-year-old (BBC). Terms used in the media such as 'old-age pensioner' suggest a grey-haired old lady, she argues, yet the reality is that many pensioners are quite different from this stereotypical view. Representations of people over the age of 50 in the media tend to conform to a very narrow stereotype which is not only unfair on these age groups but also offers a rather inaccurate representation of the reality, and lead to the reinforcement and strengthening of the stereotype.

Like most things which are shown in the media, representations of people of different ages do not always fall neatly into coherent and easily identifiable groups; rather, there is a large grey area. As media students however, you will, as you are analysing representations of age along with just about all other groupings of people or places, need to measure the representation you see against both the reality and the commonly-held stereotypes. Your ability to determine whether the representation challenges or reinforces the stereotype and the extent to which the representation has a degree of accuracy will stand you in good stead as you approach this area of the subject.

References

Cohen, S. (2002) *Folk Devils and Moral Panics* (3rd edn). Routledge.
Hall, S. (1978) *Policing the Crisis*. Palgrave Macmillan.
Whitehorn, K. *Age and Experience*. http://news.bbc.co.uk/1/hi/magazine/7942853.stm.

8 REPRESENTATIONS OF ISSUES

In this chapter we will look at:

■ Issues arising from previous representation case studies
■ Representation and issues
■ Media issues and new technology
■ Issues and audience theory
■ Case studies: representation of Roma, Gypsies and Travellers, video games and taste and decency.

What is an issue?

An issue is a point or matter of discussion and debate. It is likely to provoke strong reactions and conflict, with people arguing intensely-held opposing views. An issue is often subjective without factual rights and wrongs or a clear resolution. Due to this, issues tend to be long term – although at different times they may be more or less apparent in society – and often controversial. Issues can be global or local, are often centred on age, gender or ethnicity, and can involve individuals and professional bodies, the state and the commercial sector.

In Media Studies we may evaluate the debates involved but more relevant is the way in which those issues are represented.

Media Studies provides an excellent context for looking at issues; in fact the subject itself could be seen as part of an issue, a debate about the meaning and value of education.

Below is a selection of recent news headlines which all comment negatively on Media Studies as a subject:

Tories to tackle the Media Studies menace

(*Independent*, 16 August 2009)

A-level Media Studies is soft option for students, exam watchdog reports

(*The Times*, 22 February 2008)

Stop funding Mickey Mouse degrees, says top scientist

(*Guardian*, 10 February 2010)

The argument put forward by those who think that Media Studies is not an academic subject is based on concerns about what is studied (popular culture such as soap operas, music videos, video games, etc.) and how it is studied; the inclusion of practical and creative work as part of an academic course. There also tends to be confusion about whether Media Studies is a vocational course which trains you to work in the industry or an academic course such as English or history.

This debate over Media Studies can be seen as part of a wider issue around the future of education; that is, who should go to university, what are worthwhile subjects to study, and where the funding for education is to come from. As is quite often the case with issues, the battle can be seen as part of a wider ideological argument, in this case about funding the increasing numbers of people going to university.

ACTIVITY

Below is an article by an academic, written to defend the study of non-traditional subjects at university.

■ Read the article and identify the arguments the author uses.
■ What issues are referred to as being part of the study of the media?

continued

Beckham Studies? You're Hired!

Thursday, 14 August 2008

Professor Ellis Cashmore, 'Football Culture' Lecturer

http://news.sky.com/skynews/Home/UK-News/David-Beckham-Studies-Professor-Ellis-Cashmore-Defends-University-Mickey-Mouse-Degrees/Article/200808215077370

So what next after A levels? Is Classics not for you? The first professor of football culture or 'David Beckham studies' as it is known, argues that you should not rule out 'new courses'.

Students can study David Beckham's rise to fame

Imagine it's the late 1960s. A young graduate walks into his first job interview and hands his CV to his prospective employer. 'Now let's see. What did you study?' the interviewer asks. 'Film studies! Is this a new subject, or something? I'm guessing it's one of these new Mickey Mouse degrees that the universities are starting to invent, isn't it? Well, I'm afraid we are looking for someone with qualifications in something like the Classics. I'm afraid you are going to have to look elsewhere. Good luck, *Mr Scorsese*.'

OK, it's an imaginary scenario, but film studies was once regarded suspiciously; now it's a mainstream subject . . . and Martin Scorsese, who graduated in film and television studies from New York University in 1966, went on to become one of the world's most influential film directors.

Knowledge is organic: it grows. University education has to grow with it. There will always be a place for the traditional subjects in the university curriculum, but growing alongside them are shoots of new subjects. And, practically every time one appears, there is a stampede to make fun of it. I have personal experience.

Eight years ago, I introduced a new module: Football Culture. Think about how important football has become. It commands a bigger chunk of our time, money and energy than practically any other pursuit other than music. That was enough to justify studying the phenomenon but the clincher was the number of jobs relating to football, not just in the media, but in sports administration and management.

David Beckham's emergence as a world-famous celebrity athlete coincided with the start of the Football Culture module. Well, not just 'coincided': the manner in which Beckham was elevated represented the astonishing popularity of football. When one of the redtop tabloids ran a story on the new module, it used 'David Beckham studies' in its headline and, within hours, the course became the subject of debate, not just in Britain but all over the world.

The module is part of a wider degree programme **and it's still running**. Globalisation; gender; race and ethnicity; violence; industrialism: these are some of the issues studied through the lens of football culture – as well as the influence of Rupert Murdoch on world affairs.

In the USA, universities offer studies in Madonna (Harvard, no less), dog psychology (animal cognition, actually, at Berkeley) and, interestingly, **Oprah Winfrey** (Illinois). The latter is a good example of a new eclectic subject area: it uses the American celebrity as a living case study in entrepreneurship, racism, sexism and other areas germane to life in the twenty-first century.

Society changes constantly and universities must be supple enough to respond, developing courses and subject areas that reflect both student interests and priorities and the changing landscape of the job market.

In terms of employability, a student equipped with a degree that encompasses contemporary issues and debates is arguably better qualified than someone with a working knowledge of the Aeneid. Only yesterday, it was announced that recruitment is up 9% and that, this autumn, over 47% of school leavers will be entering universities. Their interests are diverse and universities, if they are to prosper, will adapt to them.

Puritans will object to my populist credo. Degrees are sacrosanct, they'll argue: they're too valuable to be interfered with. Some are; but we shouldn't hesitate to add and extend. Whether we like it or not, education is now a large and varied marketplace and, as such, it needs to offer the widest possible choice.

Ellis Cashmore is Professor of Culture, Media and Sport at Staffordshire University.

Identifying issues

The study of issues could begin with the identification of issues raised by texts examined in the other areas of representation: gender, age, national identity, events and ethnicity.

The representation of gender raises issues such as:

- Sexism and misogyny in the media
- The objectification of women in men's magazines
- The representation of women in tabloid newspapers
- Body image and women's magazines: Size Zero debate
- Sexualisation of images in young women's magazines.

Looking back at the work you did on representations of gender, identify which texts could be used to debate these issues.

What issues are raised by the other case studies?

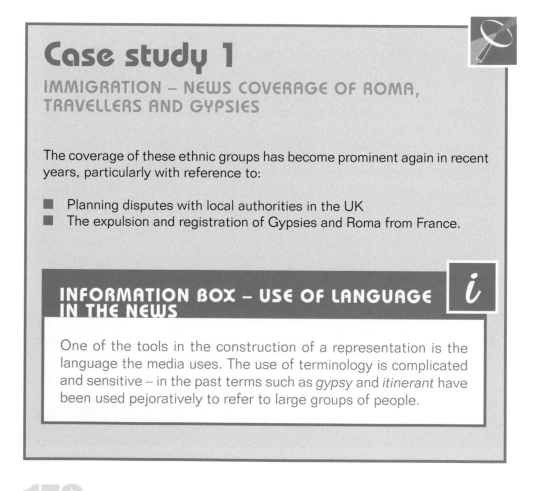

Case study 1
IMMIGRATION – NEWS COVERAGE OF ROMA, TRAVELLERS AND GYPSIES

The coverage of these ethnic groups has become prominent again in recent years, particularly with reference to:

- Planning disputes with local authorities in the UK
- The expulsion and registration of Gypsies and Roma from France.

INFORMATION BOX – USE OF LANGUAGE IN THE NEWS

One of the tools in the construction of a representation is the language the media uses. The use of terminology is complicated and sensitive – in the past terms such as *gypsy* and *itinerant* have been used pejoratively to refer to large groups of people.

GYPSY: a generic term referring to nomadic people, it is often used synonymously with Romany but the term includes other ethnic groups as well.

ROMANY: refers to a specific ethnic group whose historical origins are in India but who are now associated with Central and Eastern Europe. The Roma were the victims of genocide by the Nazis during the Second World War: 25% of European Roma were murdered by the Germans and their allies. In 1979 the West German government ruled that this persecution was racially motivated.

TRAVELLERS: in the UK media this term will usually refer to Irish Travellers (Pavees), an ethnic group with their own language and culture. The European Parliament has stated that Irish Travellers were one of the most discriminated-against ethnic groups in Ireland.

The context of persecution and racism against these particular ethnic groups is one of the reasons why the use of language is particularly important. The choice of descriptive terms in news stories is one way in which a representation or view about a particular group is constructed and transmitted to the audience. The recognition of this importance is evident in the style guides which news organisations publish. Style guides originally advised on spelling, grammar and punctuation but now also give advice on sensitive use of terminology.

In the UK the *Guardian* and *The Times* publish their guides online; the BBC's 'news style guide' is available on the companion website (or at http://www.bbctraining.com/pdfs/newsstyleguide.pdf).

In *The Guardian Style Guide* the following entries set the tone for their coverage of immigration and ethnicity issues:

Gypsies: capped: they are recognised as an ethnic group under the Race Relations Act
Travellers: capped: they are recognised as an ethnic group under the Race Relations Act; but note **new age travellers** l/c
asylum seeker: l/c. Someone seeking refugee status or humanitarian protection; there is no such thing as an 'illegal asylum seeker', a term the Press Complaints Commission ruled in breach of its code of practice.

continued

The BBC includes the following advice in the section 'Sensitivity':

> **As broadcasters you are part of the debate about what is and what is not acceptable language, and there are plenty of people who will let you know when they think you have got it wrong.**
>
> **There is a general acceptance that some words, such as crippled, spastic, Mongolism, idiot, retarded and mentally defective are no longer appropriate. It is also insensitive to refer to the deaf, the blind and the disabled, as if their physical condition was their one defining characteristic. Wheelchair users are as one in disliking the phrases wheelchair bound or confined to a wheelchair, on the grounds that wheelchairs are liberating, not confining. We must constantly be aware of terminology which might cause offence.**

Newspaper industry and self-regulation

Style guides are part of the news industry's form of self-regulation; in this case, individual newspapers set up guidelines and standards which its journalists must follow. The body for self-regulation in the industry is the Press Complaints Commission.

The Press Complaints Commission (PCC)

The PCC is an independent self-regulatory body which deals with complaints from the public about the editorial content of newspapers and magazines (and their websites). It is involved in training journalists and editors, and is particularly concerned with issues of media harassment and media intrusion.

The PCC was set up in 1991 to avoid government regulation of the industry; it is sometimes criticised for being too close to the news industry (some of the members of the PCC are newspaper editors) and for failing to enforce regulation.

ACTIVITY

The following news articles (extracts below) all deal with issues facing the Roma in Europe and appeared in different types of news-papers. The two newspapers, the *Daily Mail* and the *Guardian*, have different audiences and political perspectives; factors which are likely to shape the reporting of this issue.

Read the following articles. To develop an analysis of the issue of Roma migration make notes on the following:

- Summarise the content of the story as concisely as possible.
- What is the mode of address?
- Is there any use of emotive language? Does the use of terminology follow the guidance discussed above? Is the language used to provoke a particular response from the reader?
- Are any stereotypes or counter-types used? If so, to what effect?
- What do these articles suggest about each paper's position on: European migration, France's treatment of the Roma, multiculturalism?
- Who is the target audience for these articles (and more generally the papers they appear in)?
- Are these articles typical of the newspaper as a whole?

Roma gipsy who fled Czech Republic is the new face of British policing
By CHRISTIAN GYSIN 5 April 2008

In a city affected more than most by Eastern European immigration, a policeman's lot is not a simple one.

But 27-year-old Petr Torak finds he has fewer communication problems than most.

continued

He is a Roma gipsy from the Czech Republic, who speaks five languages; in other words, the new face of policing in multi-cultural Britain. Mr Torak, 27, a community support officer in Peterborough, will become a fully-fledged policeman in August.

He said: 'I absolutely love my job. It is what I always wanted to do and it means I can give something back to the country that has given me and my family so much.'

Since 2004, it is believed that 16,000 immigrants have flocked to the city in the Cambridgeshire Fens.

The problem was highlighted last month by the squalor of 'tent city': dozens of homeless and jobless migrants forced to live rough on wasteland.

One school, Fulbridge Primary, has seen the number of Eastern European children rise from two to 100 in the last two years, with 32 different languages spoken.

Mr Torak said: 'I believe my language skills make a huge difference.

'I understand the people from a cultural perspective and I know what they are trying to say.'

He is fluent in English, Czech, Polish, Slovak and Portuguese.

He is also learning Russian. His wife Lucia is expecting their first child.

Roma are regarded as the poorest and least educated of the Czech Republic's 10 million population. They have historically been subjected to both official and unofficial discrimination and prejudice.

During the Second World War more than 7,000 Czech Roma were killed in concentration camps as the Germans occupied Bohemia and Moravia.

Mr Torak was 18 and a promising law student when he and his family fled the city of Liberec in 1999. He and his mother had been viciously beaten after his father, a politician, protested against a wall built to separate the Roma from the Czechs.

Arriving in Britain, he had factory jobs before working as a security officer for Tesco and as a bilingual assistant.

'As long as I remember I'd wanted to be a police officer or a lawyer', he said. [. . .]

http://www.dailymail.co.uk/news/article-557355/Roma-gipsy-fled-Czech-Republic-new-face-British-policing.html##ixzz11O7j1suC.

Gypsy circus is next on France's expulsion list

After deporting many illegal Roma immigrants, Nicolas Sarkozy's government may force Europe's only Gypsy circus to close down

Figure 8.1 Musicians of the Romanes Gypsy circus play in Paris. But their future in France is uncertain. Photograph: Bertrand Langlois/AFP/Getty Images.

With its mesmerising songs and startling acrobatics, the Cirque Romanès is one of the most unusual cultural highlights

continued

of Paris: the only Gypsy circus in Europe and the only show in the French capital whose artists retreat to their caravans after the curtain falls. For 18 years it has been attracting audiences to its exotic blend of poetry and performance. In June it was deemed good enough to represent France at the World Expo in Shanghai.

But after a summer which has seen France crack down on its foreign Roma population and draw the ire of Brussels for the policy, the future of the circus and its loyal band of artists hangs in the balance. The authorities have refused to validate work permits for the five Romanian musicians whose instruments are crucial to the performances.

The French employment inspectorate insists that the cancellation of the permits has no connection with the wider political climate, which has seen around 1,000 Roma return to their home countries in nearly two months and around 200 unauthorised Roma camps cleared by police. They say there are problems with the circus's functioning, accuse its owner of underpaying the musicians and question the use of child performers.

Such claims are dismissed as 'pure invention' by Alexandre Romanès, the circus's charismatic founder. 'They're making up all these reasons. It's complete fantasy', he said, as he sipped coffee outside his caravan on the outskirts of Paris. Responding to the authorities' chief criticism – that of low pay – he added: 'They get four times the minimum wage, and they are fed and housed. When I contacted a lawyer and told her what they [the authorities] were trying to claim, she just burst out laughing.'

Romanès, a published poet and friend of the late writer Jean Genet, is unequivocal about what he believes to be the real reasons for the sudden move, taken for the first time in the circus's two decades of existence. For him, it is just another sign of France's growing hostility towards his people. [. . .]

President Sarkozy's policy of paid 'voluntary returns' for all
those foreign Roma found to be living on French soil without
permission has been denounced as unfair and unworkable by
human rights activists, foreign politicians and even members
of the president's own right-wing UMP party, one of whom
. . . enraged the government by comparing the evacuations
across France with Vichy-era roundups of French Jews and
Gypsies.

For the Romanès family, who dislike the term Roma and prefer
to be proud Gypsies, the situation is telling. Even though they
are both French citizens – Alexandre since birth – they feel
they are being stigmatised by a crackdown which is supposedly only a question of legality. This was not helped by the leak
this month of an interior ministry memo that singled out Roma
camps as the target for this summer's expulsions. [. . .]

http://www.guardian.co.uk/world/2010/sep/26/roma-gypsy-
expulsion-cirque-romanes.

Representation of the Roma in film

The stereotype of the Gypsy is still used in Hollywood cinema; recent
examples include *Drag Me To Hell* and *Wolfman*. In both films Roma Gypsies
are represented as evil, supernatural figures who can see into the future
and bring curses on to the innocent heroes.

ACTIVITY

Study the images of Gypsy characters from *Drag Me To Hell* and
Wolfman.

- .How is the lighting used to construct meaning?
- What similarities are there in the two images?

continued

- Which stereotypes do these representations draw on?
- Do you think there is a link between factual and fictional representations of Roma and Gypsies?

Figure 8.2 *Drag Me to Hell* screenshot (2009)

Figure 8.3 *The Wolfman* screenshot (2010)

Issues and audience theory

The issues discussed so far develop out of unease over the representations of particular groups – it's the subject matter which causes concern. It is clear that issues in a Media Studies context tend to be to do with one of the following:

- *Representation:* The concern that the treatment of a particular group in the real world is negatively affected by its representation.
- *Audience:* The fear that the audience – often defined by age – might be negatively affected by the media.
- *New technology:* The development of new forms of communication – which are predominantly used by young people – causes anxiety.

At times these three areas can come together creating a moral panic around specific issues such as violence and the media, online privacy (e.g. cyber bullying) and alienation (does the time we now spend online mean that we are no longer full members of society?).

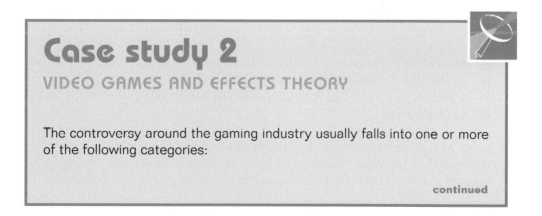

Case study 2
VIDEO GAMES AND EFFECTS THEORY

The controversy around the gaming industry usually falls into one or more of the following categories:

continued

- Effects theory: playing violent games makes the player act in an aggressive manner outside of game playing.
- Alienation: the solitary nature of game playing prevents socialisation, contributing to an increasingly fragmented society.
- Morality: the casual violence, misogyny and xenophobia of games lacks any moral code.
- Cultural sensitivity: the representation of different cultures and religions is offensive and stereotypical.

Support for some of these anxieties are found in scientific research such as 'Violent Video Game Play Makes More Aggressive Kids' by Craig Anderson (Professor of Psychology), *Psychological Bulletin* (an American Psychological Association journal), March 2010. It reports that exposure to violent video games is a causal risk factor for increased aggressive thoughts and behaviour, and decreased empathy and prosocial behaviour in youths:

> **We can now say with utmost confidence that regardless of research method – that is experimental, correlational, or longitudinal – and regardless of the cultures tested in this study [East and West], you get the same effects. And the effects are that exposure to violent video games increases the likelihood of aggressive behavior in both short-term and long-term contexts. Such exposure also increases aggressive thinking and aggressive affect, and decreases prosocial behavior.**

This argument is contested by many; arguments for the more positive effects of gaming tend to emphasise the following benefits:

- Development of fine motor skills, visual attention and spatial reasoning
- Development of logic and analytical skills through understanding complex levels and rules
- Evaluating moral choices
- Encouraging social behaviour and interaction through online gaming
- Catharsis: working through frustration and stress in a virtual world
- Entertainment.

Jane McGonical, academic and games designer, argues that the skills developed in gaming are superior to those in the 'real' world. Her academic research looks at how the attitudes and skills developed in gaming can be transferred to solving real problems. In a speech 'Gaming Can Make a Better World' she stated:

> **We do achieve more in game worlds. [We are] motivated to do something that matters, inspired to collaborate and to cooperate. And when we're in game worlds I believe that many of us become the best version of ourselves, the most likely to help at a moment's notice, the most likely to stick with a problem as long as it takes, to get up after failure and try again. And in real life when we face failure, when we face obstacles, we often don't feel like that.**
>
> (See http://www.ted.com/talks/jane_mcgonigal_gaming_can_make_a_better_world.html for video and interactive transcript of the speech.)

Many of these issues are discussed on the *Guardian's* gaming blog, *Game Theory* by Nadia Alderman (http://www.guardian.co.uk/technology/series/gametheory).

Case study 3
SIX DAYS IN FALLUJAH

The controversy over *Six Days in Fallujah* illustrates another of the controversial issues around video games – that of taste, decency and morality. *Fallujah* is a third-person shooter and was the first game to explicitly use the Iraq war as a focus for the content. The game follows the US marines during the six-day battle for the town of Fallujah. It was originally to be jointly distributed by Konami (global developer, publisher and manufacturer of video games including *Castlevania*, *Silent Hill* and the *Pro Evolution Soccer* series) but they withdrew due to the controversy; it

continued

was subsequently developed and released solely by Atomic Games. Atomic Games is a privately held US company, specialising in the real-time strategy genre with games such as *Combat* and *Breach*: 'a first-person multiplayer shooter that arms players with dozens of new ways to stun, manipulate, and eliminate their opponents through the most advanced destruction system ever released in a military shooter'.

The arguments made against the development and release of *Fallujah* can be summarised as:

■ Basing a game on warfare trivialises a serious, often tragic, subject.
■ A game is unable to deal with the complex political decisions which led to the Battle of Fallujah which means there is no context to the violence.
■ It desensitises players to the reality of war, which includes actual pain and suffering.
■ The nature of a shooter glamorises and romanticises war.
■ The Iraq war is too recent to be an appropriate subject; it is disrespectful to the surviving soldiers and the families of the deceased.
■ It's in poor taste.
■ A video game is a superficial popular culture form and therefore should never attempt to deal with serious issues.

(These arguments are reflected in the following article http://www.dailymail.co.uk/news/article-1168235/Iraq-War-video-game-branded-crass-insensitive-father-Red-Cap-killed-action.html.)

There are very few public examples of people opposing these arguments, but an editorial on IGN (Imaginary Games Network, a division of News Corporation) is explicit in arguing that *Fallujah* should be published and played:

Editorial: The Case for *Six Days in Fallujah*

Konami takes one giant step backwards.

US, 28 April 2009 by Michael Thomsen

Full text at: http://uk.xbox360.ign.com/articles/977/977518p1.html#ixzz11IRPBFET

[. . .]

The war in Iraq has been examined in every other medium imaginable. Film, radio, theater, prose, television, fiction, non-fiction, journalists and polemicists have all had a turn at trying to put the on-going conflict into a meaningful context. Apparently, video games do not have a place in that ongoing social conversation. To see the battle in Fallujah interpreted as a video game would be to marginalize it, to turn it into an adolescent entertainment.

This idea is a holdover from the old prejudice that games are toys, pastimes rather than creative expressions. [. . .]

It's sad that the video game industry continues to have to defend itself against such an inaccurate stereotype. Games are not toy-like entertainments. Gameplay is an expressive language in the same way that lighting, editing, angle, and composition formed the underlying alphabet for film a century ago. Games do more than entertain. They move us. They involve us. They require us to complete them. [. . .]

Suggestions for further work

Medal of Honor (2010, Entertainment Arts). Set in contemporary Afghanistan, the online multiplayer version included the option of taking the role of a Taliban soldier fighting against the US army. Due to the controversy the term Taliban was replaced with 'opposing forces'.

Social impact games: can video games be educational? Campaigning? The sub-genre of 'social impact games' attempts to use video games to raise awareness of global issues. *Darfur is Dying* is set in a refugee camp and puts players in the position of the victims of the war in Darfur. The game was developed by MTV. See *Darfur activism meets video gaming* at http://news.bbc.co.uk/1/hi/technology/5153694.stm for a discussion of the issues raised by social impact games.

Film and audience effects: many of the issues raised by video games are familiar from debates around film violence. Recent case studies would include the horror sub-genre of torture porn (the *Saw* franchise, *The Human Centipede*, etc.) and the controversy over the representation of violence, age and gender in *Kick-Ass*. Some suggested resources:

■ British Board of Film Classification (www.bbfc.co.uk/). The BBFC web-site includes detailed explanations behind the ratings decisions for individual films; these provide an interesting comparison with some media reporting.

continued

■ Christopher Tookey's Film Review Database http://www.movie-film-review.com/devfilm.asp?id=15578. Read Tookey's controversial review of *Kick-Ass* and the responses to it. Also includes a section of positive and negative reviews of the film.

9 REPRESENTATIONS OF EVENTS

The news media is central to the representation of events. The news media includes:

- Newspapers
- TV news
- Radio news
- News websites.

What is the news?

News is information about an event which is communicated to an audience. If we consider the number of events that may happen over a day, it is clear that not everything makes the news. So what makes an event 'newsworthy'? To be worthy of being included in the news the event needs to be of importance and interest to the target audience.

ACTIVITY

Look at the main headlines for a range of newspapers on the same day.

■ What makes these stories newsworthy?
■ Why do you think these papers have different lead stories?
■ What does the choice of leads tell us about the readership of each paper?

Selection and construction

The essence of representation is the process of mediation that takes place in creating a media product (for more on representation see Chapter 3). Media news is a construction, even though it is telling real-life stories. Someone has to make a decision about what is newsworthy, selecting the stories which meet certain demands regarding the media text, audience and institution.

News gathering

The mediation of any event commences with the news-gathering process. News producers need to source the raw material for the media, using particular methods of gathering information about events. News stories are filtered by particular agencies, producers selecting the stories which are most newsworthy to include in their text. Typical sources include:

■ Police and emergency services
■ News agencies, such as Reuters
■ Parliament
■ Courts
■ Press releases
■ Other news media.

The news sources can be differentiated between primary and secondary definers. A primary definer is usually someone who has first-hand knowledge of the event: an eye witness, journalist or the emergency services. The more credible the source, the greater the likelihood of the event being reported. The secondary definer is usually the news agencies or journalists who construct a story out of the initial event.

New technologies have had a radical impact on sourcing reports of events, as widespread ownership of mobile phones and computers enables members of the public to contribute first-hand testimonies and images easily. This can be invaluable to news producers when an unexpected event occurs and no resources are yet in place for sourcing news reports. Mobile phones provided some of the most vivid and immediate images of the aftermath of the London bombings in 2005 whereas 'crowdsourcing' software is used to compile user-generated reports of incidents. This has become a useful tool in tracking the unfolding of catastrophic events in the Third World, such as the Haiti earthquake, involving the wider public in news reporting.

Figure 9.1 Mobile phone picture: 7/7 tube bombings

CROWDSOURCING: sourcing information and knowledge from the wider public, drawing on their experiences and eye-witness accounts.

ACTIVITY

Look at a news website such as those of the BBC, Sky or CNN.

- What use do they make of user-generated content?
- Why do you think producers like to make use of such content?

A radical use of new technology in sourcing news has been the comparatively recent emergence of Wikileaks, a website which leaks documents regarding international news stories to the general public. This development allows anonymous sources to place controversial material in the public domain – for example, leaked material concerning the war in Afghanistan.

The producers have to make a decision about what to include in their version of the event, and what to exclude. This process of editorialising is essential to constructing the narrative of the news. Producers make decisions such as:

- What would interest the audience
- Who are the key characters
- Who to interview
- What are the most newsworthy aspects of the event.

The complexities of how an event arose, the impact of the event and the many people involved are not of interest to most of the audience, and would prove next to impossible to condense into the required length for a news bulletin or newspaper article. In reporting an event such as the visit of the Pope to the UK, the majority of the news media will not dwell on why the visit took place, the lead-up to the event, the impact on different faiths and institutions within the country along with the significance for Catholics, and so on. Ultimately the possibilities for reporting this story are endless, as such an event has boundless implications and effects. This would require too much space, and would not appeal to a mass audience.

News selection

In order to help understand what is valued as newsworthy and how the news is reported, it is useful to apply the concept of news values. The two researchers analysed news stories from around the world and analysed what factors these stories had in common, and what seemed to make these stories most important in the news agenda. News producers will prioritise the news according to its values and ideologies. Harcup and O'Neill developed a list of the values and criteria which dominate the news agenda.

News values	Description
The power elite	Stories involving powerful people or organisations
Celebrity	Famous people
Entertainment	Stories that feature human interest, sex scandals, show business or animals; opportunities for humour, photographs, headlines, etc.
Surprise	Stories which contain an element of unexpectedness or which contrast with other stories which are currently in the public sphere
Bad news	The majority of news tends to be bad news as this is what is judged to attract audiences and engage their interest
Good news	Heroic rescues or cures for illnesses are examples
Magnitude	The size of an event in terms of the number of people affected or potential for impact
Relevance	Stories featuring issues, social groups or countries that are seen to be relevant to the target audience
Follow-ups	Continuation of stories that have already been in the news, and have engaged public interest
Media agenda	Stories which fit in with the producer's own agenda on a range of issues, especially its stance on politics, social affairs and culture

Harcup and O'Neill's research is useful in developing an understanding of why certain events are represented in the news, and how they are represented. News values are applied in the selection of stories, in order to suit the purpose of the media text and its audience. Different news organisations will have their own differing interpretation of news values, taking their target audience, medium and ideological standpoint into consideration. A local newspaper will have a different news agenda from a national newspaper, featuring events, people and places that are of relevance to a specific target audience, defined by geography. The popular press will place more emphasis on celebrities and entertainment, whereas the quality press tends to rely a little less on such news values.

Popular press: smaller 'tabloid'-sized newspaper, appealing to a mass audience, with a tendency towards sensationalism. Often referred to as 'red-top' – for example, the *Sun, Daily Star, Daily Mirror* and *News of the World*.

Mid-market: smaller 'tabloid'-sized newspaper, with sensationalised news reporting, balanced with slightly more detailed coverage of 'hard' news stories; black-top masthead – for example, *Daily Mail, Daily Express*.

Quality press: hard and soft news, with more space given to news regarding politics, the economy, foreign affairs; more formal presentation and register – for example, *The Times, Daily Telegraph, Guardian, Independent, The Financial Times* and the *Observer*.

Pick an example of the popular press, a mid-market paper and the quality press, and consider the following questions:

■ What are the leading news stories of the day?
■ Which news values do they adhere to?
■ How much space are the same stories given in different newspapers?
■ What do you notice about the news values applied by different newspapers?

With less newsworthy stories editors will seek an angle to interest their target audience. With a predictable story such as the release of A level results a typical approach could be to:

- Focus on negative aspects such as suggestions of declining standards or boys' underachievement
- Personalise the story by focusing on specific students who have a remarkable story
- Use appropriate visual images to catch attention – for example, photogenic girls crying with joy or hugging each other.

Figure 9.2 The *Guardian*, 'Comprehensives lose out to elite schools in race for coveted A*'

Impartiality and bias

IMPARTIALITY: not partial or biased; unprejudiced

BIAS: a tendency or preference towards a particular perspective; prejudice; preferring one side over another

- Do you always believe what you hear and see in the news? Is the news to be trusted? Is it possible for the news to be impartial?

News reporting strives to appear to be a 'window on the world', yet inevitably on closer inspection it can often be seen to be far from transparent. It is very important for the news to appear to be impartial, that is, objective and therefore trustworthy. Producers will strive to seem to be balanced and not to be overtly biased in their reporting.

Public service broadcasting requirements, fundamental to the broadcasting remit of the BBC, and to a varying extent of the other terrestrial channels, demands that television news should endeavour to be impartial. As far as possible it should represent both sides in any conflict, and should avoid any bias. In contrast, the newspaper industry is self-regulating, with the concept of the 'freedom of the press' seen as being vital to the health of a democracy. The Press Complaints Commission was set up by the newspaper industry to ensure that newspapers adhered to a Code of Conduct, but has been criticised for being ineffectual and serving the interests of the industry, rather than the public. The press is also subject to a number of legal statutes as to what it can and cannot report, including libel laws and the Official Secrets Act.

We have seen that the news is the result of a process of selection and construction; it is a representation of an event. Inevitably there will be a preferred reading encoded in the news text which is the result of various factors. The news will construct a picture of events, yet analysis can reveal various values and beliefs that colour the representation.

Figure 9.3 The *Mail on Sunday* headline, 'EU to ban selling eggs by the dozen'

AS MEDIA STUDIES: THE ESSENTIAL INTRODUCTION FOR WJEC

This bias is often apparent in British newspapers, which often have a very explicit political agenda. The headline story in the *Mail On Sunday* tells how the European Union is going to outlaw the sale of eggs by the dozen, describing the move as 'bonkers' and 'absolute madness'. The article expresses indignation at the destruction of British traditions and way of life. But within a couple of days it transpired that this was not the truth of the situation, and that we will still be able to buy a dozen eggs. The *Daily Mail* reported this as a climb-down on behalf of the EU, as the result of the British 'backlash', even though the newspaper had actually misreported the legislation. This subsequent article is buried on the website, not appearing in the actual newspaper. Such reporting reveals a political agenda, in this case opposition to the European Union, which fits in with the *Daily Mail*'s overall position as a newspaper which supports right-wing, traditional values as upheld by the Conservative Party.

INFORMATION BOX – *FOX NEWS* *i*

Fox News, the US 24-hour rolling news channel, was the subject of the documentary *Outfoxed* in 2004. The documentary argued that *Fox News*'s agenda was to support the Republican administration under George Bush, and that its news reporting was biased with little attempt to be balanced and impartial.

Figure 9.4 *Fox News*, 'Michelle Obama finally proud of U.S.A.'

Fox News openly campaigned against Barack Obama during the 2008 presidential election, and has continued to maintain this political bias in its broadcasting. In 2009 hostilities between the White House and *Fox*

continued

> *News* came out into the open when Obama refused to appear on *Fox News*, 'because the most-watched cable news channel in America dealt in rightwing propaganda, not news' according to a White House spokesperson (http://www.guardian.co.uk/media/2009/oct/13/fox-news-obama-white-house).
>
> In 2010 News Corporation, the media conglomerate which owns *Fox News*, donated $1 million to the Republican Party.

ACTIVITY

- Read through a range of national newspapers, paying particular attention to the editorials and headlines used.
- For each paper what are the core beliefs and opinions regarding current affairs and politics?
- Are there substantial differences in the reporting of the same events between different papers?

In Britain the broadcast media is legally required to be politically impartial; all reporting should endeavour to be balanced, representing different points of view regarding events. This remains a problematic area, with regular accusations of bias from political parties in particular. The Glasgow Media Group, a respected media research organisation, have pointed out that the news cannot help but represent the establishment's viewpoint. Most journalists are products of the establishment, the majority coming from privileged middle-class backgrounds, and having been trained within established organisations representing the elite, including the major broadcasters and news agencies.

News as entertainment

The media is an increasingly competitive environment, as digitalisation and the impact of the internet means that there are more news providers seeking an audience. Newspapers have seen a dramatic decline in circulation and 24-hour news channels have undermined the necessity to watch the terrestrial channels' news bulletins or read an evening paper. News providers have sought to shore up their audience share by:

- Focusing more on celebrities
- Shifting the emphasis away from 'hard' news (current affairs)

- Relying on visual images and soundbites to make news more attention grabbing
- Promotional gimmicks (free CDs)
- Developing news websites.

Case study 1
ALTERNATIVE NEWS REPORTING

Alternative voices to the conventional news have found a home on the internet, where they are able to reach an audience and operate beyond the reach of regulators. *Schnews* is an alternative newsletter, which focuses on environmental and social issues/struggles in the UK and internationally, which are largely unreported elsewhere. A weekly newsletter is distributed to subscribers and other interested parties, but the majority of readers access it on the internet. The organisation is run by volunteers, relying on donations for its income.

ACTIVITY

Go to the website for *Schnews*: www.schnews.org.uk. This section will focus on the back issue 728.

- Make notes on the use of colour, fonts, layout and headlines.
- What are the main news values?
- Make notes on the language, tone and content of the articles.
- Is the reporting balanced and impartial?
- Who is the target audience? What uses and gratifications would they seek to gain from this text?

continued

Weekly SchNEWS

www.schnews.org.uk

Friday 25th June 2010   Free/Donation   Issue 728

OSBORNE SAYS DATA SUPPORTS TOUGH BUDGE AUSTERITY MEASURES

WELL IT WON'T BE ME FEELING THE PAIN OF THESE CUTS...

DATA   OSBORNE

CUTTING 'N' RUNNING

WHO WILL TORONTO THE LINE AT THE G20 MEETINGS AS AUSTERITY TOPS THE AGENDA..?

So 'austerity' took shape this week as George 'where were you hiding during the election campaign' Osborne went for broke on Tuesday with his hard-hitting 'fuck the poor' budget.

Yes, taxes & VAT are going up and almost every type of benefit is being slashed (and tied into being available for whatever work they deem you fit for), but hey! it's not all bad news - corporation tax is being reduced!

Well someone's gotta pay for all those huge profits, bonuses and debt screw-ups – and it might as well be the less well off. After all there's so many more of them. Easier to take say £100 a year off 30 million relatively powerless people (bringing in £3bn) than try and take half a million each off the richest 60,000 (and just think – the deficit is hundreds of billions!).

Events in Greece (see below) have lead to a few tight sphincters around the European elites – how best to avoid similar scenes in their own countries? A fashion for economic hair shirts has swept Europe with Germany, Spain, France (a bit) and many others joining in to see who can self harm the most. But it is a big gamble. Opinion amongst leading economists is split as to whether excessive blood letting is actually more or less likely to lead to another longer, more severe depression. And many in the US, included Obama's most trusted advisers, err on the side of less austerity now.

Not that we are flag waving one way or the other for methods to prop up a failing, structurally flawed exploitative system – but it all means that this week's cosy get-togethers of world leaders at the latest G8 and G20 meetings might be the scene of more disagreements than usual. Don't worry, we're sure they'll cordially agree to differ here and there and come out for the usual photo-opportunities afterwards.

Both summits are being held in Canada (G20 in the centre of Toronto, G8 in a more remote luxury 'resort' in Huntsville, Ontario) – where the conservative Government is currently introducing its own programme of heavy public cuts. But somehow they were still keen to pitch for the chance to host the 'Austerity' round of meetings – and demonstrate their own commitment to penny pinching by spending a jaw-dropping $1.1bn on wining and dining the World's most powerful for a week. Well it's not cheap to get 20,000 police to shut down, clear out and create a impenetrable 'ring of steel' in the middle of your capital city.

Not that all the cash has gone on a huge overblown security operation - despite the media being full of footage of uber-riot gear cops sporting serious weapons up to and including a 'sonic cannon'. A spokesman for the Canadian secret service reported no particular intelligence of very large scale protests or extremist threat – but don't worry though, there is an officially-sanctioned 'protest zone' miles away from the action. No, nearly $200m dollars has been spent on creating a artificial lake out by the media centre, presumably to provide a more picturesque backdrop to those handshaking photo calls. Well Canada is the country with the highest number of natural lakes in the World, so it obviously badly needed a new fake one.

Such utter wastefulness did not go completely unnoticed by the Canadian public and media, and it will be interesting to see if that swells numbers as a week of whatever-protest-is-still-possible is set to begin with the largest likely to be Saturday (26th)'s 'People First!' union / socialist alliance type shindig.

Yesterday saw a protest in the financial district – up against the giant security fence erected across downtown Toronto - where oil-dowsed protesters spilt through the streets decrying the many shortcomings of a black gold worshipping World, whilst others handed out '$1bn' bills to passers-by.

There was also a 1000-strong march in support of the First Nation peoples, who of course have been treated like shit since the European invaders first nicked their country. And not only historically – as well as numerous unanswered land claims, they claim that hundreds of their women have been murdered or disappeared in the past decades as part of a deliberate strategy to dwindle their numbers down to extinction. see www.defendersoftheland.org

* A convergence and full program of resistance events is planned for the whole week – for details see www.g20.torontomobilize.org

UP SHIT GREEK

The tide of strikes and general disorder continues across Greece (see SchNEWS 720) as austerity measures begin to bite.

The Ministry of Public Order was shown exactly how orderly the Greek public currently are when a bomb went off on its 7th floor yesterday (24th), killing a senior ministerial aide. Previous bombings have targeted prisons and courthouses.

In the past week alone there's been several smaller public sector strikes, most impressive of which was the Piraeus dockworker's strike. Organised mainly by PAME (middle of the road Communists), the dockworkers prescribed a 24hr blockade on the country's main port last Monday (14th).

In retaliation the courts declared the action illegal, leading to PAME blocking all entrances to the port again on Wednesday (23rd). All tourist boats had to cancel their trips to the islands.

PARTY & PROTEST
For events listings updated weekly see
www.schnews.org.uk/pap

Asked by the tourist cartel why the dockworkers were not treated "as the law requires", the Ministry of Public Order claimed that "such problems are not solved by means of repression". Elsewhere industrial action against the austerity measures has included a 24hr strike by journos which saw all TV, Radio and internet news unplugged for the day and a complete public transport strike in Athens.

Another general strike looms. In preparation, this week began with the abstention of markers from the final exams. On Wednesday (23rd) a law attacking social insurance was due to be voted in parliament. Grassroots trade unions alongside GSEE and ADEDY (garden variety trade unions) held demonstrations in Athens with hundreds in attendance. The voting has now been postponed for Monday. As seems to be the fad, hospital doctors went on a 24hr strike across the country. At the same time railway workers will be engaging in rolling two-hour stoppages throughout the week that are predicted to periodically interrupt all major train journeys in the country.

Meanwhile the government is hesitating to bring its new anti-labour laws before Parliament for a vote as the PM is fearful of his rule collapsing. You don't say...

EDO TRIAL UPDATE

After sixteen days of evidence the EDO Decommisioners trial is near to the end. After closing speeches the jury is expected to be sent out as early as next week. The defence closed (apart from character references) with eyewitness testimony from Sharyn Lock, who was on the ground in Gaza during the Israeli attacks in 2009 (see SchNEWS 661). She described how the hospital she was working in was struck by missiles and white phosphorus. Video footage of Sharyn's blog, (http://talestotell.wordpress.com) documenting the effects of the bombardment were shown to the jury. She closed her evidence by saying that she had no doubt that those who armed the Israeli airforce 'had the blood of children on their hands'.

Smash EDO told SchNEWS "Whether the verdict is guilty or not guilty our resistance against EDO/ITT will continue... We will be here until EDO are not! We are planning to hold a demonstration as soon as the verdict is known. Keep an eye on this site for updates. If you'd like to receive an update about the verdict and about the demonstration please send your email address or mobile number to smashedo@riseup.net".

* See www.smashedo.org.uk
http://decommissioners.co.uk

INFORMATION FOR ACTION Copyleft Published in Brighton since 1994

Figure 9.5 Issue 728 of online newsletter *Schnews*

GREEN VILLAGE PRESERVATION SOCIETY

Democracy Village and the camp which has occupied Parliament Square since Mayday is into the second week of the High Court battle – Democracy Village vs Boris Johnson (who wrongly assumed he had default power over the square – see SchNEWS 727). The judge will decide next Tuesday whether to issue a possession order to the GLA London council and, if that goes ahead, bailiffs could arrive for an eviction within days. In the 6-8 weeks there's been over 20 arrests including those for direct action rooftop banner drops and three arrests for climbing parliament.

The village are arguing on various fronts to win the case, including the need to have a public space and forum to discuss unlawful govt actions, such as illegal military adventures. Then there's four European human rights convention laws about freedom of expression, free assembly, religion and the right to legally question govt activites; Also the fact that traditionally, the land around Westminster Abbey was a mound which was the site of the Goreshedd of Tothill, a place of free speech, bardery, and festivities, enshrined by Richard I "Lionheart" in 1189, ratified by parliament in 1858 and never repealed.

There is still a call out to come to the square, and there will continue to be the regular events, including the talking circle on Wednesdays at 7pm, poetry and music from 5pm on Fridays, and the Peoples' Assembly on Saturdays at 5pm. The whole camp is in fact a peoples' assembly - a discussion forum - which became known as Democracy Village. It has side-stepped SOCPA laws (see SchNEWS 612) by saying it is a discussion not a protest. Even if there is an eviction, nothing can stop the continuation of peoples' assemblies if it's new people or those not named on injunctions.

The court case which began on June 14th has been a lopsided battle between an unsympathetic judge – backed of course by extreme political weight – versus 19 uppity and up-for-it defendants aided by some top human rights lawyers and supporters. The judge got so pissed off with the defendants after being vigorously questioned about common law which he obviously didn't know, and being reminded of state war crimes, he declared that the public would no longer be allowed in, only the defendants and the press.

He also disallowed an expert on war legalities and the rights to assemble – because he's not a lawyer, even though he's spoken on government committees. But Monday (21st) saw star witness Tony Benn, who came out for the village and their right to hold the government to account, saying it was 'an integral part of the democratic process'.

As an interim measure the GLA have allowed tents at the Great George Street corner on the paving – on a license for an undefined period - so this could go on for some time yet.

So it's not over yet it needs new people - bring food, tea, tents, climbing gear, cake, skills to share and good vibes. If a possession order is issued next Tuesday, look out for call-outs to help defend the village, and make plans for the future.

* See www.democracyvillage.blogspot.com and www.democracyvillage.org or see Facebook site. Site mobs 07981877462, 07722444146

* This Tuesday (22nd) saw a day of actions at the square against the austerity measures which will effect the poor not the war effort, and Ed Milliband was confronted about whether he voted for the Iraq War – which he refused to respond to, as he was whisked off by a minder to avoid some activists who wanted to citizens arrest him for war crimes.

TOME RAIDERS

Occupying an abandoned shopfront in the gentrified playground of Stokes Croft, Bristol, anarchists have set up a library. On May 22nd, the bookish radicals set up a free library with cafe and internet facilities to celebrate the Stokes Croft street festival in style. They told SchNEWS that they wanted "any radical literature which people care to share with their community".

Zines and books are to be read on site, though all legalities of book sales have been made on rare occasions. These include the overpriced sales of stolen Banksy books to local scenesters with proceeds being put aside to be invested in zine-printing.

The landlord is still in a state of shock since wandering into the free library in search of his own shop. His mental health may well have been permanently affected as he has suggested to the anarchists that they continue their good work but be sure to pay the electricity bills. Now in its second month of existence and resistance the bookshop has become the seventh autonomous space on the same road. It hopes to continue the fight against the yuppification of the croft.

If you happen to be passing through, feel free to pop by for a browse and a brew (nothing special). Don't be fooled by the grumpy faces. These individuals are community and communally loving radicals. The shop's at 40 Stokes Croft opposite Classics the freeshop. It's neon pink and black "and you couldn't fucking miss it if you tried..."

ISRAEL IN THE DOCK

The port of Oakland in the US has refused to allow an Israeli ship from being unloaded in protest against Israel's blockade of Gaza and attack on the Freedom Flotilla. Over 800 activists intercepted the gates of the docks (6th largest port in the US), encouraging workers to refuse to cross the picket lines where they were scheduled to unload the Zim Lines ship - which they did.

Protesters stood by the four gates of the Stevedore Services of America from 3:30am to 9:30am chanting "Free, free Palestine, don't cross the picket line" and "An injury to one is an injury to all, bring down the apartheid wall." An emergency arbitration was held around 9am to decide whether it was unsafe for the workers to cross the picket line or not. The ruling proved to be in favour of the workers not crossing without disciplinary measures taken against them. This was greeted by boisterous cheers of "Long live Palestine!", Jess Ghannam of the Free Palestine Alliance said "This is truly historic, never before has an Israeli ship been blocked in the United States!"

Oakland's reaction is the beginning of several protests and strikes planned around the globe, including Norway, Sweden and South Africa

* www.indybay.org/newsitems/2010/06/20/18651361.php

...and finally...

Manchester cops this week slammed a mystery Moss Side rapper, who has made over seven hundred 999 calls in the last three months alone.

A one-man campaign bringing 'no justice, no peace' (or quiet) back to the police, he bombards the switchboard with calls in which he raps, preaches and plays loud music to the helpless operators - who aren't supposed to hang up in case vital information comes out.

Obviously not Hip Hop fans, fuming top brass have complained about the caller wasting police time and that it's not even real music – all shouty, no singing. Despite attempts to track the man down – he has used and discarded over 60 mobiles - so far they haven't found anyone to take the rap.

Police are now appealing to the public to track the 999 spitter down so they can lay down some fresh beats of their own. Will the real SIM Shady please stand up?

Disclaimer

SchNEWS reminds all readers - that the Tories are really distraught and upset about having to make these cuts. It's killing them. Honest.

RAZED BEDS

Brighton County Court issued an eviction order against the Lewes Road Community Garden (see SchNEWS 727) this Monday (21st). A 40-strong solidarity demo was held outside court.

Gardeners Ron Edwards and Duncan Blinkhorn were told to vacate and hand over keys by 4.30pm next Monday (28th) or be held liable for costs, estimated at £6,800 and counting.

Following the verdict, a garden moot on Tuesday saw a highly reluctant vote to quit the land in order to support the named individuals.

But that's not to say the garden will fall fallow. One laughing gnome told SchNEWS: "We're not just going to roll over with this one. Tesco can fek off and so can the betting shop come to that. Who in their right mind wants another friggin supermarket or somewhere else people can go and get totally fucking alienated." Look out for another garden in the area sometime soon.

In the meantime planters and bigger items are to be moved to Fairlight and St Martin's schools, Saunders Park, The Patch and possibly other derelict sites in the area. "In this way the garden will live on in the physical world as well as in our hearts – a garden in exile," said Duncan. Well not exactly Tibet but yeah we get where you're coming from.

Brighton Council is coming in for more flak as it comes to light just how little consultation residents were offered. The original planning applications back in '08-'09 proposed a 3-storey building including four flats. Residents in the area are now demanding a meeting with the council.

* An Anti-Tesco demo will be held outside the garden on Monday 28th June between 5-7pm.

* See http://lewesroadcommunitygarden.webs.com

STICKY WIKI

US intelligence analyst and alleged Wikileaks source, Bradley Manning, has been arrested while serving in Iraq, taken to a US military prison in Kuwait, and held for three weeks without charge. He allegedly leaked the infamous 'Collateral Murder' video showing a 2007 US helicopter strike as well as unseen footage of the 2009 Garani massacre in Afghanistan which killed over 100 people – mostly children - in an airstrike. It is also claimed that he leaked 260,000 diplomatic cables, which Manning reportedly said would expose "how the first world exploits the third, in detail".

Wikileaks have rather cagily said claims they are in possession of the cables are "as far as we can tell, incorrect" but admitted they are working on the release of the Garani footage. 'Collateral Murder' shows US Apache helicopters gunning down 12 Iraqis and two Reuters journalists, causing a media storm when it was released in April. Wikileaks have said they don't know if Manning leaked it as they never collect records on sources, but that if he did then he is a "national hero." They have now sent a three man legal team to Kuwait help Manning but have so far been denied access to him.

Wikileaks have been earmarked as a major threat to US 'national security', as revealed in a recent classified US Army Counterintelligence Centre report discussing them. They are appealing for support by people setting up local "Friends of Wikileaks" groups. Email friends@sunshinepress.org

* For the full story see www.schnews.org.uk/archive/news/727.php

---

SUBSCRIBE! Get SchNEWS free every week by email in pdf or text file - visit our site, or send us stamps and we'll post it to you. Copy and distribute! Keep SchNEWS free with donations (via website or cheques payable to Justice?). Posted free to all prisoners.
SchNEWS, Tel +44 (0)1273 685913 Email mail@schnews.org.uk Web www.schnews.org.uk

continued

TEXTUAL ANALYSIS

Schnews uses a newsletter format, with low production values and limited use of pictures, graphics and colour. The two pages are tightly packed with articles, organised in a very conventional style, using a conventional sans serif font. This style of presentation and layout suggests a very serious and blunt approach to the news, creating the expectation of detailed and earnest reporting of events. Nevertheless, the serious tone is dissipated by the play- ful title 'SchNEWS', suggesting an unconventional approach to the news. This anarchic tone is further enhanced by humour, juxtaposing the photo of George Osborne, Chancellor of the Exchequer, with a *Star Trek* character, and the ironic use of headlines. The headlines use language techniques typical of tabloid newspapers, relying on puns, irony and rhyme to create a playful mode of address, yet this is in stark contrast to the radical tone of the news stories themselves. This radical representation of events is signalled in the masthead, with the tagline 'WAKE UP! IT'S YER ALWAYS UNDER BUDGET . . . SCHNEWS', playing on the idea of awakening our awareness, and referring to the lead story of the recent budget. The use of 'yer' is typical of the colloquial tone of the text, which balances a sophisticated lexis (typical of an upmarket broadsheet) with more frank, street-wise language, often using expletives to signal anger and frustration.

NEWS VALUES

This edition is typical of the news sheet in having a very rigid news agenda, featuring only nine stories, all of which share a common concern with social issues and activism. The news values of the publication are unconventional, reporting events that were largely unreported within the mainstream press, such as the EDO decommissioners' trial, and giving an alternative per- spective on political and international events. The focus is on hard news, reporting events in countries such as Israel and Greece which are not elite nations, but also reporting news that is of specific interest to a local reader- ship in Brighton, where *Schnews* is published. In contrast to conventional news reports, the stories lack simplicity, there is no attempt to balance the composition of the publication beyond a mix of local, national and inter- national news, and there is no attempt to personalise the stories.

BIAS

Schnews has an explicit political agenda, and so does not set out to be impartial in its representation of events. The leading article on the Toronto G20 Summit is typical of the reporting style, in forming a critical com- mentary, more typical of an editorial. Traditionally the editorial is the place in a newspaper where judgement and opinion can be aired on the events of the day. Only one source is mentioned in the article, 'a spokesman for the Canadian secret service', with no attempt to create a balanced report by giving space to the representatives of government. In this respect the text has more in common with a tabloid in its approach to news reporting, taking an overt political position on events, rather than the rather more covert bias of broadsheet newspapers. The language used is highly emotive in parts, creating a passionate, highly charged mode of address, balanced with use of statistics throughout to create a more informed tone (although no sources are given). Readers are given the opportunity to find out more or to take action with details of websites and mobile numbers.

The internet has radically challenged traditional methods of news reporting, having undermined audience size for both newspapers and television. There has been a growth in the number of partisan news sites, often giving a very partial interpretation of events, some commentators seeing this as threatening the future of impartial news reporting.

AUDIENCE: ENCODING/DECODING

Schnews has a very direct mode of address, clearly appealing to a readership who share the values and opinions of the producers. There are clear assumptions about the values and attitudes of the intended reader, with an expectation that they reject the main political parties and capitalist values, and wish to make a contribution to social change. There is a strong sense of a common culture with the clearly defined news agenda which takes an overt political stance. The distribution of the news sheet through the website and in specially selected outlets for the target audience means that most of us would be unaware of its existence; only those who would be sympathetic to its values, or who generally accept the preferred reading would have access to it. Nevertheless the text takes a very controversial and radical position which would result in an oppositional reading outside the target audience; *Schnews* takes a radical position regarding dominant values within society. This is a text speaking directly to a political and cultural minority, which would be found deeply offensive by the majority of readers of most daily newspapers, particularly those that support the Conservative Party. The language and tone is uncompromising, not seeking to reach an audience beyond its niche.

continued

Case study 2
THE SUN

The *Sun* is Britain's best-selling newspaper, selling in excess of three million copies a day. It is a tabloid newspaper and is part of Rupert Murdoch's multinational media conglomerate, News Corporation. The *Sun* is infamous for its sensational news reporting, partisan political stance and page 3.

Figure 9.6 The *Sun*, 'Beckhams' staff massacre'

continued

The front page of the *Sun* of 20 August 2010 was dominated by the headline story about the Beckhams making cutbacks to their staff. A story about the latest European Union legislation is pushed to the side of the page, while a promotion for Tesco is splashed prominently around the masthead. Adjacent to this is a puff featuring a smiling Cheryl Cole, inviting us to buy the paper to find out more about her and the phenomenally popular TV show, *X Factor*. A second puff, in rather more muted colours, creates a further enigma around the offer of an award to find a 'killer' of a 'war hero'. The overall effect is bold, bright and attention-grabbing, suggesting a direct, no-nonsense approach to news reporting. The masthead stands out with the white sans serif title emboldened by the red background. The page is dominated by colour pictures, with headlines using large typeface. The £5 Tesco offer is given the largest typeface, signifying that this may be of more interest than the news to the prospective buyer. The colour scheme is predominantly cheery bold colours: the majority of which are red, white and blue, connoting patriotism.

NEWS VALUES

The news agenda for the *Sun* is dominated by a fascination with celebrity, with the Beckham report being the headline story, in addition to the Cheryl Cole report. The lead story also satisfies the news values of personalisation, being a human interest story, and negativity, as the Beckhams sack a number of staff. This reliance on celebrity and sensation to appeal to the readership, in preference to hard news, is typical of tabloids. Broadsheet newspapers on the same day led with stories reporting the withdrawal of American troops from Iraq, the shortage of university places, and record profit margins for banks.

SENSATIONALISM

The main headline 'BECKHAMS STAFF MASSACRE' is sensational and emotive, suggesting a hideous crime, with the Beckhams as the villains of the piece. A smaller font and lower case is used to add further detail: 'Couple sack 14 of their servants', assuring the reader that no violent crimes have taken place, but suggesting criminal intent on behalf of the celebrity couple. The reader is positioned to take sides against the Beckhams, with the use of emotive language, as is typical of the tabloids. Words such as 'massacre', 'sack' and 'servants' suggest that the Beckhams are uncaring employers, cynically disposing of their staff. The short article emphasises the wealth of the Beckhams, implying that they are selfish by having so much yet sacking so many staff: 'The couple, worth £115 million, axed a third of those employed at their homes in England, LA, Dubai and France.' The verb 'axed' continues the suggestion that a brutal crime is taking place.

The only source evident in the article is the 'friend' who is quoted, suggesting that *The Sun* has intimate contacts with celebrities such as the Beckhams, but providing little in the way of hard facts as a basis for the report. The article is continued within the paper, with the aforementioned 'friend' remaining the only quoted source within the whole article. This reliance on hearsay and gossip is typical of tabloids' approach to reporting stories. The story is one-sided, not attempting to provide an impartial report, but building on the public's continuing fascination with celebrities, and our desire to be kept informed of the excess that characterises their lives.

PHOTOGRAPHIC IMAGERY

The article is accompanied by headshots of the Beckhams which have been cropped from library images. David Beckham looks directly at the camera, with narrowed eyes and a slight smile, creating direct eye contact with the reader, seeming straightforward and friendly, with a suggestion of smugness in association with the brutal headline. Victoria Beckham is behind David, echoing their status in the public eye regarding their comparative popularity. She is bronzed and groomed, with bare shoulders, connoting glamour and wealth, yet she looks down, not meeting the reader's eye. This, in conjunction with a half-smile, makes her seem scheming and uncaring in the context of the news story.

Audience: uses and gratifications theory

By applying uses and gratifications theory we can understand how tabloid newspapers appeal to audiences, in terms of the stories and events they choose to report, and their style of news reporting. (For an explanation of uses and gratification theory see pp. 96–9.) The focus on the Beckhams on the front page gratifies the audience's need for surveillance; lives of celebrities are structured into narratives, and we wish to follow the next instalment, the triumphs and disasters involving these mythical figures. In this ongoing narrative, Victoria Beckham is often represented as the villain, being criticised for her body, clothes, facial expression and lifestyle, while David Beckham, England's footballing icon, is represented as a hero who is exploited by his fame-hungry wife.

The article also satisfies the audience's need for diversion, as we are entertained by this celebrity narrative, with its two key participants who are so well known that the strapline need only refer to them using the more informal 'Posh and Becks'. The need for personal identity is also gratified

continued

by such celebrity stories, as the reader is encouraged to aspire towards the fairy-tale glamour of celebrity lifestyle, with the fabulous wealth and many homes of the Beckhams, yet feel reassured as we learn about the sordid realities and supposed suffering that is part of the myth of celebrity. This story positions us to be scornful of the mean-spirited penny-pinching of the Beckhams, as the public struggle with the economic realities of the credit crunch.

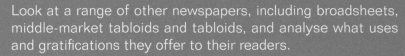

ACTIVITY

- Look at a range of other newspapers, including broadsheets, middle-market tabloids and tabloids, and analyse what uses and gratifications they offer to their readers.
- Compare how different newspapers represent a celebrity story. What sources are used? Are they impartial or biased?
- Undertake an analysis of types of stories featured in one edition of a tabloid. Use the results to develop a profile of the typical reader, considering lifestyle, attitudes, values and demographic factors.

Case study 3
BBC NEWS AT SIX, 24 AUGUST 2010

BBC news is the biggest broadcasting news organisation in the world, generating television and radio news throughout the day, in addition to its news website. The BBC often has to fight charges of political bias in its news coverage from interested parties, yet is independent of the government, being a public service broadcaster with a remit granted by Royal Charter. The Charter requires the BBC to be objective and to operate free from political and commercial bias.

The *News at Six* is the second most popular TV news broadcast in the UK, with 4.3 million viewers (compared to the 4.7 million viewers for the BBC's *News at Ten*).

Figure 9.7 *BBC News at Six*, 24 August 2010 (six screenshots of report)

continued

Watch an edition of *BBC News at Six*, and consider the following questions:

- Analyse use of technical codes and *mise en scène* in the opening title sequence. What is the intended impact on the viewer?
- Which news values are given greatest priority?
- To what extent is the reporting of the lead story made impartial?

Sample analysis

TECHNICAL CODES AND *MISE EN SCÈNE*

The title sequence makes use of sophisticated graphics with images of the globe swirling around, with the names of significant cities signifying the global nature of the news and the BBC's status as an international news operation. The futuristic music with its insistent beats enhances an image of technical wizardry and urgency, building suspense as the audience is led into the first news story.

NEWS VALUES

The lead story of this particular edition of the *News at Six* concerns the new revelation that a Roman Catholic priest was responsible for an IRA bomb that killed nine people in 1972. In terms of news values it demonstrates:

- Negativity: in terms of the revelation that there had been a cover-up involving the Church and the government.
- Proximity: the bombing was in Northern Ireland, and the UK government was guilty of a cover-up.
- Size: nine people had died in the bombing.
- Predictability: the report into the investigation was due to be released on this day, therefore the BBC could plan its coverage and resources in advance.
- Personalisation: interviews with people directly affected by the bombing.
- Visual imperative: library footage from 1972 showing the aftermath of the bomb.
- Timing: the new revelations had emerged that day.

This story is very much 'hard news' that does not seek to entertain but to inform the audience. This fits in with the BBC's image as a serious and authoritative news organisation, which has more in common with the news values of a broadsheet newspaper than a tabloid. The coverage of this story is detailed and lengthy, taking just over eight minutes out of the 30 devoted to national news. It is a complex story, involving an event that took place nearly 40 years ago alongside religion, politics and the long-running Northern Ireland conflict.

IMPARTIALITY

The report uses a range of storytelling devices to engage the audience and to harness the events into a compelling narrative. At the same time the BBC has to endeavour to be balanced and objective by representing the key points of view. Hence the report includes archive footage from 1972, footage of the press conference featuring relatives of the victims, interviews with a survivor, an archbishop, the Northern Ireland Secretary and an authority on the conflict in Northern Ireland. Graphics, photos and a map are used to provide further visualisation of the story, in addition to various location shots of the town of Claudy.

The sources for the content of this story are made explicit, with frequent references to the report published that day, which is shown in close-up, with quotes from relevant documents incorporated into the graphics, alongside detail of the source itself.

This attention to attaining balance and credibility gives the report greater authority and gravitas, in keeping with the BBC's remit to be objective and impartial. Nevertheless, the report endeavours to appeal to viewers by using emotive language and personalisation. News anchor Kate Silverton introduces the story with a blunt statement, using strong language: 'The British government, the police and the Catholic Church colluded to cover up the suspected involvement of a priest in a bomb attack on the village of Claudy.' The report dwells on the 'youngest victim of the bomb', an eight-year-old girl, accompanied by a moving close-up image of a smiling young girl, followed by a clip of her brother speaking of how 'betrayed' he felt by the government.

It is inevitable that journalists and other representatives of powerful institutions generally gain more credence in such reports. They are trained public speakers, often talking with greater confidence and authority, with a more sophisticated vocabulary, often without a regional accent, and formally dressed. Members of the public may seem to be less authoritative and credible in contrast to the 'professionals'.

continued

In terms of news values the programme as a whole attempts to achieve a balance across the categories of news stories. There is an emphasis on negativity and stories that are of immediate concern to the target audience, but also coverage of a couple of international events that are of sufficient scale to be included, such as the devastating floods in Pakistan. There are just two stories featuring elite people, which are more typical of a tabloid news agenda: the arrival of the prime minister's new baby, and the trial of George Michael for driving under the influence of drugs.

Audience issues: mode of address

The *News at Six* establishes a tone of authority and formality throughout the programme, as is evident from close analysis of the opening sequence. The opening medium-shot of news anchor Kate Silverton establishes the tone of the programme. She is formally dressed in a suit and wears glasses, with smartly groomed hair and a hint of glamour suggested by her earrings. She appears businesslike and, as a consequence, authoritative, as is signified by her serious facial expression and vocal delivery. The formal tone is enhanced by the urgency of the music, with its insistent beats signalling the announcement of the main stories of the day. Silverton is simultaneously authoritative and reassuring, serving to engage the viewer. Her suit is a soft pink, connoting femininity and glamour in combination with her well-groomed appearance.

At this point in the programme Silverton is seated behind a desk, further enhancing her position of authority, whereas the audience is positioned as the client, passive and listening while the professional takes control. A hierarchy is created by this positioning, and we are directly engaged as the newsreader speaks directly to the camera, and to us, giving her further power and authority. The backdrop framing the newsreader is a futuristic office setting, dominated by metallic silver and high key lighting.

Even though the news is dominated by conflict and suffering, the news-reader is a reassuring presence. Kate Silverton is a familiar face, who the viewer knows and trusts as an experienced newsreader. The music, title sequence and setting are all familiar to the audience, signifying the authority of a respected institution which relies on its reputation as the guardian of the nation's broadcasting.

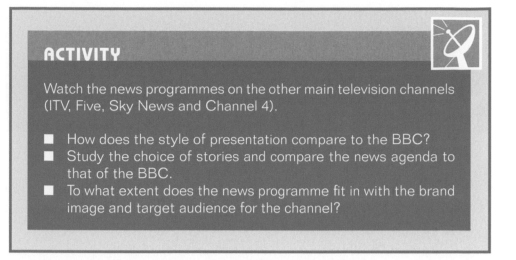

Summary

When considering representation of events you need to analyse:

■ The selection of events for news reporting
■ The sources used for reporting an event
■ How the representation of an event is constructed for the target audience
■ To what extent the representation tries to be impartial
■ The impact of the news medium on the reporting of the event.

Reference

Harcup, T. and O'Neill, D. (2004) 'What is News? Galtung and Ruge Revisited' in
   P. Rayner, P. Wall and S. Kruger (eds) *Media Studies: The Essential Resource*.
   Routledge.

REPRESENTATIONS OF NATIONAL AND REGIONAL IDENTITY

10

Key terms: national and regional identity

The concept of identity refers to the way in which different groups (family, friends, schools, government, etc.) in society see us and the way in which we see ourselves. The factors affecting our identity include gender, race, religion, class, sexuality and nationality which are interlinked and have become more and more complicated.

The concept of national identity is the idea that who we are can be defined – at least in part – by our nationality. This suggests that there are identifiable characteristics that belong to a nation which can be identified in a population. The concept of national identity is a complex one because not everyone in a population will agree about what the national characteristics are, or even if they exist at all.

The definition of national identity is further complicated by the idea of regional identity; for some people this might be more important in describing who they are than national identity. Regions are not necessarily clearly marked by boundaries and places; a region might be a county but it might not have such a specific definition, referring instead to a general area – North and South, Essex, Yorkshire, etc.

Evaluating national identity

How important is your nationality in defining your identity? How do you define yourself? Scottish? British? European? What do you think is more important to your definition of yourself – nationality, age, gender, race, family, friends, religion?

One of the ways in which the identity of a nation is constructed – for audiences both at home and abroad – is through the media.

ACTIVITY

What ideas about Britain do you think audiences in other countries would get from the following texts (or choose your own examples):

- *The Queen* (Frears, 2005)
- *This Is England* (Meadows, 2006)
- *Shameless* (C4, 2004–present)?

You should consider setting (city, country, England, Wales, Scotland, Northern Ireland?), characters (gender, age, class, appearance, nationality, etc.?) and subject matter (realistic, comic, whimsical?).

ACTIVITY

Study the images in Figures 10.1 and 10.2 and make notes on the following:

Film poster

- Which typical codes and conventions of a film poster are present in the *Essex Boys* poster?
- How are these codes and conventions used to create expectations for the viewer?
- Who is the target audience for this film?
- Using your notes from the previous responses, write a paragraph which describes the representation of regional identity in the poster.

continued

Figure 10.1 *Essex Boys* film poster (2000)

Figure 10.2 *Essex Life* magazine, August 2009

Magazine cover

- Which typical codes and conventions of a magazine cover are present in *Essex Life*?
- Define the mode of address of the cover.
- Who is the target audience for this magazine?
- Using your notes from the previous responses, write a paragraph which describes the representation of regional identity in the cover.

Looking at your responses it will be clear that these two texts represent the Essex identity in very different ways. In thinking about the reasons for these differences, you should consider the influence of:

- *Audience:* how are representations selected to target different audiences?
- *Media forms:* how are representations shaped by the media form in which they appear?

In the example of representations of Essex, it is clear that there are 'competing representations': Essex as a beautiful, coastal county with a sophisticated culture and heritage or Essex as an offshoot of London, characterised by gangsters and

Some points to consider:

■ While English is the dominant language, people in Britain speak Welsh, Hindi, Punjabi, Arabic, Gaelic, etc.
■ In addition to the Churches of England, Scotland and Wales and the Catholic Church, the major religions of the world (Buddism, Hindu, Muslim, Jewish, Sikh) are represented in Britain.
■ Many people have no religious beliefs or are not practising members of a church.
■ Britain is a multicultural and multiracial society.
■ Britons live in different regions and countries, belong to different social classes and also define themselves with reference to gender and sexuality.

For statistics on all aspects of the make-up of Great Britain, go to National Statistics Online at: http://www.statistics.gov.uk/default.asp.

A further complication in defining Britishness is that the very terms *British* and *Britain* are quite vague. They are often used interchangeably with other terms such as *Great Britain*, *United Kingdom* and even *England*. It is important to be aware of the specific political and geographical definitions of the variety of terms:

■ *Great Britain* is the collective name for the three countries of England, Scotland and Wales.
■ *United Kingdom* refers to Great Britain and Northern Ireland.
■ *British Isles* is a geographical definition and includes Great Britain, Ireland, Orkney, Shetlands, Inner and Outer Hebrides, Isle of Wight, Isle of Man, Lundy, Channel Islands.
■ *Devolution* is the transfer of power from the British government to individual countries. The Scottish government and the Welsh Assembly legislate on a range of areas which have been devolved from the UK government. These include health, education, asylum and immigration and the justice system (Scotland only). The Scottish National Party and Plaid Cymru are campaigning further for independence for their nations.

National identity as construction

As with other examples of identity (gender, sexuality, ethnicity, etc.) the concept of national identity is a construction – a representation based on a particular view of what it means to be British. The idea of a nation has been described as an 'imagined community' (Anderson, 1983). It is impossible for everyone in a nation to know everyone else; instead they share a recognition of certain characteristics and values which supposedly make their nation distinctive. This 'imagined' nation is constructed through the media, arts, politics, education, etc. Television plays an important role in 'uniting' the nation through special events. Examples include coverage of sports (e.g. football and rugby World Cups, Olympics) and royal occasions such as weddings and funerals, where there is a clear assumption of shared national values.

For some theorists any attempt to define a nation promotes nationalism: the belief that one nation is superior to another, which is a racist ideology. The debate about the link between nationalism and racism can be explored in media coverage of sport – specifically football.

Sports coverage and national identity

Figure 10.4 The *Sun*, 'Their finest hour (and a half)'

The front page of the *Sun* (Friday, 18 June 2010) uses a range of references to English national identity as part of the buildup to England's match against Algeria in the World Cup. England had made a poor start to the competition and needed to win against Algeria to be confident of progressing.

In analysing the construction of national identity in the media, it can help to categorise the representation under the following headings:

- Iconography referring to the nation
- References to a nation's history
- Representations of gender, race, sexuality and regional identity as they cross over with nationality.

It is also important to consider the way in which the media form, in this case a tabloid newspaper front page, and target audience affects the representation.

National iconography

There are several visual references to England on the front cover of the *Sun*: the small St George's flag in the top right-hand corner of the title box and on the crisp packet at the bottom of the page, the flag draped over Rooney's shoulders and the three lions badge on his England football strip. The photograph of Winston Churchill can also be defined as English iconography: the cigar and V for Victory salute are directly linked to the nation's history. (Churchill, despite being the British prime minister during the war, is now often used to represent just one of the British nations – England.) Overall, the front cover, from the title box to the puffs, uses the red and white colours of the English flag. There are no visual signifiers for the opponents Algeria, just the statement 'England v Algeria, 7.30pm'.

National history

The historical context of the Second World War provides the theme for the front page and this is a fairly common convention in tabloid coverage of important football matches. These references are more usually made when England plays Germany and previous coverage has been controversial in its representation of Germans (see the *Daily Mirror* Euro 96 front page, 24 June 1996). At the time of the Second World War, Algeria was a French territory and fought with the allies; therefore it is difficult to construct the usual battle metaphors about conflicts between nations. One of the reasons for the minimal reference to the opponents might be the limited recognition that Algeria has among an English audience, which makes constructing stereotypes very difficult.

The war references draw on a very low point for Britain: the period in 1940 after the invasion of France and before the US had entered the war. This choice of period is probably due to the relative anonymity of the opponents and the difficult situation England find themselves in at this point in the tournament. The phrase 'Their Finest Hour' was part of a speech given by Churchill in the House of Commons before the Battle of Britain and is imagining how future generations will look back on this time. In other words, it is a rousing speech imagining the future rather than commenting on actual events. The concept of the underdog fighting back against the odds has become a dominant part of the English national identity and is often referred to, in another wartime signifier, as the Dunkirk spirit.

Representation of masculinity and national identity

The selection of Wayne Rooney as the focus for the front page links a certain type of masculinity to the concept of English national identity. In analysing the meaning of a persona, it can help to analyse the change in meaning created if a different person had been used.

> ## INFORMATION BOX – COMMUTATION TEST *i*
>
> The commutation test was developed in semiotics and refers to the way in which the meaning of a text can be analysed by substituting one sign for another and seeing how it would alter the meaning. In Media Studies this has most commonly been applied to the study of film stars; John O.Thompson (1978) illustrated the way in which stars bring specific meanings to films by 'replacing' one star with another, demonstrating the importance of a star persona in constructing meaning for the audience.

In this case Wayne Rooney has been chosen over other recognisable English players such as John Terry, Peter Crouch, Frank Lampard and even the captain Rio Ferdinand (who didn't play due to injury). This selection suggests that Rooney fits in with the representation of national identity constructed by the *Sun* in a way in which the other players do not. In the image, Rooney looks straight at the reader, his head lowered slightly as if ready to charge. His expression is serious and determined rather than friendly. With the flag wrapped around his shoulders, the overall impression is of a soldier about to go into battle. In interpreting this image of Rooney, the reader also brings contextual knowledge of him. Despite being a millionaire and sporting celebrity, Rooney's persona represents down-to-earth values through his working-class background, regional identity (Liverpool), close family ties and happy marriage to his childhood girlfriend (newspaper revelations about his life which may have affected this persona came out after the World Cup). His 'brawn over brains' representation is usually seen as a positive quality in contrast to a more intellectual or sophisticated approach to life and sport. These elements are emphasised to construct a traditional representation of masculinity, one which values strength, power and the ability to protect others over vulnerability and sensitivity. In the context of the *Sun* front cover, the interconnection of gender, class and national identity presents Rooney as a human 'British Bulldog', representing the nation.

Media form

The conventions of a tabloid – and specifically the *Sun* – front page are also important in analysing the construction of identity. This front page conforms to many tabloid conventions: emphasis on visual elements rather than words to tell the story and create a mood; the use of a pun in the headline; emphatic language to exaggerate the importance of events. The tabloid style means that stories have to be simplified and easily understood; hence the reliance on stereotypes and generalisations; it does not attempt to be nuanced or ambiguous. The conventional tone of a tabloid is also important here – the address is often humorous with a direct, informal relationship to the readership.

Audience reception

The mode of address of the front page of the *Sun* is direct and informal, with a close relationship between the paper and its readers. There is an assumption on the part of the producers of the *Sun* that their audience will understand the references and approve of the meaning. Regular readers of tabloids will understand the address and the element of humour in the use of the pun in the headline, realising that the comparison to the Battle of Britain isn't to be taken literally. An oppositional reading of the front page may come from readers outside the target audience who are less familiar with tabloid style. This group may feel that the linking of a football match to war is out of proportion and tasteless; the signifiers of English identity may seem more sinister with the link to white working-class culture having connotations of racism and extremist groups.

Of course it isn't only the English media which uses references to war in the representation of national identity. The front page of the *New York Post*, over the page (like the *Sun* it is also owned by News Corporation) references the War of Independence to convey the USA team's achievement of drawing with England. Bunker Hill was a pyrrhic victory for the British; they lost so many soldiers defending their territory that it could be seen as a defeat. This historical 'tie' is used to contextualise the drawn result in a game which England were expected to win easily.

Public Service Broadcasting and national identity

Public Service Broadcasters (PSB) are financed by the public, for the public. Public Service Broadcasting is neither commercial nor state-owned; it should be free from political interference and pressure from commercial competition. Through the PSB, the public is informed, educated and also entertained. In the UK the BBC is the main PSB (although Channel 4 and ITV also have to adhere to a public service remit) and is funded by the licence fee which is compulsory for everyone with a TV. Because of this direct link the BBC have an explicit role to represent the nation.

Read the following extract from the BBC Charter:

NEW YORK POST

LATE CITY FINAL

SUNDAY, JUNE 13, 2010 / Partly sunny, 79-85 / Weather: Page 34 ★ ★   **SUNDAY**   www.nypost.com $1.25

WORLD CUP SHOCKER

USA WINS 1-1

Greatest tie against the British since Bunker Hill

PAGE 7 AND SPORTS

Figure 10.5 *The New York Post*, 'USA wins 1-1'

BBC Public Purpose remit: Representing the UK, its nations, regions and communities

You can rely on the BBC to reflect the many communities that exist in the UK. These communities may be based on geography, on faith, on language, or on a shared interest such as sport. You can expect the BBC to stimulate debate within and between the communities of the UK, and to encourage people to get involved with their local communities.

What the BBC will do to achieve this Purpose

1. Represent the different nations, regions and communities to the rest of the UK.

Across the range of its network output, the BBC should portray and celebrate the range of cultures and communities across the UK at national, regional and local level.

2. Cater for the different nations, regions and communities of the UK.

The BBC should provide a range of output, including original content, designed to meet the needs of the nations, regions and communities of the UK.

3. Bring people together for shared experiences.

The BBC should broadcast individual programmes that bring together a very wide range of people – for example, great state occasions, important national sports events and high-quality entertainment.

4. Encourage interest in, and conversation about local communities.

The BBC should provide engaging output that gives an accurate picture of the many communities that make up the UK and that informs understanding and stimulates discussion about their concerns.

The BBC should provide forums in which these communities can debate among themselves and with other UK communities.

5. Reflect the different religious and other beliefs in the UK.

The BBC should give people opportunities to understand the beliefs of others, and to examine their own beliefs critically.

6. Provide output in minority languages.

In its output, the BBC should support the UK's indigenous languages where appropriate. It may also provide output in other languages used by licence fee payers in appropriate contexts.

To attempt to represent the nation, the BBC seems to be trying to do two things:

- Celebrate the differences between communities in the UK (these might be regional, ethnic, religious, etc.).
- Bring the audience together through shared values.

Sunday evening TV: representing the nation?

The TV schedule is an important context in analysing representation as it is indicative of the target audience and their values. Different parts of the week have become synonymous with different types of programme – for example, Saturday early evening is for mass appeal family viewing while Sunday has become associated with traditional dramas and documentaries (often travelogues), which can be seen as safe and cosy (this could be a positive or negative description depending on your taste).

The late afternoon/evening schedule for BBC1 on Sunday, 19 September 2010:

17:30 Songs of Praise

Peckham Praise

The Prince of Wales visits All Saints in Peckham, south London, to see how the church was saved from closure and became a key part of the local community once more. Diane Louise Jordan also introduces a selection of hymns and worship songs, including 'All Hail the Power of Jesus' Name' and 'Leaning on the Everlasting Arms'.

18:05 BBC News; Regional News and Weather

18:30 Countryfile

Matt Baker and Julia Bradbury visit the Cheshire towns of Knutsford and Alderley Edge. While Matt explores a network of ancient mines, Julia learns how bats and newts cope with the noise generated by jumbo jets at Manchester Airport. Elsewhere, John Craven investigates a recent increase in rural crime, and Adam Henson hosts a day out for horse owners at his Cotswold farm.

19:30 Antiques Roadshow

Series 33. Episode 2/30: Beverley Minster 2

The team pays a second visit to Beverley Minster, East Yorkshire, where the objects up for scrutiny include a pair of medical leech jars, a ring containing a highly valuable lock of hair, and a distinctive sideboard that contains some very well-hidden drawers. Presented by Fiona Bruce.

20:30 Inspector George Gently

Series 3. Episode 1/2: Gently Evil

A young woman's body is found in a seemingly idyllic Northumbrian coastal village in 1966, and the subsequent investigation leads Gently and Bacchus to suspect her estranged husband is responsible for the killing. However, they soon come to realise her disturbed family is hiding an even more shocking secret. Starring Martin Shaw and Lee Ingleby.

■ What different genres are included in this schedule? Which are fictional and non-fictional?

- Who do you think the audience is for BBC1 on a Sunday evening? Is there a dominant demographic throughout the afternoon/evening schedule?
- Note the different references to regional and national identity in the programmes. How would you characterise the representation of national identity constructed? To help with your analysis you could compare the range of representations here with those on the radio homepage.

The Antiques Roadshow is typical of BBC1 Sunday evening television. The credit sequence signifies traditional references to Britain (England?) through the images of stately homes, vintage cars, bone china, pastoral landscapes and old masters. The opening credits can be viewed on YouTube.

- Is the BBC1 schedule typical of the terrestrial channels on a Sunday evening? Compare the same time slots on ITV1 and Channel 4 in terms of genre and representations of national identity.

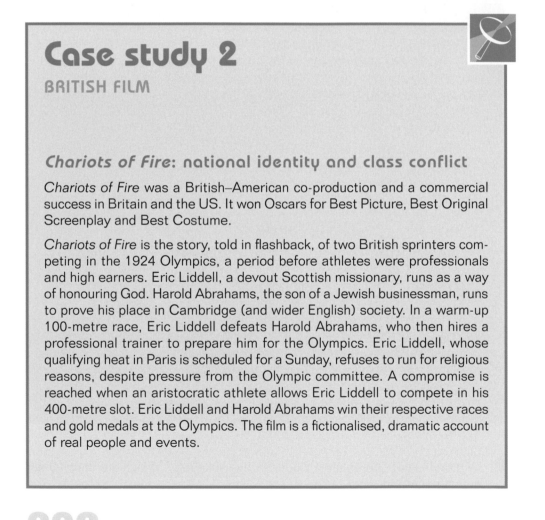

Case study 2
BRITISH FILM

Chariots of Fire: national identity and class conflict

Chariots of Fire was a British–American co-production and a commercial success in Britain and the US. It won Oscars for Best Picture, Best Original Screenplay and Best Costume.

Chariots of Fire is the story, told in flashback, of two British sprinters competing in the 1924 Olympics, a period before athletes were professionals and high earners. Eric Liddell, a devout Scottish missionary, runs as a way of honouring God. Harold Abrahams, the son of a Jewish businessman, runs to prove his place in Cambridge (and wider English) society. In a warm-up 100-metre race, Eric Liddell defeats Harold Abrahams, who then hires a professional trainer to prepare him for the Olympics. Eric Liddell, whose qualifying heat in Paris is scheduled for a Sunday, refuses to run for religious reasons, despite pressure from the Olympic committee. A compromise is reached when an aristocratic athlete allows Eric Liddell to compete in his 400-metre slot. Eric Liddell and Harold Abrahams win their respective races and gold medals at the Olympics. The film is a fictionalised, dramatic account of real people and events.

ACTIVITY

Watch the first 10 minutes of *Chariots of Fire* and note down the different signifiers of class evident through the *mise en scène* (particularly setting and costume), characters and action.

The setting quickly establishes an upper-middle-class milieu:

- Playing cricket in the ballroom
- The accents and manner of speech of the main characters
- Cambridge University.

As the film develops there are further references to the hierarchy of social class through the Masters of Caius (pronounced Keys!) college, Lord Birkenhead (chair of the Olympic committee) and Lord Lindsey.

Choose three scenes from the film which illustrate the characteristics of the Masters, Birkenhead and Lindsey. What do these representations suggest about the view of Englishness in the film?

The concept of Englishness is often constructed through the contrast with Scottishness in the film – symbolised by the figure of Eric Liddell.

ACTIVITY

In *Chariots of Fire* there are clear oppositions between the English and Scottish nations.

- After watching the film, draw up a list of the characteristics of the English and Scottish as represented in the film.
- What do these differing representations tell us about the values of the film?

continued

Some points to consider:

Englishness is represented as male, upper class and traditional through the *mise en scène* of Cambridge halls, stately homes, the college dash, the Masters and the members of the Olympic committee. These powerful groups are shown to be hypocritical, racist (casual verbal attacks on Jews, the French and a belief in Britain as the greatest nation) but also decent and generous through the character of Lyndsey.

In contrast *Scottishness* is signified through images of nature, family, community and references to God. The character of Liddell, who states 'I am and will remain a Scot' is represented as a man of integrity (therefore the English upper classes don't understand him). The scenes in Scotland construct an image of innocence and authenticity; working-class culture is reflected in country fairs and working men; people think of others rather than of themselves.

Harold Abrahams

The main character in the film doesn't fit into either of the oppositions outlined above – this is a common position for the hero in film narrative. Abrahams is an outsider who, although technically English is shown not to fit into English upper-class society – something he has in common with Liddell. This position as an outsider can be seen in the following areas of identity discussed in the film: class, nationality, religion and race, and culminates in his speech to Aubrey about his experience of anti-Semitism in England. In fact Abrahams seems to have far more in common with the US athletes, whose professionalism symbolises the future, than with the traditional culture of England.

Reception of the film

Chariots of Fire is set (mostly) in the 1920s, was produced in 1981 and released in 1982 when Margaret Thatcher was prime minister. The Falklands War between Britain and Argentina began in spring 1982. The context of the Falklands War meant that *Chariots of Fire* was often interpreted as a patriotic, nationalistic film when in fact the central characters are 'outsiders' rejected by British society. What may have been intended as a liberal film attacking the racist and snobbish attitudes of Englishmen was received and promoted as a celebration of Britishness (although the film emphasises the differing experiences of the English and the Scottish). This suggests that the meaning of a film within the culture is not always the one intended by the film makers. The film continues to be watched in constantly changing contexts.

For further discussion of heritage cinema in the 1980s and 1990s see Cooke (1999).

Suggestions for further study of national and regional identity in film

This Is England (Shane Meadows, 2007) (The C4 series (2010) produced by Shane Meadows would also be relevant here.)

In *This Is England*, Shane Meadows draws a link between the jingoistic (English) response to the Falklands War in politics and the media with the racist policies of the British National Party. Throughout the film the cross of St George is used as a symbol of national identity – one which has inherently racist connotations.

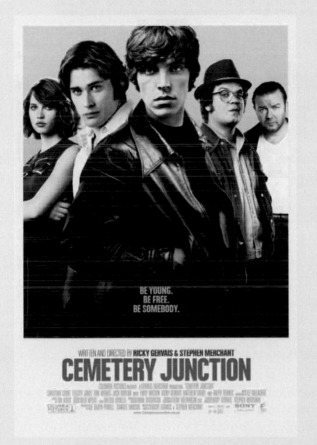

Figure 10.7 *Cemetery Junction* film poster (2010)

continued

Cemetery Junction (Gervais and Merchant, 2010): set in Reading in the early 1970s, *Cemetery Junction* uses the conventions of a coming-of-age film to represent the English suburbs as stultifying and repressive. It has been compared to the British new wave movement of the 1960s (e.g. *Saturday Night Sunday Morning* (Karel Reisz, 1960) and A *Taste of Honey* (Tony Richardson, 1961).

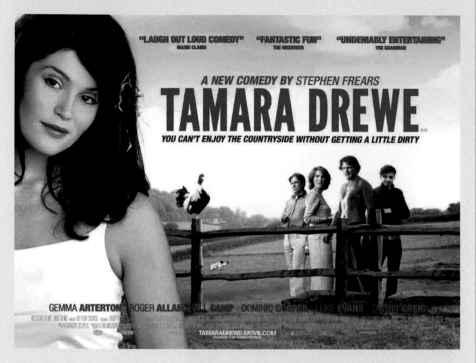

Figure 10.8 *Tamara Drewe* film poster (2010)

Tamara Drewe (Frears, 2010): based on a graphic novel and with reference to the novels of Thomas Hardy, *Tamara Drewe* constructs a range of comical representations around local, regional and national identities. The film is particularly interested in the gap between the romantic ideal and the reality of English country life.

British cinema has also examined national identity with reference to the changing racial, cultural and religious mix of society. These issues have been discussed in a range of styles from social realism to comedy, aimed at niche and mass audiences. A study of any of the following films would make an interesting area to consider in an attempt at defining Britishness.

My Son the Fanatic (Prasad, 1997): this film deals with several identity and social conflicts and is a good example of the way in which these conflicts intertwine. The central character is Parvez, an immigrant from Pakistan who lives in Bradford and has integrated into British society. Farid, his son, is a student who rejects the values of Western society and becomes a fundamentalist Muslim. The conflicts include those between the different generations and between religions. The film raises difficult questions of national identity – who is defined as British and who is not.

Yasmin (Beaufoy, 2004), *Bullet Boy* (Dibb, 2004) and *Dirty Pretty Things* (Frears, 2002) all focus on questions of national identity with specific emphasis on ethnic and religious identities.

In This World (Winterbottom, 2003) and *Last Resort* (Pawlikovski, 2000) both use realist techniques to examine the lives of refugees and the conflicts arising from fears of 'invasion'.

Grow Your Own (Laxton, 2007): a typically British comedy of cultural conflict – set on an allotment – about the reaction of an English community to the arrival of a refugee family.

References

Anderson, B. (1983) *Imagined Communities: Reflections on the Origin and Spread of Nationalism*. Verso.

Cooke, L. (1999) 'British Cinema: Representing the Nation', in J. Nelmes (ed.) *An Introduction to Film Studies*. (2nd edn) Routledge.

Thompson, J. O. (1978) 'Acting: Screen Acting and the Commutation Test', *Screen* 19(2): 55–70.

11 PASSING MS1: MEDIA REPRESENTATIONS AND RESPONSES

In this chapter we will look at:

- What to expect in the exam
- How to prepare for the exam
- How to cope with the exam
- Useful revision techniques
- What makes a good answer.

What to expect:

- The exam is worth 50% of the AS level
- It is 2.5 hours long
- There are three compulsory questions.

INFORMATION BOX

Past papers are available to look at on the WJEC website. Familiarise yourself with the layout, questions and language used in the exam papers. Have a go at some of the questions, even if you just bullet point your ideas for answers.

The exam paper

Question 1 requires an analysis of an unseen text, either print or moving image. It is worth **40 marks**.

You are not expected to be familiar with the specific example chosen but you should know the codes and conventions of the form. For example, the unseen text might be the front pages of the *Independent* and the *Mirror* – you may not have studied those in class but you will have studied (and revised!) newspapers.

WJEC suggests that 25–30 minutes will be allocated to the viewing and study of the unseen texts, leaving 45–50 minutes of writing time.

Questions 2 and 3 will be based around audience and representation issues, with question 2 being broken down into shorter questions, while question 3 requires a longer essay-style answer. You will be required to use your own examples of texts to answer the questions. Each question is worth **30 marks**.

WJEC suggests that between 35 and 40 minutes should be allocated to each of the two questions – remember that they are worth the same amount of marks. The 'stepped' question will allocate the marks between the shorter answers, giving you an idea of how much to write.

There are 100 marks available in total.

Preparing for the exam

1. Familiarise yourself with the exam papers. Your teacher will be able to help you with this, but you can also visit the WJEC website as suggested above.
2. Coordinate your notes. You need to make sure that your notes are complete, and that there is nothing missing. It is also important that you organise your notes so that you know exactly what is required to revise for each question. One way of doing this could be to organise notes into the following sections:

    (a) Media language, codes and conventions for media texts, narrative structure and genre conventions (Question 1).
    (b) Audience theories: key points for each theory, arguments for and against the usefulness of the theory.
    (c) Representation case studies: age, gender (male and female), ethnicity, identity, issues and events.

3. Ensure you have two or three texts you can write about for each representation case study; these must be from a range of media forms. Revisit these texts and add to your notes, considering:

■ how they compare to each other
■ which issues and debates they raise.

Make sure you know these texts really well, making a list of key words for each text which summarise the points you need to make.

Example: revision summary for a news programme – *BBC News at Ten*

Visual codes:

- Colour in opening sequence: red, grey and white; gender neutral, serious and calm
- Graphics: CGI, fast-moving, abstract shapes suggesting speed and urgency
- 'Costume' and body language of news reader: formal suit, upright posture
- Iconography, props and set: glass and reflective surfaces, hard, clean lines, very large, curved desk, suggests latest technology (sci-fi genre?). Laptop, flat screen in 'wall', pen in newsreader's hand ready to record the latest developments.

Technical and audio codes:

- Music: recognisable 'theme tune', electronic, regular, intense beat; sound of chimes introduces each headline
- Voiceover: newsreader summarises each story over the images
- Each story summarised by images – report, graphics, etc. – variety of shot styles
- Mid-shots, straight-ahead framing dominates in studio setting.

Genre conventions:

- Credit sequence: music, graphics, sound
- Newsreader: recognisable presenter, male, middle-aged, white
- Stories listed according to hierarchy of news values
- Narrative structure: newsreader introduction, report, two-way, newsreader, etc.
- Narrative structure: domestic news, foreign news, sport, light story, local news, weather.

Develop your revision by posing – and answering – questions relating to the following concepts:

Audience:

- Who is the audience for *News at Ten*?
- What uses and gratifications are available for the audience?
- Does the audience accept news stories as true?

Representation:

- Gender: male-dominant form? (presenters, reporters, editors), older male/younger female pairing of news readers
- National identity: construction of British identity through selection of stories covered
- Ethnicity: how are different ethnic groups represented in the news? How does the hierarchy of news values affect this representation?

Issues and debates:

- Has the news become another form of entertainment? (celebrity as news, etc.)
- Can the news be objective?

MS1: A Practice Paper created by the authors

See the WJEC website for past papers.

Answer all three questions

Figure 11.1 *Sex and the City 2* film poster (2010)

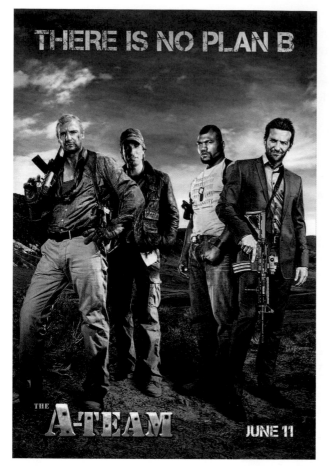

Figure 11.2 *The A-Team* film poster (2010)

Question 1

1. Analyse the two film posters commenting on:

- Visual codes
- Layout and design
- Genre conventions. [40]

Exam tips: how do you make notes?

Remember you must structure your analysis around the bullet points (usually three from the following):

- Visual codes, technical codes, narrative codes, genre codes

---

Therefore it makes sense to use these to organise your notes. You might use a mind map, columns, spider diagram – whatever system you find most effective.

The second stage is to SYNTHESISE your notes with your ideas about:

■ PURPOSE and EFFECT

In writing an analysis you need to explain why a particular form has been used; what the PURPOSE and EFFECT is. It isn't enough just to describe the text.

Summarise your notes

Visual	■ SATC: main characters grouped together, low-angle shot, eyeline straight at viewer. ■ Costume: limited colour range, mostly plain, silky material, diaphanous, floaty scarf waves across the women, stiletto shoes. ■ Setting: sand and sky, almost blank, very little detail.
Purpose and effect	■ Composition reinforces the selling point of the film – the four female friends; emphasises their closeness, eyeline makes direct contact with the viewer – this is an intimate, emotional film experience. ■ Costume is sophisticated and expensive looking; one of the pleasures of the film will be seeing the fashionable clothes the characters are wearing. Relative plainness of the costume means that the focus is on the recognisable faces of the four stars. Costume also reveals the muscular arms and shoulders of the women. ■ The setting is in contrast to the title with its reference to the 'city'; suggests a journey for the characters – in keeping with the demands of a sequel.

continued

Shaping your analysis

Once you've made your detailed notes you need to write your analysis:

- Structure the analysis around the bullet points – but use formal essay style, not notes.
- Begin with a statement or overview of the text/s which shows you have considered the codes, purpose and effect.
- If there is something unconventional about the text/s this would be a good place to start.
- Avoid starting with 'I'm going to analyse the text with reference to. . .'.

2. (a) Choose **one** of the film posters. Suggest **two different** audiences for this film. Give brief **reasons** for your choice. [6]
   (b) Using **either** of the film posters explain how the **main** audience for the film has been targeted. [9]
   (c) What **different uses** are available to a **range of audiences** from different media texts? Refer to **your own detailed** examples. [15]

Exam tip: following instructions

In this exam paper the questions move from a focus on the exam texts to asking you to refer to your own examples. It's very important that you follow these instructions; if you base your answer on the exam texts when you've been asked to refer to your own examples you can only receive a low mark.

It is worth highlighting the instructions about use of texts before you start making your notes.

3. With reference to **your own detailed** examples, explore the **different representations** of **gender** in the media today. [30]

Exam tip: exam essay writing

Writing essays in an exam can be broken down into the following stages:

- read and analyse the essay title
- plan your answer
- write up your answer.

Exam essays must address/answer the question:

- Essays which summarise everything you know about an area without addressing the question explicitly will only gain a low mark.
- It is very important to spend time planning your essay in an exam – it's time well spent.

Read and analyse the essay title

It is important to read and analyse essay titles carefully. See if the title can be broken down into a number of parts or questions. **Underlining the key words and phrases** is an ideal way to start. This will help you identify **what** you are being asked to discuss and **how** you are being asked to discuss it. You know you will be asked about a specific topic area. However, you also need to note whether you have been asked to analyse, describe or evaluate or to compare texts.

Once you have carefully analysed the title allow yourself some time to write down **any and all ideas** which you think are associated with it. This free flow of ideas is sometimes described as a **thought shower**. Don't worry about getting them in any order or making them completely clear. The idea is to simply **gather your thoughts** in one place.

Plan your answer

An essay consists of three parts: an **introduction, main body and conclusion**.

The introduction: although approaches to this part of the essay can vary, here is an approach which is particularly effective in putting the person reading your essay (the examiner) at ease.

continued

First, show clearly that you're **responding** to the **essay title**. State what you are going to do in the essay in a few short, clear sentences. This will help to give your essay a **clear structure**. Finally, tell the reader what you are going to **argue or conclude**.

The main body of the essay: this is the major part of your essay, as your introduction and conclusion should only be one paragraph each. Typically, you might have **three or four points** of discussion in the body of an essay although this can vary depending on the essay. For each point of discussion explain clearly the subject under discussion. You should assume that your reader is 'intelligent but uninformed', so you need to explain each point you make. Also, show how this line of argument is **directly addressing the essay title** and how it is related to what you are going to argue or conclude.

In each paragraph try to follow the '**main point, plus supporting evidence and conclusion**' structure. That is, state the main point that you are making at the start of the paragraph; then give your evidence and/or reasoning in support of this point; and then refer back to the main point again as you conclude your paragraph.

The conclusion: this should be brief and to the point, and no more than a paragraph in length. You should aim to summarise your essay by gathering the most important of the points that you have made. This summary can then be used to justify your main argument or conclusion, as stated in the introduction.

Question 2

In your answer to this question you need to demonstrate your understanding of the concept of audience.

(a) This part of the question requires you to focus on one of the two texts and apply your knowledge of audience segmentation and ways of categorising a target audience. The question also requires you to give reasons for your answer, for which you need to make close reference to the text itself, but also use your awareness of secondary and alternative audiences for media texts.

Possible target audiences for the *Sex And The City 2* poster could include:

- Women aged mid-twenties upwards – fans of the television series and of the previous film
- Younger fashion-conscious audience: female, late teens and upwards; their boyfriends

- Female
- Gay men.

(b) This second part of the question requires detailed reference to the same poster to elaborate on your answer to the previous question. There are more marks available for this question, requiring you to go into greater detail to get the marks.

A possible answer on the *Sex And The City 2* poster could include the following points (assuming the main audience is women aged between their twenties and forties):

- Use of established female characters with whom the audience are familiar
- Use of eye contact to engage reader
- Emphasis on glamour created by high-fashion costumes
- Poster employs codes familiar from women's magazines: the fashion shot
- Soft pastel shades
- Aspirational appeal for older women
- Use of tilt and dynamic body language to convey excitement
- Upbeat feel created by broad smiles.

Now apply these questions to the poster for *The A-Team*.

(c) The final section of the audience question requires a short essay-style answer which is centred around texts you have studied. Your answer should show an understanding of the relevant audience theory, but must be based around analysis of the texts. It is expected that you should write about **two or three texts**, and to show an awareness of the different possible audience uses. Your texts should be from different media and be reasonably contemporary.

You will need to choose two or three contrasting texts which enable you to compare and contrast in your answer. A possible answer could involve discussion of:

- *Grand Theft Auto*
- 50 Cent website
- The *Sun*.

This would allow you to discuss the various uses and gratifications available for different target audiences, involving discussion of different media forms, texts and possible audience uses.

Question 3

This question is worth 30 marks and requires an extended response, structuring your points in the form of an essay, using the techniques outlined earlier in the chapter. A good answer will:

- Demonstrate an understanding of representation theory
- Illustrate your points using detailed analysis of texts
- Choose two or three appropriate contemporary texts from different media (use different texts from those chosen for Question 2)
- Show understanding of issues and debates surrounding the representation of gender
- Analyse the process of selection and construction which produces the representational focus.

Revision and exam preparation summary

- Revise and prepare three or four texts for each area of representation.
- Your total choice of texts should cover all the media forms listed by WJEC.
- Check your understanding of the theory behind the representations – for example, why does representation matter?
- Revise the key audience theories.
- Be familiar with the exam rubric and layout of the paper.

part 3

PREPARING FOR MS2:
THE PRODUCTION PROCESS

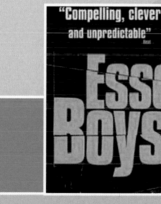

"Compelling, clever and unpredictable"
Heat

Essex Boys

PRODUCTION WORK,
EVALUATION AND
REPORT

12 PRODUCTION WORK, EVALUATION AND REPORT

In this chapter we will look at:

- What the coursework involves
- Effective research strategies
- Planning your pre-production and production work
- Effective approaches to the production task
- Evaluation of your production
- Writing the report.

The coursework is responsible for 50% of your overall marks for AS Media Studies. There are specific skills which you develop and utilise in your coursework, such as practical skills, planning, research and evaluation skills which make it distinct from your preparation for the exam. Interpersonal skills are also very important, as you may need to work closely with others, particularly if you are doing group work. This can be one of the greatest challenges of the coursework!

On the other hand, the success of your coursework depends on your understanding and knowledge of the media that you have gained through your Media Studies lessons. In this respect the other chapters of this book are important to your efforts, particularly the chapters on Media Language, Audience, Representation, and Narrative and Genre. These fundamental concepts will be at the heart of your coursework in planning, researching, producing and evaluating your product.

What does the coursework involve?

The WJEC gives very specific guidelines as to what you will need to produce:

Candidates will be required to produce **three** pieces of **linked** work. These will comprise:

- a **pre-production** reflecting research and demonstrating planning techniques
- a **production** which has developed out of the pre-production
- a **report** of 1200–1600 words.

It is important that you bear in mind the marks allocated to each of the three pieces. The coursework is worth 100 marks in total, which is divided as follows:

- Pre-production (20)
- Production (40)
- Report of 1200–1600 words (40).

According to the specification, the assessment objectives require you to:

- Apply knowledge and understanding when analysing media products and processes, and when evaluating your own practical work, to show how meanings and responses are created.
- Demonstrate the ability to plan and construct media products using appropriate technical and creative skills.
- Demonstrate the ability to undertake, apply and present appropriate research.

The report is just as important as the actual production piece so it is important not to overlook it and leave it to the last minute. The temptation can often be to devote most of your time to the production, bearing in mind that it can be very time consuming. You do need to be preparing for the report while working on your production work, making a record of research and important decisions.

The WJEC emphasises that the three pieces must be linked in some way. This means that you will focus on one specific area of the media in terms of genre or product. An example could be:

Pre-production: a script for an opening sequence for a new thriller

Production: the opening sequence of the new thriller

OR

Pre-production: storyboard for a trailer for a new soap opera

Production: a double-page spread on the new soap opera for a TV listings magazine

OR

Pre-production: mock-up of a website for a new band

Production: radio feature on the band.

There are more examples available on the WJEC website.

Starting out

You may be set a specific brief by your teacher, or you may be given more choice over the type of product you undertake. Consider your choice of brief carefully, thinking about your strengths and weaknesses, and whether you are more suited to group work or to individual tasks. Video work can seem more exciting than other choices, but entails much hard work and attention to detail. Nevertheless, it is important that you not only choose a brief that interests and appeals to you, but that you also try not to be over-ambitious.

Before you start out on your coursework, make sure you are clear about:

- How much time have you been given for each stage of the work? When is the deadline?
- What resources do you need?
- What research do you need to do?
- Are you familiar with the software you will be using?
- Will you be working as part of a group for the production stage?
- Will you be able to use equipment off the premises if you need to? Will you be able to use it outside your lessons?

The pre-production

The pre-production is worth 20% of the overall marks for the coursework. You will need to produce a piece of work that demonstrates:

- Research into your chosen product/industry
- Research into your target audience
- Planning skills
- Technical and creative skills
- Written skills (where appropriate).

Essentially the pre-production should be an artefact which demonstrates planning skills, as would be used in the media industry. Examples include:

- Storyboard
- Script
- Mock-up of magazine/website.

As in the examples given earlier in the chapter, there must be a link between the pre-production and your main product.

The first step

Consider your own technical skills in deciding on what artefact to produce. If you lack confidence in your artistic skills and feel you have stronger written skills, you may wish to choose to produce a script, for example. Make sure that you know what the conventions are for the differing artefacts, this being an important area in which to demonstrate your research skills.

Developing your ideas: coming up with your initial ideas for your pre-production and production can be quite challenging. You may be overwhelmed by ideas, or struggling to come up with anything. You need to be able to demonstrate:

- Technical skills
- Creativity
- Knowledge of textual conventions
- Narrative coherence and clarity
- Genre conventions.

The best source of ideas is other media texts. You need to research other examples of the product, making notes on ideas and conventions that you can adapt in your own work. Many actual products are strongly based on ideas from other texts – for example, the 2007 thriller *Disturbia* is fundamentally a remake of the 1950s Hitchcock film *Rear Window*, except it is set in contemporary America with a teen cast. Another good source for ideas can be your own experiences or stories you have come across in the news or magazines. Ultimately it is not the originality of the story that matters so much as your ability to develop and realise the idea, demonstrating the appropriate research, skills and knowledge.

It is very important to keep a record of your research, as it will inform what you write in your report. Try to be organised and have a way of keeping notes so that they will make sense to you when you come back to them. One possibility is to create a chart to record your observations, such as the one opposite which is in preparation for a mock-up for a front cover for a new high-quality women's magazine. The research could involve a detailed textual analysis of three comparable products.

Figure 12.1 *Harper's Bazaar*, October 2010

MAGAZINE	Language	*Mise en scène*	Mode of address	Types of stories
Harper's Bazaar (October 2010)	Alliteration used in cover lines; focus on celebrities and fame; generally informal yet sophisticated tone; 'Harper's Bazaar' suggests an exotic range of delights.	Slim, young model: couture clothing; surroundings alternate white/red classic bold font on white background; face centred on page; opened mouth creates sensual appeal.	Cover model looks directly at the reader; sultry expression; face and gaze is emphasised as directly beneath masthead; informal, fun yet sophisticated.	Cover lines focus on A-list celebrities and iconic places (e.g. Karen Elson, Alexa Chung). Revelations and insights into the lives of the famous; fashion and beauty advice.
Vogue				
Tatler				

Audience research

Audience research is an essential element of your production work. Not only will your pre-production and production work benefit from effective research into your target audience, but you will also need to demonstrate what research you have undertaken and how it has informed your work when writing your report.

It would be a good idea to form a clear idea of your target audience before you go any further (see Chapter 4 which explores the media and audiences). You may approach this by considering demographic and psychographic factors; as a starting point these may include:

- Gender
- Age range
- Lifestyle
- Attitudes and interests.

You may also wish to consider the way in which your target audience will consume the text – for example, how, where and when? This should be fundamental to how you approach the production, as you will need to construct the text with the manner and method of consumption in mind. For example, an advertising campaign needs to be designed with a clear sense of where and when the adverts will be displayed, and how they are going to actually reach their target audience. A magazine advert for a new fragrance would need to be placed where it will reach the social grade, gender and age group it is targeting – would it be targeting the readership of *Heat* or *Vogue*, for example?

Audience research techniques

The following methods can produce some valuable primary research for your production. It is important you plan your research strategy wisely and target appropriate representatives of your target audience.

Questionnaires: you will need to make sure that your questionnaire is going to provide you with relevant and useful material, which you can use in forming your decisions for your work. Avoid closed questions requiring 'yes' or 'no' answers as you need to encourage a fuller discussion to provide you with useful information of relevance to your coursework. As an example of how to frame useful questions, the following could be used to gain information about the target audience for a new horror film:

- Which are your favourite horror films?
- What do you find appealing about these particular films in comparison to others?
- What do you think makes an effective trailer for a horror film (give examples)?
- What is most important to you when deciding whether to see a new horror film – for example, the characters, suspense, mystery, the actors, the director?
- How are women represented in horror films?

Figure 12.2 *Eden Lake* film poster (2008)

■ Why do you think most contemporary horror films target a young adult audience?

Focus groups: a focus group is a means of having a structured discussion with a small group of representatives of your target audience. It is a way of developing a fuller response to your areas of research, as you will get discussion between the different members of the group. It is important that you prepare for it carefully, making a considered list of possible questions, perhaps open-ended ones in the style of the examples above. Be flexible though, as the discussion may develop some other useful ideas which you can use in your coursework. You could take along some examples of relevant comparable products to prompt discussion – for example, screening three examples of horror film trailers to accompany a discussion of what makes an effective horror film. One idea may be to record the discussion so that you can listen back to it and take notes, as you may find this difficult to do while chairing your group. Useful quotes could be taken from the discussion to use in your report.

Secondary research: you could undertake further research into audience ratings by looking up audience research that is already available in the public domain. A website such as www.imdb.com has breakdowns of audience ratings for films creating a profile of the target audience in terms of age and gender. Some magazine publishers place profiles of their magazines' target audience online in order to attract advertising, as can seen from the following profile of readers of FHM:

Audience profile

Men, aged 18–35. FHM is broad in its appeal, and has a wide range of readers and users, typified by mid-twenties 'work hard, play hard' guys. In the early stages of their careers and with an eye to the future, FHM readers are typically professionals, office workers and university-educated. They may be dating or living with a girlfriend, but they still take holidays with their mates. With good incomes and few financial commitments, these are high-value consumers, eager to invest in fashion, grooming, gadgets, travel and cars.

http://www.bauermedia.co.uk/Brands/FHM/

Figure 12.3 *FHM*, October 2010

Storyboards

The storyboard is a planning tool, in which the moving image sequence is planned, frame by frame, visualising exactly how it will be filmed. A storyboard should aim to show:

- Which characters are in the frame, and how they are moving
- What the characters are saying to each other, if anything
- The timing of each shot
- Camerawork
- An understanding of the target audience.

Researching texts: start out by researching sequences similar to the one you are going to storyboard. If you are going to plan opening sequences for a new thriller, watch a few examples. Ask your teacher for ideas to start with, but you can use websites such as imdb.com to research examples of film genres. YouTube can be a good place to view sequences if you are not able to get hold of a copy of the film.

ACTIVITY

Watch one minute of an example of the moving image text you are going to be planning.

- Count the number of transitions.
- What do you notice about the types of shots used and how they follow on from each other?
- What types of transitions are used?

Have a go at sketching a storyboard of the sequence to develop your understanding of how a film sequence is structured in terms of shots and transitions.

If you are not a very confident artist, you could use detailed stick figures or photographs in the storyboard. You are not assessed on artistic skills, but need to demonstrate a clear visualisation of the sequence. Have a look at examples of storyboards for ideas regarding presentation and style (try websites such as www.thestoryboardartist.com).

Below are some examples of students' storyboards.

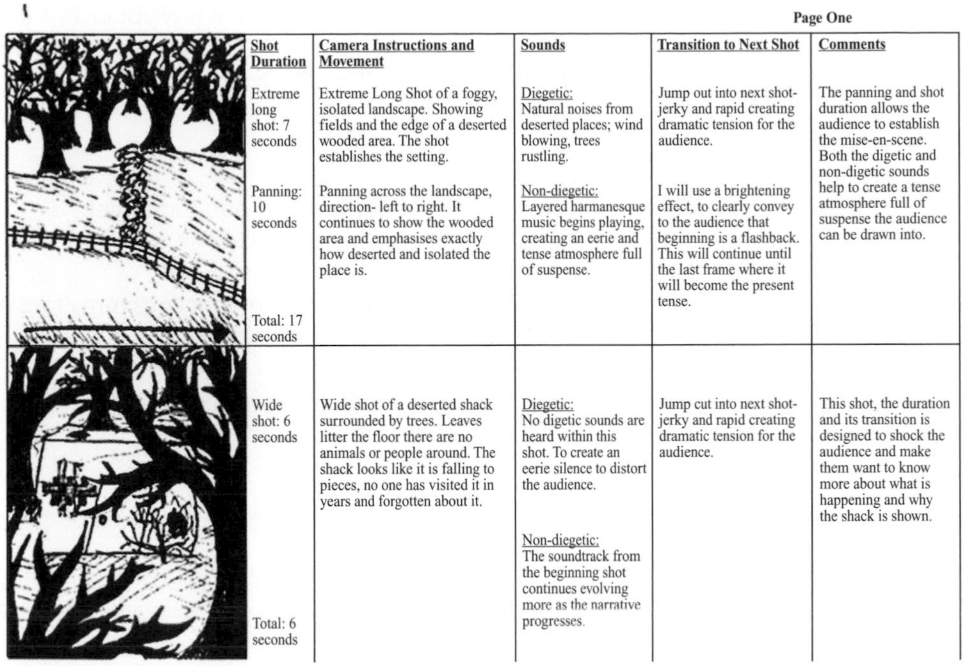

Page One

	Shot Duration	Camera Instructions and Movement	Sounds	Transition to Next Shot	Comments
	Extreme long shot: 7 seconds Panning: 10 seconds Total: 17 seconds	Extreme Long Shot of a foggy, isolated landscape. Showing fields and the edge of a deserted wooded area. The shot establishes the setting. Panning across the landscape, direction- left to right. It continues to show the wooded area and emphasises exactly how deserted and isolated the place is.	Diegetic: Natural noises from deserted places; wind blowing, trees rustling. Non-diegetic: Layered harmanesque music begins playing, creating an eerie and tense atmosphere full of suspense.	Jump out into next shot- jerky and rapid creating dramatic tension for the audience. I will use a brightening effect, to clearly convey to the audience that beginning is a flashback. This will continue until the last frame where it will become the present tense.	The panning and shot duration allows the audience to establish the mise-en-scene. Both the digetic and non-digetic sounds help to create a tense atmosphere full of suspense the audience can be drawn into.
	Wide shot: 6 seconds Total: 6 seconds	Wide shot of a deserted shack surrounded by trees. Leaves litter the floor there are no animals or people around. The shack looks like it is falling to pieces, no one has visited it in years and forgotten about it.	Diegetic: No digetic sounds are heard within this shot. To create an eerie silence to distort the audience. Non-diegetic: The soundtrack from the beginning shot continues evolving more as the narrative progresses.	Jump cut into next shot- jerky and rapid creating dramatic tension for the audience.	This shot, the duration and its transition is designed to shock the audience and make them want to know more about what is happening and why the shack is shown.

Figure 12.4 Example student storyboard (1)

Credit Courtesy of Amy Roberts

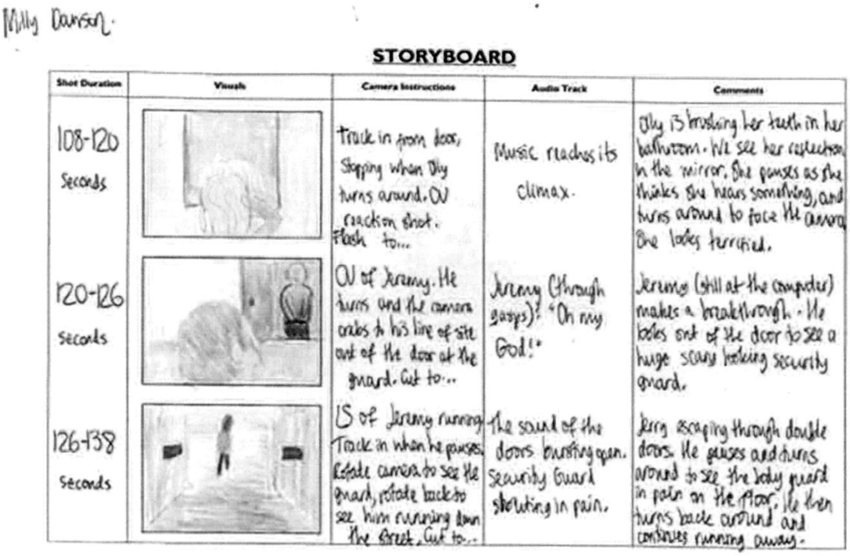

Milly Dawson.

STORYBOARD

Shot Duration	Visuals	Camera Instructions	Audio Track	Comments
108-120 Seconds		Track in from door, Stopping when Olly turns around. CU reaction shot. Flash to...	Music reaches its climax.	Olly is brushing her teeth in her bathroom. We see her reflection in the mirror. She pauses as she thinks she hears something, and turns around to face the camera. She looks terrified.
120-126 Seconds		CU of Jeremy. He turns and the camera crabs to his line of site out of the door at the guard. Cut to...	Jeremy (through gasps): "Oh my God!"	Jeremy (still at the computer) makes a breakthrough. He looks out of the door to see a huge scary looking security guard.
126-138 Seconds		LS of Jeremy running. Track in when he pauses. Rotate camera to see the guard, rotate back to see him running down the street. Cut to...	The sound of the doors bursting open. Security Guard shouting in pain.	Jerry escaping through double doors. He pauses and turns around to see the body guard in pain on the floor. He then turns back around and continues running away.

Figure 12.5 Example student storyboard (2)

Credit Courtesy of Milly Dawson

There are certain conventions regarding the written content of a storyboard which you will need to adhere to in order to demonstrate your understanding but also to ensure that your ideas are made clear:

- A new frame for each shot
- The duration of each shot, in seconds
- The camera instructions: choice of shot, angle, framing and movement
- Type of transition between shots, i.e. cut, fade, wipe, dissolve
- Details of sound: dialogue, sound FX, music
- Other useful information, e.g. lighting, character movement/gesture/facial expression, significant details regarding *mise en scène*.

(See Chapter 1 to revise relevant aspects of media language; pay attention to the abbreviations for shot sizes on p. 15.)

COURSEWORK TIP

Make sure that your drawings match up with the accompanying written annotation: if you describe the shot as being a close-up, then the picture needs to show a close-up!

Screenplay

The screenplay (or script) is another planning tool which concentrates more on the *mise en scène* and dialogue than a storyboard. A good screenplay pays close attention to detail, displaying a thorough visualisation of the sequence, through the medium of words rather than pictures.

Preparation: after watching examples of sequences similar to the one you are going to script, have a look at a range of different screenplays. Your teacher may have examples of film scripts, but there are a range of resources online which could help you, including:

- http://www.bbc.co.uk/writersroom/: this has advice for writing film, radio and TV scripts.
- http://www.screenwriting.info/: gives you advice for developing ideas, and also on how to present TV and film scripts.

ACTIVITY

Watch the opening of *Waterloo Road* – series 1, episode 1 – up until 1'
54". Having looked at a couple of scripts, draft the script for the sequence
before looking at the actual script that was used (as given below).

- How does the script create an impression of setting?
- What do we learn about the characters from the script? How important is dialogue in this sequence?
- What do we learn about the possible storyline of the episode and
  series?

WATERLOO ROAD

EPISODE 1

BY ANN MCMANUS & MAUREEN CHADWICK

PREQUEL

EXT. WATERLOO ROAD PLAYGROUND – DAY

JACK, TOM, BRIAN VAISEY, ESTELLE, ANDREW, NS PUPILS, NS
BARMAID

IT'S BREAK TIME AND THE PUPILS ARE HANGING OUT IN THE
PLAYGROUND – A ROWDY BUNCH OF MIXED RACES, WEARING
MARKET COPIES OR KNOCKED OFF ITEMS OF THE LATEST GEAR
WITH ONLY A FEW CONCESSIONS TO SCHOOL UNIFORM,
SUPERVISED BY DISILLUSIONED AND SOMEWHAT SHABBILY
DRESSED DEPUTY HEAD **JACK RIMMER** & ENGLISH DEPT 'MR
FIT' **TOM CLARKSON**.

JACK SURVEYS HIS CHARGES WITH A LOOK OF DESPAIRING
FRUSTRATION – A GANG OF TEENAGE GIRLS SPORT TIGHT T-
SHIRTS WITH SLOGANS LIKE 'FCUK LIKE BUNNIES' AND 'TOO HOT
TO HANDLE', INCLUDING A HEAVILY PREGNANT 16 YEAR OLD; A
BUNCH OF BAD BOYS COVERTLY SWAP CASH FOR A STASH;
SOME YOUNGER BOYS KICK A BALL AGAINST A GRAFFITI-
COVERED SCHOOL WALL.

continued

AS THE BALL STRAYS TOM'S WAY HE KICKS IT BACK TO THEM WITH FLAIR, TO ADMIRING GIGGLES FROM A COUPLE OF HIS 12-YEAR-OLD GIRL FANS. TOM TAKES A BOW.

THEN THERE'S A WHOOSHH! – AS A STACK OF BOX FILES COMES CRASHING DOWN FROM ON HIGH INTO THEIR MIDST – CRRUMPP! – JUST MISSING BRAINING ONE OF THE FOOTBALL PLAYERS . . . GIRL PUPILS SCREAM, THE KIDS SCATTER, PAPERS FLY LOOSE – IT'S LIKE A DIRTY BOMB'S JUST BEEN DROPPED. AND ALL HEADS REEL UPWARDS – TO SEE THEIR ELDERLY HEADMASTER, **BRIAN VAISEY**, CHUCKING OUT MORE FILES FROM HIS UPPER STOREY OFFICE WINDOW, HIS FACE TWISTED WITH PANIC AS HE YELLS DOWN AT THEM.

BRIAN
Who keeps soiling all this paper? I haven't got a dirty bum, I'm the head!

This is my school, not a toilet! I've got to get rid of all this rubbish . . .

HE DUCKS BACK INSIDE AND ANOTHER LOAD OF FILES IS HURLED OUT OF THE WINDOW. AND JACK RIMMER PALES – OH FCUK. THE PUPILS RUN FOR COVER, BUT SCREAMS AND GASPS TURN TO SNIGGERING.

PUPILS
Sir's gone muppet/He's a nutter/
Trying to kill us/ Call the pigs / & etc.

JACK NUDGES TOM.

JACK
Get the hell up there and gag him.

TOM GULPS AND DASHES INTO THE BUILDING, AS JACK BARKS AT THE KIDS.

JACK
Right, back inside! Now! Move it!

Script conventions

It is important that you can demonstrate that you have researched the conventions of the form, and use them consistently throughout. The conventions include:

- Each scene should start with a **scene heading**. This should indicate whether the scene is inside or outside, day or night, and where it is – for example, EXT. WATERLOO ROAD PLAYGROUND. DAY or INT. BRIAN'S OFFICE. DAY. (EXT: exterior; INT: interior)
- A scene heading should be followed by a **description of scene action**, that is, a description of the characters' actions and events. For example:

    It's break time and the pupils are hanging out in the playground – a rowdy bunch of mixed races . . .

- Characters' **names in capital letters**, unless mentioned in dialogue.
- Name of character who is speaking should be in the middle of the line above their dialogue.
- **Actor direction** can be added in brackets underneath the character's name. This can be used occasionally to indicate the way in which they speak, or to whom.
- **Dialogue**: the actual speech.

Note: scripts do not typically include directions for camerawork and editing.

Tips:

- Redraft to check that every word is essential and is helping to develop the action.
- Always check that your layout is accurate.
- Make sure that you use appropriate conventions for the genre and product you are creating.
- Does the script have a clear narrative?
- Is there a strong sense of your target audience?

Other pre-production artefacts

You may have been set the task of a mock-up for a magazine, newspaper, website, etc. A mock-up means a very detailed draft of a media product. The exam requests a minimum of two pages, which need to demonstrate research into a range of similar products, specifically:

- Clear understanding of the relevant codes and conventions
- Clear sense of target audience
- Clear narrative purpose

- Genre conventions
- Understanding of relevant aspects of media language.

Do not make the mistake of thinking that a mock-up is merely a sketch, and use original photographs rather than 'found' images.

Production

The production is worth 40% of the coursework marks, and must be linked to your pre-production piece, as explained earlier in the chapter. Your coursework may be in one of the following three forms:

- *Audio-visual*: can be produced individually, or as part of a group (of up to four). If you are working as part of a group you will need to choose one member's pre-production as the basis of your production. The finished piece should be up to three minutes in duration, although this is dependent on size of group, and nature of production.
- *Print*: individual work; a minimum of two pages of original material (including pictures).
- *Interactive media*: individual work as above; minimum of two pages of original material.

The mark scheme requires evidence of:

- Ability to construct media products
- Technical skills
- Creative skills
- Good written skills (where appropriate).

There are some very straightforward rules for producing good production coursework:

1. Planning: the product itself, resources and use of time
2. Research
3. Proficiency in using technology
4. Attention to detail
5. EFFORT!

The research that you have undertaken for your pre-production should inform your work. Your study of comparable products will be essential in helping you demonstrate these skills. Your production should aim to use appropriate:

- Technical codes
- Generic codes

- Narrative codes
- *Mise en scène* and
- . . . *a clear sense of your target audience.*

Audio-visual production work

PLANNING

The pre-production artefact will be the starting point for your production, but may well benefit from being adapted and extended in order to prepare for the actual filming. Your group will need to ensure that you have planned up to three minutes' worth of filming. As a group you will need to spend as much time as possible planning your filming. If you are working from a script, you will need to start developing a storyboard, visualising the filming of the sequence. In planning the filming, try to be as detailed as possible in considering the fundamental elements; that is:

- Camera shots
- Setting
- Costume
- Props
- Actors
- Time of day.

Not only will this assist you in planning out your sequence, but it should alert you to what needs to be done to prepare for the shoot in terms of organising of resources and time.

You will also need to produce a script to plan the dialogue and action. It would be useful to ensure that all members of the group and actors have a copy of this.

After this initial planning of your production you need to plan the logistics of your coursework. A useful tool for this is a shooting schedule, which allows you to plan what needs filming where, when and involving who. This encourages you to make sure that you don't have to return to the same set too many times, as you will do all the filming based there in one go. An example of a shooting schedule is shown below.

Shooting schedule: *Betrayed*

Date	Location	Scene	Actors	Costume	Props	Other info.
Monday, 15 October: pm	Castle Park	Scene 10: Steven meets Kate	Robbie (Steven) Jess (Kate)	Casual clothes – Steven in dark colours, Kate: bright primary colours	Ipod	Need a park bench for S. to sit on.
		Scene 17: Steven returns to park to find Kate	Robbie Bradley (Steven's friend: Tom)	Casual clothes – need to be different to indicate a different day		Same bench
Tuesday, 16 October: am	College: outside main entrance	Scene 8: Steven's argument with Tom	Robbie Bradley	Casual clothes: sombre colours for Steven	Books and bag for Tom	

Ensure that everyone has a copy of the shooting schedule. You will have to adapt it as you progress with the work, and ensure that everyone is up to date with changes. The shooting schedule will make clear to you how much filming you have to do, and how you are going to fit it into the time you have available.

ROLES FOR GROUP WORK

> **Eighty percent of success is showing up.**

(Woody Allen – *US movie actor, comedian and director*)

The WJEC state that each student in a group should make 'a significant and definable contribution' to the production. This could either be by taking a specific role, or by taking responsibility for specific scenes. Typical roles are:

Cinematographer in charge of the camera and lighting

Sound takes responsibility for organising sound equipment, checking sound levels, organising sound effects and music

Editor responsible for overseeing and directing editing.

TOP TIP!

Make sure you have mobile phone numbers for all members of crew (including actors); you need to be able to contact each other if there are any problems, especially with turning up at the right place, and at the right time.

BE PREPARED!

Actors: you will need to select appropriate actors for your production. Make sure that you have considered how appropriate each actor is for the role in terms of age, appearance and acting experience. You are not assessed for performance, yet casting and poor acting can detract from the overall production. It can be worth trying to find friends who have performing experience, but remember that they need to be available to fit in with your schedule and, above all, they must be reliable.

Locations: it is worth researching appropriate locations which will fit in with the desired atmosphere and setting, as well as being consistent with the generic conventions. Ensure you have sought permission to film when you plan to use other premises, such as shops or other privately-owned properties. It is worth being imaginative in your choice of location, but make sure that it is accessible. You may find that your footage for a specific location is incomplete or inappropriate, in which case you will need to be able to go back to do more filming. This could be a problem if the location is not easily reached.

Take the time to plan the actual set, making sure that you have made as much effort with lighting, props and *mise en scène* as possible. This is where it would be useful to have a set designer who is specifically charged with this responsibility.

EQUIPMENT

Make sure that you have booked the equipment you need for the filming: camera, tripod, microphones and lighting equipment. It is very important that you are familiar with how to use the equipment before you start filming. Check everything is in full working order, and batteries are fully charged, before travelling to your location.

Good planning and a reliable group go a long way towards ensuring success. Nevertheless, there are certain techniques and tips to follow:

■ Rehearse each shot before filming in order to identify any problems.
■ Don't move the camera around, or zoom in and out, too much when filming.
■ Use a tripod all the time, unless going for a deliberate handheld effect.
■ Get a good variety of shots – always film several takes of the same shot to give you more to choose from when editing.
■ Film close-ups to cut into a sequence when editing – for example, of facial expression, gesture, props; don't go more than three shots without a close-up!
■ Let the camera run for a few seconds before and after the planned shot.
■ Film more than you think you need! It will always come in handy when editing.
■ Consider the lighting of the shot – is it too dark? Is it appropriate for the scene?
■ Shots of scenes with nothing happening, or nothing being said, can be very effective at times in building atmosphere.
■ Make sure you have no distracting details in the shot – such as passers-by or a stray camera bag.
■ Check that you have the right amount of sky and background in the shot.
■ Don't film anywhere with lots of background noise – you will find that this will be all you can hear when you play it back.
■ If you can, use a separate microphone.

A useful website for advice on camerawork is http://www.bbc.co.uk/videonation/contribute/tips.

POST-PRODUCTION: EDITING

Editing is the process of organising and assembling your film footage, selecting appropriate and effective shots, and ultimately discarding the majority of your raw material. The editing process is a matter of crafting your footage into the final product, adding elements such as sound, special effects, transitions and titles to create the finished effect.

Never underestimate the time you need to allocate for editing. Editing is a very time-consuming and often frustrating process, yet it is also an opportunity to demonstrate creativity and sophisticated technical skills.

As part of your planning for your production you need to have researched the editing style which characterises similar products. This should include:

■ Use of continuity editing
■ Distinctive editing techniques – for example, montage, dissolves, fades, jumps, wipes
■ Pace of editing

■ Use of editing in constructing time/place for narrative – for example, flash-backs.

Have a look back at Chapter 1 to refamiliarise yourself with editing.

The most important preparation you can do is to familiarise yourself with the editing software. Your teacher or technician will be able to give you some guidance to get you started, yet you need to build up some experience in order to find out just what you can do with the software. Most software packages offer online manuals and advice, with video tutorials to support you.

Most editing programmes follow the same basic rules:

1. Capture footage (uploading on to the computer)
2. Assemble into rough order
3. Cut out excess footage
4. Fine-tune order and sequence of edits
5. Add any special effects
6. Add music and sound effects
7. Render into final product.

EDITING TIPS

The majority of film and television products will be making use of **continuity editing**. This is when shots are edited together to create seemingly continuous action, even though they will have been filmed at different times. Shots are edited together to create this effect. Most edits are straight cuts (see Chapter 1) unless more stylised transitions, such as wipes or jump cuts, are a distinctive feature of the product, and are particularly suited to the effect you are seeking.

Editing software offers an immense variety of effects and transitions that could be applied to your product. Restraint is essential as overuse of such features can detract from the impact of your final piece.

■ Ensure the pace of editing suits the atmosphere and mood you are seeking to create.
■ Always match an action: if a character leaves the frame on the right they should enter the next shot on the left.
■ Ensure you maintain the 180° rule: all shots that are edited together should be from the same side of an imaginary line, as shown in Figure 12.6.
■ Edit shots so that characters' eyelines are matched – for example, a taller character should be looking down towards a shorter character in the next shot.
■ Use cutaway shots (close-ups of specific details or objects relevant to the action) to develop the detail and fluency of your production – they can also help conceal any jumps or weak points in your footage.
■ Capture your footage regularly so that you can review its quality – and also as security, just for if the camera's hard drive is wiped.

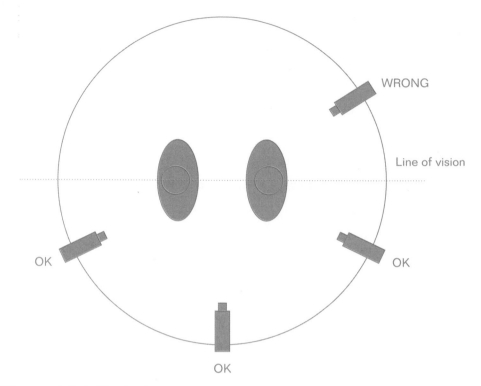

WRONG

Line of vision

OK

OK

OK

Figure 12.6 180° rule diagram

© Media Education Wales

http://www.mediaed.org.uk/posted_documents/Filmplan.html

■ Don't overuse effects on transitions: dissolves and fades can be very effective used sparingly and appropriately; wipes can seem tacky if not used with good reason!

■ Try not to cut on movement; wait until camera movement, or action within the shot has moved out of frame or stopped, before cutting.

FINAL TOUCHES . . .

Having edited together the footage you have selected for your product, play it through to other people who have not been involved in your group, and ask for their feedback. It's important that you listen to what they have to say, as a different pair of eyes can be useful in directing your attention to aspects of your work which could be improved. Don't lose heart when facing criticism; ultimately no product is ever really perfect or complete, but your task is to get the best possible mark, bearing in mind the task you have been set.

Once you are happy with the editing you will need to consider adding **text** and any other sound that is required. If you are producing a title sequence, advert or trailer, textual content may well be essential in proving your knowledge and research into the product. Not only do you need to consider what should be contained in the captions, but also the choice of typeface, colour font and placing of the captions. The editing software will allow you to make choices regarding how you want the text to appear on the screen. Try to respect the conventions of your type of product as much as possible.

As part of your research into the product you need to pay attention to the use of **sound**. If you are making a music video, this should be something to consider before you do any editing, as you may well want to edit your shots to the rhythm of the music track (rhythmic editing). Does your text require a voiceover? If so what kind of voice do you need considering the type of text, genre and target audience? Do you need to add any sound effects?

When adding a **music track** you need to consider what music to use, and when to use it. Don't be afraid to have silence, or just ambient sound; this can be a very effective and atmospheric device, rather than overusing a music track. Likewise, don't get carried away by using your favourite track, turning your sequence into a music video.

Spend time researching what music to use. It is a good idea to go beyond the obvious, and use the internet, your library and even your college's music department to source some suitable atmospheric music if this is required.

Production work: print products

Print work has to be produced individually, and should consist of at least two pages of original material, including photographs. Possible products could include:

- Magazine front cover and double-page spread
- Advertising campaign
- Newspaper front page and double-page spread
- DVD cover and posters for a new film release
- CD cover and accompanying adverts for a new music artiste
- Two pages from a website for a new radio station.

PLANNING

Your pre-production work will have helped you form ideas and gather relevant research for your chosen area. Nevertheless, you may well be producing a different product and will have to undertake further research into examples of the product, in particular its codes and conventions. As for your pre-production, you need to demonstrate research into your target audience in all your choices in constructing your product.

In your research you will need to pay particular attention to codes and conventions regarding:

- Layout
- Typeface

- Language and register
- Mode of address
- Use of colour
- Images
- Overall style and design
- Industry elements – for example use of bar code, price, logo
- Brand image
- Narrative codes.

Case study
FILM POSTER

One possible piece of production work is a film poster. You will have made decisions about the genre and target audience for your poster when planning your pre-production work. One possible approach could be to design a poster for a new thriller (perhaps alongside a DVD cover). A starting place for your planning will be to look at examples of thriller posters in order to research their codes and conventions.

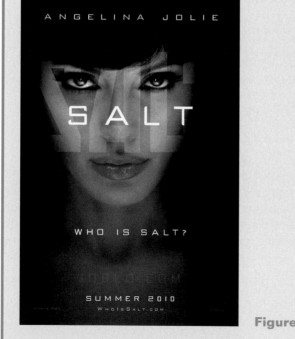

Figure 12.7 *Salt* film poster (2010)

The teaser poster (*Salt*, 2010): the teaser poster has a simplicity which lends itself to student production work. The layout is very straightforward, with minimal written text, centred in the frame, as is the close up of Angelina Jolie, who engages the audience by looking directly out of the poster, demanding our attention.

The title of the film is placed in the middle of Jolie's face, but is also shadowed behind the main title, covering her face. The title becomes inescapable as the audience are initially drawn to Jolie's gaze, which is caught up in the letters. The thriller genre is enforced by the sombre use of colour, as darkness frames Jolie's face, in contrast with the flesh tones of her skin and the sensual pink of her lips. The typeface is all in white, using a straightforward, sans serif font with connotations of espionage with its anonymous square lettering.

Thriller conventions are also evident in the use of enigma as the tagline is a question 'WHO IS SALT?' which is centred across Jolie's neck, inviting us to watch the film to find out the answer. Teaser posters rely on enigma to intrigue the audience to want to find out more about the film. Other film poster conventions include the date of release (although a teaser tends to state a general time of release – for example, 'summer 2010'), a website address and production company logos. The unique selling proposition of this film is made clear with the star's name being the main attraction for the audience, her face being instantly recognisable. The sensuality of her expression helps attract a male target audience, in addition to a female audience who may wish to watch a film with a strong female central character. Of course the target audience will be dominated by fans of her former roles, in particular that of Lara Croft, another enigmatic and strong female character.

Theatrical release poster (*The Expendables*, 2010): in contrast to the teaser poster there is much more written text on the main theatrical release poster for a film. Certain conventions are common to both, with the emphasis being on the stars of the film and the title being the most prominent detail, set in a larger typeface and centred across the bottom of the poster. The stars are the main selling point of the film with the names being listed across the top of the poster, with the biggest stars being depicted as their names are repeated above the title. This film appears to be an action/adventure thriller, as would be expected from the stars involved. The muscular masculinity of the three characters depicted is highlighted by the backdrop of a hellish inferno. The characters are unconcerned by this, one of them calmly holding a large weapon, and all dressed in dark clothing, presumably ready for action. The Stallone character is impassive

continued

Figure 12.8 *The Expendables* film poster (2010)

and confrontational in the foreground, his arms folded, brandishing his impressive muscles, a large cigar in the corner of his mouth and aviator sunglasses creating an air of mystery. All three of the characters look coolly out of the poster, as if they are sizing up the audience.

The sans serif typeface uses red and orange in places to continue the explosive feel of the poster. The poster suggests a narrative that revolves around violent conflict, appealing largely to a male target audience who would be familiar with other films featuring these stars. The title of the film is important in signifying the genre with 'The Expendables' suggesting a life-and-death situation, as is made vivid on the poster.

All theatrical release posters have a credit block across the bottom, which includes detailed credits regarding cast, crew and production companies, including relevant logos. The actual release date stands out underneath, using an orange typeface and a larger font size.

It is important that you use the appropriate conventions for the text you choose to work with – paying attention to detail such as the difference between the teaser poster and the subsequent theatrical release version. The same film may have very different posters for each stage of its advertising campaign, as you can see on a website such as www.imdb.com.

From looking at these two posters, among others, you may gather ideas about what to include on your poster, how to structure and style it, how to appeal to your target audience and how to use appropriate genre and narrative codes.

After having established the relevant codes and conventions, and having revised your research into your target audience, the next stage would be to produce a mock-up of your text(s). This involves a full-size handwritten draft of the layout, indicating images, style and key headings. The more detailed and thorough this is, the more useful it will be. Show the mock-up to members of your target audience and get their feedback before producing the final product.

THE PRODUCTION

Whatever text(s) you are producing you will need to use an appropriate software package, such as Photoshop. Make sure that you are confident with the software before you start, seeking appropriate support from your teacher and/or technician. There are also some useful tutorials online if you visit websites for the software.

Images: one of the key elements in making your product successful will be the images that you use, which you will need to create, whether they are photos or graphic images. These images need to be meticulously planned. If you are going to be taking photos, make sure you have planned:

- Composition
- Setting
- Lighting
- Framing
- Props
- Choice of 'model'
- Costume
- Colour.

Take a range of shots using different angles and shot distances in order to have some choice over what will work best for your purposes.

Written content: research the style and register of similar products, taking into consideration your target audience. Don't overlook the importance of the written content as it needs to demonstrate your knowledge of the product and the audience. Make sure your mode of address, layout and structure are appropriate for the type of text.

Finishing: it is important to allow time for final checking and feedback. Print off your work in draft quality before printing a final high-quality version. This will allow you to spot any problems or errors before you submit it. It would be a good idea to show it to members of your target audience to get any last feedback – they may notice something that you have overlooked! Make sure you use a good-quality printer for your final draft.

Below is an example of student print production work – posters and a DVD cover for a new thriller.

Figure 12.9
Example student print production work – poster (1)

Figure 12.10
Example student print production work – poster (2)

Figure 12.11 Example student print production work – DVD cover

Courtesy of Liam Mahon

The report

The report is worth 40 marks, the same amount of marks as the production. The WJEC's guidance states that It must be:

- 1200–1600 words
- Individual work.

According to the WJEC, the report should include:

- a discussion of the most significant research findings which informed the pre-production
- a brief justification of the target audience for the production
- an evaluation of the production which highlights its strengths and weaknesses through, for example, a comparison with existing media products.

The report can be submitted as either:

- an illustrated report;
- an essay; or
- a suitably edited blog.

The mark scheme halves the marks available between:

- demonstrating independent research skills; use of research to inform the pre-production
  and
- ability to apply knowledge and understanding in evaluating the product, with reference to comparable media products.

These two sections are quite different from each other, as the first half is based on research skills, whereas the second half is marked for evaluation skills. One way to approach writing this would be to write the first half after having completed the pre-production, and then the second half when you have finished the product. There may be quite a long break between completing the two pieces, so it would be best to write about your pre-production while it is fresh in your mind. Allow roughly half the word count for each section, given the equal split in marks between the two.

Research and the pre-production

In this section you need to write concisely about the research you have undertaken, and how this has informed your decisions about the pre-production. In preparation for your first draft you may find it helpful to consider the following questions:

- What comparable texts did you use for research?
- How did you adapt the codes and conventions from these texts for your pre-production artefact?
- What research did you undertake into your target audience?
- How did you use the results of this research in forming your artefact?

It is very important that you keep a record of your research to help you organise your ideas for the report.

Start the report by outlining your brief, before going into more detail about the pre-production, as in the following example:

> For my coursework I decided to plan a storyboard for a new reality TV show before going on to work as part of a group and filming the opening sequence. As part of my research into the genre I watched a range of reality TV shows, with three in particular being important in forming my

ideas for my storyboard: *Wife Swap, The Family* and *Come Dine With Me. Wife Swap* was important in forming the narrative of my reality show, with the concept of swapping places and living someone's life, while I decided I wanted to use the fly on the wall observational documentary style of *The Family. Come Dine With Me* inspired the use of an ironic voice-over in my production, and the idea of people from different backgrounds having to spend time together.

As this example illustrates, it is important to refer to specific aspects of the texts you have researched and relate them to the decisions you have made in forming your pre-production work.

Evaluation

This section is centred on evaluating your final production piece, demonstrating your knowledge and understanding of the relevant codes and conventions. Again, the mark scheme requires you to make reference to your research, by comparing your production to comparable products. A good starting point would be to get some audience feedback, preferably from the audience you are targeting with your work.

Make a list of the strengths and weaknesses of your production work, in comparison with specific examples of comparable products. Consider:

- Media language
- Genre conventions
- Narrative codes and conventions
- Use of representations
- Technical sophistication
- Targeting of an appropriate audience.

A straightforward way to start this section is to outline your role in the production work; this is of greater importance if you work as part of a group. Your evaluation should then focus on your contribution to the overall production. You may well want to make comments about the overall effectiveness of the product, but take care to analyse your work in particular, whether it be lighting, cinematography or editing, for example. A possible structure for the report could be:

- Outline your role
- Summarise overall effectiveness of final product
- Indicate strengths and weaknesses, in relation to relevant aspects of comparable products
- Outline effectiveness of techniques used to engage target audience
- Summarise response of target audience.

Don't get sidetracked into merely describing what you did, or dwelling on the various problems that occurred along the way. You will gain marks for demonstrating your knowledge and understanding of the media in your evaluation of the production process and the media text(s) you have produced. The following example of the beginning of an evaluation shows how you should aim to analyse and evaluate, rather than describe:

> My group decided to develop my storyboard for a title sequence for a new soap opera *Mersea Folk*, and my role was to take charge of the camerawork. Having studied a range of soap operas we decided to depart from typical conventions in having a pre-title sequence which followed on from the cliff hanger of the previous episode. The camerawork was kept static deliberately, relying on the editing to involve the audience as in all conventional soaps. A range of still shots of the different characters and settings were used to create a montage for the title sequence. The characters were photographed against a blank wall in a variety of shots and poses, as in the title sequence for *Hollyoaks*. This worked well in establishing the characters, although it would have been more effective if we had used a greater range of character types, to indicate the range of storylines that are typical of a soap opera.

A good report will try to make use of appropriate terminology, making use of your learning from elsewhere on your course in proving your knowledge of the media concepts. Remember you are being assessed for the structure, accuracy and quality of your writing as well. Finally, make sure that you stay within the stipulated word count. Too few words would suggest that you needed to go into greater detail, but it is equally important not to exceed the maximum length.

EPILOGUE: IS THAT IT? A LOOK TO THE FUTURE

In reading the final part of this book, you are now most likely doing one of two things. Either you are reading this having completed or are just about to complete the AS level course and are wondering what the future may hold for you, or you are in fact not at that stage at all and are simply thumbing through the book and have stumbled across this final section. To be honest, whichever of these is the case, there is never a bad time to consider your future options and the part you want Media Studies to play in that future.

The fact is that you are now only half-way through your studies, assuming you have recently or will soon be completing the AS course, half-way, that is, towards completing the complete advanced course of study. This is an exciting time as you ponder moving up to A2 level in a subject area which is linked to one of the fastest-growing sectors in the UK economy, albeit one of the most competitive as well – the media. There will always be a need for talented media professionals to fill those posts, which do become available both within and outside the media industries, and to take the subject further through innovation and creativity. The subject and those related to it have also experienced growth in higher education and if you fall into the category of a student who has decided to follow either or perhaps both of these paths in the future, then the importance of continuing to work hard and meeting the demands of A2 level are clear.

However, for many students, the summer holiday lies between you now and the commencement of the A2 course – and not forgetting those examination results in August. If you have completed the AS course, there really isn't much you can do to affect those results now, but if you haven't, then perhaps you should give some consideration to a final push before the exams start. However, there is no time like the present to reflect on the subject and ask what the subject has brought you in terms of skills and experience and what it can offer you at the higher A2 level.

So what has the subject done for you so far?

- You have learned how to read a range of media products (arguably the subject's core skill) using semiotic devices.
- You have explored audience issues attached to a range of media and considered who consumes media products and how they are consumed.
- You have considered how the media represents people, places and things and how representations are often based upon stereotypes by either challenging or reinforcing them.
- You have researched a media type of your choice and planned your own production based upon your research.
- You have tried your hand at practical production which was based upon your research findings; seldom in any academic field do you find a more important or relevant task than 'finding something out' and then 'applying your findings creatively'. Your production will have been more refined, polished and professional than any you might have done at GCSE.

And here's what you can expect at A2 level:

- A more focused research task based upon an area of media of your choice and one which invites you to structure your own research, answer an issue you have identified and complete deep analytical study into media products which are relevant to your research topic.
- Complete a research essay based on your findings and present it in a manner befitting second-year advanced study.
- Apply your research to a further practical production which this time requires you to illuminate your findings creatively and appropriately.
- Look more closely into the area of media industry and examine issues surrounding technology, regulation, ownership and control of media organisations.
- Develop your studies from the AS course into text and audience and prepare for an exam which requires you to have detailed knowledge of at least nine different media texts drawn from three media types and to be able to answer three questions: one each on text, industry and audience.
- In terms of challenge, you will see an upward step from AS level as you are encouraged to take more responsibility for your own learning and to become more independent while at the same time showing skills of synopticity in which you draw upon your prior learning and use the key concepts and tools of the subject with regularity and ever-increasing confidence.

And now you should look forward to the day when as a second-year advanced level student, you open up the pages of your copy of *A2 Media Studies: The Essential Introduction for WJEC* (Bateman, Bennett, Casey Benyahia and Wall, 2010) for the first time and begin to thrive and blossom in your final year as a second-year Media Studies A level student, unless of course your enthusiasm and conscientiousness has inspired you to read it over the summer holiday. . . .

GLOSSARY

action code A narrative device by which a resolution is produced through action; for example, a shoot-out.

actuality Recordings of images and sounds of events made on location as they actually happen for inclusion in news reports or documentaries.

agenda setting Selection of important news events.

anchorage The fixing or limiting of a particular set of meanings to an image. One of the most common forms of anchorage is the caption underneath a photograph.

bias To lean towards a particular point of view; to demonstrate a prejudice.

binary oppositions The presence of opposing forces or qualities such as light and dark, good and evil, etc. A key means of acquiring understanding in media products.

breaking news A news story, the details of which are unfolding as the story is being reported.

bricolage The way in which signs or artefacts are borrowed from different styles or genres to create something new.

catharsis A purging of the emotions through pity and terror, leaving an audience less likely to behave horribly because they have experienced the results vicariously.

chiaroscuro effect The effect caused by a strong contrast between light and dark on an image.

cinéma vérité A documentary form which combines realism with cinematic styles of camerawork and editing.

codes Rules or conventions by which signs are put together to create meaning.

connotation The meaning of a sign that is arrived at through the cultural experiences a reader brings to it.

content analysis A method of collecting, collating and analysing large amounts of information about the content of media products, such as television advertisements, in order to draw conclusions about such issues as the representation of gender roles.

continuity editing System of editing which uses specific techniques to create the effect of continuous action.

conventions Typical characteristics of a media form.

convergence The coming together of different communication technologies such as the telephone, the computer and the television.

countertype A representation which counters the commonly shared stereotype.

crowdsourcing Sourcing information and knowledge from the wider public, drawing on their experiences and eye-witness accounts.

cut (straight cut) Straight edit from one shot to another.

decoding The process of reading the meaning encoded in a media text.

denotation What an image actually shows and what is immediately apparent, rather than opposed to the assumptions an individual reader may make about it.

diegesis The environment created in a fictional moving text.

disequilibrium The disruption of normality within a narrative.

dissolve Film term for the transition between two images whereby one 'dissolves' into the next.

docu-soap A hybrid genre in which elements of documentary and soap opera are combined to create a series about the lives of real people.

effects model Theory concerning the impact of the media on people's behaviour and thinking.

encoding A process by which the media constructs messages.

editorialising Process undertaken by media producers in deciding what to include, and exclude, in a news report.

end credits At the end of a film or television production, a detailed list of all the people who contributed to the production, from producers and directors to actors and technical, administrative and support crews.

enigma A narrative device that teases the audience by presenting a puzzle or riddle to be solved.

equilibrium The 'normality' that exists at the beginning of a narrative, which is disrupted.

ethnicity Characteristics of a social group having racial, cultural and religious traits in common.

feature In newspapers this is generally an article that concerns itself with a topical issue while not having any hard news content.

feminism Movement to gain equal rights for women.

foley artist The person responsible for artificially creating the sounds used in a film or TV programme.

gatekeeping Controlling which events are reported in the media.

genre The term used for the classification of media texts into groups with similar characteristics.

hard news News that is important and is happening at the time it is reported. A rescue attempt on a cross-Channel ferry, the death of an important national figure or a rise in mortgage interest rates could all be classified as hard news.

hegemony The concept used by the Marxist critic Antonio Gramsci to describe how people are influenced into accepting the dominance of a power elite who impose their will and worldview on the rest of the population. Gramsci argues that this elite is able to rule because the rest of the population allow it to do so. It can be argued, therefore, that the ideological role of the media is to persuade us that it is in our best interests to accept the dominance of this elite.

horizontal integration This involves the acquisition of competitors in the same section of the industry. It might be possible for one company to seek to control all of the market – a monopoly position – but most capitalist countries have laws to prevent this from happening.

hybrid A cross between at least two different genres or formats.

hypodermic needle theory A theory which suggests that the media 'injects' ideas into a passive audience, like giving a patient a drug.

hypothesis An assumption or question about something that the research will investigate and, it is hoped, either prove or disprove.

icon A sign that works by resemblance.

iconography Those particular signs that we associate with particular genres, such as physical attributes and dress of actors, the settings and 'tools of the trade' (for example, cars, guns).

ideology A system of beliefs that determines how power relations are organised within a society.

impartiality Not showing any bias; balanced point of view.

independents Companies (usually relatively small ones) that maintain a status outside the normal big-business remit and therefore tend to focus on minority-interest products.

interpellation The process by which a media text summons an audience in much the same way as a town crier would ring a bell and shout to summon an audience for an important announcement.

intertextuality The way in which texts refer to other media texts that producers assume audiences will recognise.

linear narrative A plot that moves forward in a straight line without flashbacks or digressions.

media imperialism The idea that powerful and wealthy countries can exercise economic, cultural and social control over others through control of media industries.

media industries The industries and businesses which produce, distribute and exhibit media texts.

media saturation A term used to describe the extent to which our experience of the world is dominated by the media, not only at an individual level but also nationally and globally.

mediation The process by which a media text represents an idea, issue or event to us. This is a useful word as it suggests the way in which things undergo change in the process of being acted upon by the media.

methodology The system or manner used to carry out research; the different ways in which 'data' can be captured.

mid-market tabloids Tabloid-sized newspapers, balancing news values of the popular press with more serious news reporting.

mise-en-scène A term which literally means 'put on stage' (from 1920s theatre terminology), this has come to mean 'put in scene' in media. It refers to the creation of the visual elements in a moving image such as lighting, costumes and props.

mode of address The way in which a particular text will address or speak to its audience.

montage A sequence of different shots edited together which are juxtaposed to create a specific effect or message.

moral panic A mass response to a group, a person or an attitude that becomes defined as a threat to society.

multi-tracking The process whereby different instruments and voices are recorded separately and then mixed together in a recording studio.

narrative The way in which a story is told in both fictional and non-fictional media texts.

narrowcasting The opposite of broadcasting. Where texts are aimed at very small, special-interest groups.

negotiated reading A response to the text which is only partially that intended by the producers, with some disagreement with encoded readings.

news agencies Organisations dedicated to gathering news items, and selling them on to news producers.

news values The values applied by a news producer in determining the news agenda.

newsworthy An event which is judged of sufficient importance as to be reported in the media.

niche market A small target audience with specific interests, for example, DIY, classic cars or royalty.

open questions Those that start with 'what', 'where', 'why', 'when', 'how' or 'who'. These encourage the interviewee to 'open up' and talk freely.

oppositional reading Response to media text which is in conflict with that intended by producers.

parallel action A narrative device in which two scenes are observed as happening at the same time by cutting between them.

patriarchy Society dominated by male power.

polysemic The way in which a text has a variety of meanings and the audience is an important component in determining those meanings.

popular press The tabloid-sized mass market press, otherwise known as 'red-tops'.

postmodernism The social, political and cultural attitudes and images of the late twentieth and early twenty-first century.

preferred (or dominant) reading The reading closest to that intended by the producers of the media text.

pre-production, production, post-production The different stages and processes involved in the construction of a media text.

primary media Where we pay close attention to the media text, for instance, in the close reading of a magazine or newspaper, or in the cinema where we concentrate on the film in front of us.

PSB (Public Service Broadcasting) Introduced in the UK in the 1920s by Lord Reith, later Director General of the BBC, with a remit to 'inform, educate and entertain'. The yearly licence fee was payable first to cover radio sets and then, after the Second World War, to include televisions, too. This form of financing meant that the service was not reliant on outside commercial backing and could therefore, in principle, remain unbiased. PSB is designed to ensure a balanced coverage of different types of programme.

qualitative research A type of research that attempts to explain or understand something and may necessitate much discussion and analysis of people's attitudes and behaviour. It usually involves working with small numbers of people or 'focus groups'.

quality press Newspapers reporting more serious, 'hard' news, using a more formal presentation and register.

quantitative research A type of research, usually based on numbers, statistics or tables, that attempts to 'measure' some kind of phenomenon and produce 'hard' data. It often involves working with large groups of people.

realism Representation by the media of situations or ideas in such a way that they seem real.

representation The process by which the media presents to us the 'real world'.

secondary media Where the medium or text is there in the background and we are aware that it is there but are not concentrating on it.

semiotics The study of signs and sign systems.

sensationalism Reporting which highlights and exaggerates the more sensational aspects of an event.

sign The sign consists of two components: the signifier and the signified. The signifier is a physical object, for example, a sound, printed word or advertisement. The signified is a mental concept or meaning conveyed by the signifier.

situated culture A term used to describe how our 'situation' (daily routines and patterns, social relationships with family and peer groups) can influence our engagement with and interpretation of media texts.

social media Web-based and mobile technologies which promote interactive communication, for example, Facebook, Twitter, etc.

soundbite A snappy and memorable quotation that can easily be assimilated into a broadcast news story.

spin doctor A person who tries to create a favourable slant to an item of news such as a potentially unpopular policy.

stereotype A 'typical' representation, which is widely accepted; a simplified, and possibly judgemental representation.

structuralism This approach argues that identifying underlying structures is all-important in undertaking analysis. In linguistics, for example, it can be argued that all languages have a similar underlying grammatical structure, which we are born with the capacity to learn. Similarly, certain social structures, such as the family unit, may be common to many cultures.

sub-genre A sub-division of a genre; for example, the vampire film is a sub-genre of the horror genre.

symbol A sign that represents an object or concept solely by the agreement of the people who use it.

syntagm A single piece of action in a moving image.

tabloid A compact newspaper, half the size of a broadsheet, designed to appeal to a mass audience. Tabloids, particularly at the lower end of the market, are associated with sensationalising trivial events rather than with comprehensive coverage of national and international news.

technical codes Refers to the use of camerawork, lighting, editing and sound in audio-visual media and graphic design elements for print-based and interactive media.

tertiary media Where the medium is present but we are not at all aware of it. The most obvious examples are advertising hoardings or placards that we pass but do not register.

text In Media Studies this term is used to refer to all media products.

user-generated content Media content placed in the public domain by members of the public, using new media.

uses and gratifications theory The idea that media audiences make active use of what the media offers. The audience has a set of needs, which the media in one form or another meets.

utopian solution The fantasy element and escapism from daily routines and problems provided by entertainment genres.

vertical integration This involves the ownership of every stage of the production process (production + distribution + exhibition), thereby ensuring complete control of a media product.

BIBLIOGRAPHY

Blumler, J. G. and Katz, E. (1974) *The Uses of Mass Communication*. Sage.

Bordwell, D. and Thompson, K. (1996) *Film Art: An Introduction* (5th edn). McGraw-Hill.

Branston, G. with Stafford, R. (1999) *The Media Student's Book* (2nd edn). Routledge.

Coad, D. (2008) *The Metrosexual, Gender, Sexuality and Sport*. State University of New York Press.

Cohen, S. (2002) *Folk Devils and Moral Panics* (3rd edn). Routledge.

Comolli, J. and Narboni, J. (1977) in J. Ellis (ed.) *Screen Reader 1*. London Society for Education in Film and Television.

Dyer, R. (1993) *The Matter of Images: Essays on Representation*. Routledge.

Earp, J. and Katz, J. (1999) *Tough Guise: Violence, Media and the Crisis in Masculinity*. Media Education Foundation.

Hall, S. (1978) *Policing the Crisis*. Palgrave.

Hall, S. (1980) 'Encoding/Decoding' in S. Hall *et al.* (eds) *Culture, Media, Language*. Unwin.

Hall, S. (1997) 'The Work of Representation' in *Representation: Cultural Representations and Signifying Practices*. Open University Press.

Iverson, P. (1994) *The Advent of the Laugh Track*. Hofstra University Archives.

Lacey, N. (2002) *Media Institutions and Audiences: Key Concepts in Media Studies*. Palgrave.

Lacey, N. (2009) *Image and Representation: Key Concepts in Media Studies*. Palgrave.

Lazarsfeld, P., Berelson, B. and Gaudet, H. (1968) *The People's Choice*. Columbia University Press.

McElroy, W. (1995) 'From A Sexually Incorrect Feminism' in *Penthouse* magazine, July.

Morley, D. (1992) *Television, Audiences and Cultural Studies*. Routledge.

Mulvey, L. (1975) 'Visual Pleasure and Narrative Cinema' in *Screen*, Autumn.

Perkins, T. (1997) 'Rethinking Stereotypes' in T. O'Sullivan and Y. Jewkes (eds) *The Media Studies Reader*. Hodder.

Phillips, P. (1996) 'Genre, Star and Auteur' in J. Nelmes (ed.) *An Introduction To Film Studies*. Routledge.

Radner, H. (2000) 'New Hollywood's New Women' in S. Neale and M. Smith (eds) *Contemporary Hollywood Cinema*. Routledge.

INDEX

Media Studies: The Essential Resource

Edited by Philip Rayner, Peter Wall and Stephen Kruger

A unique collection of resources for all those studying the media at university and pre-university level, this book brings together a wide array of material including advertisements, political cartoons and academic articles, with supporting commentary and explanation to clarify their importance to Media Studies. In addition, activities and further reading and research are suggested to help kick-start students' autonomy.

The book is organized around three main sections: Reading the Media, Audiences, and Institutions and is edited by the same teachers and examiners who brought us the hugely successful *AS Media Studies: The Essential Introduction*.

This is an ideal companion or standalone sourcebook to help students engage critically with media texts. Its key features include:

- further reading suggestions
- a comprehensive bibliography
- a list of web resources.

ISBN13: 978–0–415–29172–9 (hbk)
ISBN13: 978–0–415–29173–6 (pbk)
ISBN13: 978–0–203–64440–9 (ebk)

Available at all good bookshops
For ordering and further information please visit:
www.routledge.com

Communication, Cultural and Media Studies

The Key Concepts

Third Edition

This book provides a topical and authoritative guide to
Communication, Cultural and Media Studies, ideal for students of Advanced Subsidiary or Advanced Level courses.
It brings together in an accessible form some of the most
important concepts that you will need, and shows how
they have been – or might be – used. This third edition of
the classic text *Key Concepts in Communication and
Cultural Studies* forms an up-to-date, multi-disciplinary
explanation and assessment of the key concepts and
new terms that you will encounter in your studies, from
'anti-globalisation', to 'reality TV', from 'celebrity' to 'tech-
wreck'.

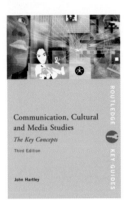

This new edition includes:

- Over 70 new entries
- Coverage of recent developments in the field
- Coverage of interactive media and the 'new economy'
- An extensive bibliography to aid further study

John Hartley is Professor and Dean of the Creative Industries Faculty at
Queensland University of Technology, Australia. He is author of many books and
articles on television, journalism and cultural studies. His most recent books
are: *Popular Reality* (1996), *Uses of Television* (1999), *The Indigenous Public
Sphere*, with Alan McKee (2000), *American Cultural Studies: A Reader*, edited
with Roberta E. Pearson (2000) and *A Short History of Cultural Studies* (2003).

ISBN 978–0–415–26889–9 (paperback)
ISBN 978–0–203–44993–6 (e-book)

Available at all good bookshops
For ordering and further information please visit
www.routledge.com

Communication Studies: The Essential Resource

Edited by Andrew Beck, Peter Bennett and Peter Wall

This book brings together a huge range of material including academic articles, film scripts and interplanetary messages adrift on space probes with supporting commentary to clarify their importance to the field. *Communication Studies: The Essential Resource* is a collection of essays and texts for all those studying communication at university and pre-university level.

Individual sections address:

- texts and meanings in communication
- themes in personal communication
- communication practice
- culture, communication and context
- debates and controversies in communication.

Edited by the same teachers and examiners who brought us *AS Communication Studies: The Essential Introduction*, this volume will help communications students to engage with the subject successfully. Its key features include:

- suggested further activities at the end of each chapter
- a glossary of key terms
- a comprehensive bibliography with web resources.

ISBN13: 978–0–415–28792–0 (hbk)
ISBN13: 978–0–415–28793–7 (pbk)

Available at all good bookshops
For ordering and further information please visit:
www.routledge.com

Film: The Essential Study Guide

Edited by Ruth Doughty and Deborah Shaw

Providing a key resource to new students, *Film: The Essential Study Guide* introduces all the skills needed to succeed on a film studies course.

This succinct, accessible guide covers key topics such as:

- Using the library
- Online research and resources
- Viewing skills
- How to watch and study foreign language films
- Essay writing
- Presentation skills
- Referencing and plagiarism
- Practical filmmaking

Including exercises and examples, *Film: The Essential Study Guide* helps film students understand how study skills are applicable to their learning and gives them the tools to flourish in their degree.

ISBN13: 978–0–415–43700–4 (pbk)
ISBN 3: 978–0–203–00292–6 (ebk)

Available at all good bookshops
For ordering and further information please visit:
www.routledge.com